The Cinematic Muse

The Cinematic Muse
Critical Studies in the History of French Cinema

Allen Thiher

University of Missouri Press
Columbia & London, 1979

Library of Congress Cataloging in Publication Data

Thiher, Allen, 1941–
    The cinematic muse.

    Bibliography: p. 207
    Includes index.
    1. Moving-pictures—France. 2. Moving-picture
plays—History and criticism. I. Title.
PN1993.5.F7T47   791.43′0944   79–1560
ISBN 0–8262–0277-2

    The author wishes to thank the following for permission
to reprint photographic stills:
from *La Grande Illusion*, *La Règle du jeu*, *Les 400 Coups*,
    Jules et Jim, and *Un Chien andalou*; courtesy of Janus
    Films, Inc.
from *Un condamné à mort* and *Deux ou trois choses que je sais d'elle*;
    courtesy of New Yorker Films.
from *Alphaville*; courtesy of Corinth Films.
from *Feu Mathias Pascal*; courtesy of the Museum of Modern Art.
from *A Nous la Liberté*; courtesy McGraw-Hill Book Co.
from *Tirez sur le pianiste*; courtesy of François Truffaut.
from *L'Année dernière à Marienbad*; courtesy of
    Les Éditions de Minuit.

To the Ronell clan,
with thanks.

Acknowledgments

I should like to thank the editors of *Boundary II*, *Dada/Surrealism*, and *Literature/Film Quarterly* for permission to reprint those parts of this study that have appeared in these periodicals.

I should also like to thank Avital Ronell, Roger Shattuck, Roland Simon, Mary Ann Caws, among others, for their encouraging readings of various parts of this work.

Finally, I should like to express my gratitude to the John Simon Guggenheim Memorial Foundation for a year of free time during which I was able to complete this work.

Contents

Aber was heisst denn ein blosses Spiel, nachdem wir wissen, dass unter allen Zuständen des Menschen gerade das Spiel und nur das Spiel es ist, was ihn vollständig macht und seine doppelte Natur auf einmal entfaltet?
——Friedrich Schiller

Vive la muse cinématographique!
——Jean Cocteau

Jean Cocteau: "Vive la muse cinématographique!"

Feu Mathias Pascal: Mathias facing his double, a shot Buñuel remembered in *Un Chien andalou*.

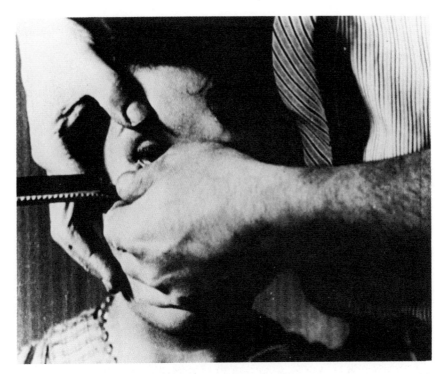

Un Chien andalou: Cinema is designed to open one's eyes.

A Nous la Liberté: The beginnings of an industrial empire (and an ironic view of how sound should be used in film?).

Prisoners and guards in *La Grande Illusion*: Before the castle, the aristocrat looks over the men of whom history has given him charge.

The hallway of La Colinière in *La Règle du jeu*: Renoir's theatricalized world, framed by overlapping proscenium arches, where master and servant imitate each other.

The four prisoners in *La Grande Illusion*: Escape as theatrical entertainment.

The two women in *La Règle du jeu*: Wife and mistress conferring about their costumes for the evening's entertainments.

The escape in *Un condamné à mort*: Preparing for a leap of faith.

The young prisoner in *Un condamné à mort*: A traitor or an agent of providence?

The two boys in *Les 400 coups*: Free from school—free to invent games.

Parents and boy in *Les 400 coups*: Punishment, the result of too quick an imagination.

The player and the piano in *Tirez sur le pianiste*: The low-angle shot reveals Edouard trapped behind his piano.

Edouard and Theresa in *Tirez sur le pianiste*: Husband and wife playing at being customer and waitress—or playing at being husband and wife.

Catherine by the Seine in *Jules et Jim*: She refuses
to join Jules and Jim as they try to categorize women.

Jules in the café in *Jules et Jim*: Truffaut recreates La Belle Epoque. (Note
the homage to Vigo in the newspaper headline.)

Woman in hotel room in *L'Année dernière à Marienbad*: The image offers a hypothesis about the room that might have been.

The formal garden of *L'Année dernière à Marienbad*: The ordered
world that the narrator's desire menaces.

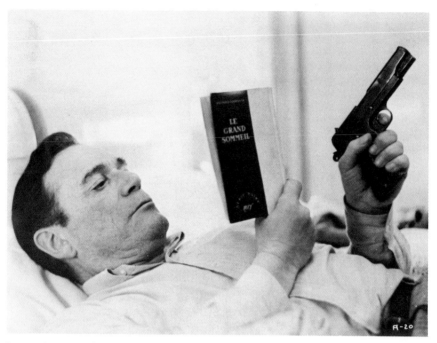

Lemmy Caution with gun in *Alphaville*: *The Big Sleep*—required reading for a pop private eye.

Window shot of Anna Karina in *Alphaville*: Can the language
of poetry attain the transparence of glass?

Arkansas newspaperman in *Deux ou trois choses que je sais d'elle*: The camera
eye can be a voyeur as well as a chronicler of prostitution.

Introduction

The following studies undoubtedly propose something that is akin to a theory of film or at least a tentative search for one. Film theory is only one focus of this work, however, and if theoretical inconsistencies are found among the various essays, they should perhaps be attributed to the exigencies of explicating the singularly rich films that I have selected to study. True, it is my hope that these critical essays will stimulate discussion of a theoretical nature about film and film aesthetics. But I also hope to show that film criticism can be as full in scope and as culturally significant as the criticism that is given to literature and painting. The dual aims of this book are reflected in what I take to be the two axes, the one conceptual, the other historical, that underlie the essays. Before I turn to some comments on these axes, I should like to make a few observations about the general nature of this book.

It was once platitudinous to assert that film suffered from a paucity of good criticism, and I must readily admit that my first impulse in undertaking this book was to come to grips with precisely that lack, especially with regard to French film. Having come to grips with a great deal of critical thought about film, I am not certain that the platitude is justified. I have certainly profited greatly from reading such intelligent critics as André Bazin, Barthélemy Amengual, Susan Sontag, Stanley Cavell, André Gardis, to name a few who immediately come to mind. And if it does seem true that much film criticism is mediocre, it is just as true that much criticism of other media, be it of literature, theater, or painting, is also mediocre. What is curious about film studies, however, is that, by and large, theoretical studies on the subject are generally intellectually superior to either critical or historical studies of film. Indeed, my first impulse was to write a history of French film, but given the material difficulties one encounters in such a project, I now wonder if it is even possible to write an intelligent history of film. Indeed, my point here is not to bemoan a lack of intelligence on the part of film critics and historians, but rather to suggest that it is easier to theorize about film in general than to do practical studies of individual works, of the dozens of films that may make up a director's oeuvre or of the hundreds of films that make up a given cinematic history. It is in fact extremely difficult to see the films one wants to see when one wants to see them and to see them the number of times necessary to write perceptively about them.

The following essays do represent something of a critical history of French film, a kind of personal history born of the circumstances that have allowed me to see and study certain films as I desired to study them. Of course, I have partially shaped those circumstances, especially in that, as a teacher of film, I have often been able to choose those films to which I wanted to have access. But these essays also reflect the availability of certain films in large cities; thus they are a product of what the marketplace has decided will be living film history. Films do disappear from circulation, and no amount of leg work around New York or Paris will ever turn them up again—unless, by chance, a copy is discovered in some studio attic or stored away in some corner of the Cinémathèque. Catching films in the Village or at midnight on Montreal television is not quite as easy as checking out a book from the local research library, and so we might all be a little more indulgent the next time we read a critic or historian who has (as we recall) confused scenes in one film with scenes in another or, even more typically, made a complete shambles of the plot. These are perhaps the least of sins when it comes to writing about film.

The films I have written about are thus films that are accessible, but I should also add that I have had access to the films I wanted to see—often by sheer luck. For example, a local Parisian cinema had a Bresson festival that allowed me not only to see the Bresson films I had not yet seen, but also to see *Un condamné à mort* three times in a row. (This happened, I might add, after Langlois told me that he had sent Bresson's *Le Journal d'un curé de campagne* to Spain and did not know when, if ever, it was coming back to the Cinémathèque.) In general, then, those films not accessible for intensive viewing were not the films I should have cared to write about. Some readers may maintain that a study or two of other directors or films should have been included. Gance, Feyder, Melville, Chabrol, Malle, Rohmer, to name a few, are all directors who have made at least one film of some historical importance. But I believe none of them to be as important as the directors and films that I have studied here; furthermore, in nearly all cases, my critical approaches to the films I have written on can be applied to those favorite directors and films that are missing.

To anticipate what may be a further criticism of these studies, I should state that I am well aware of the "literary" bias that might be attributed to these essays. I do not believe this is a very serious objection, for it is precisely the point of these essays to explore how some major French films are grounded in the cultural context of their time and to show that they often share the same aesthetic axioms that gave rise to major works of literature. The notion that film can be studied only in terms of some idea of cinematic purity is, I feel, an unreasonable methodological restriction. Though I understand why some film critics react against those studies that make of film a kind of second-rate literature, cinematic purity is really a myth, and a damaging myth at that, because it isolates film from the rest of our intellectual and cultural concerns.

At this point it is appropriate, then, to discuss the conceptual grids that make up the axes that give this book its coherence. (Readers having no taste for theoretical matters are advised to skip over to the book's first section, where they will find practical criticism.) Some readers, especially those who dislike a "literary" approach to film, are likely to wonder why I use the concept *mimesis* throughout this book. From the outset, then, I should like to say that mimesis must be taken here in as broad a sense as possible, encompassing the full range of meaning of representation and imitation that the term has traditionally had. Mimesis, understood correctly as the imitation of an action, can help us understand how film transforms a mechanical projection of the world into an aesthetic gestalt that is capable of having meaning. Except to those Platonists who are afraid of the power of art, mimesis has never meant a mere duplication of some preexisting reality, a reality superior to the work of art. Rather, it means imitation (or embodiment) of a guiding principle, an action, that gives coherence and meaning to every part of the work. As used here, and as I think Aristotle used the concept, mimesis is what many critics would call a formalist notion that suggests how individual parts derive meaning from a whole. Mimesis suggests that individual parts of a work, such as images, can have semantic import only if they are integrated into a total action.

This use of the term *mimesis* is coupled with frequent appeal to concepts taken from semiotics. Or perhaps it would be more accurate to say that some of these essays utilize a semiotic understanding of films as a sign system while, at the same time, they do not hesitate to use other critical methods of explicating film. There can be no doubt that film is, on one level at least, a sign system, but let me hasten to assure the dubious reader that the often arbitrary formalization of such systems will not be undertaken here. Semiotics does propose a coherent model for understanding film as a communication system, and it is my hope that in some of these essays I have suggested a way of integrating semiotics into a critical practice that is historical in orientation. Moreover, the use of semiotic models is consonant with a view of film as mimesis precisely insofar as semiotics allows us to see how the imitation of an action converts every element in a film into a signifying element, how it converts projections of the world into signs.

To utilize semiotic models is to utilize models derived from structural linguistics. The danger in applying such models to film is, of course, in applying metaphorically models that in linguistic usage are to be taken only as an operational description. Nothing is more emblematic of this kind of mis-guided use of linguistic models than those recent discussions that attempted to liken the image to a word. With this analogy in mind, the theorist could then seek to see how the image could be described in terms of the double articula-tion that is characteristic of all languages. What concerns us here, then, is the misguided use of metaphors; for in one sense it is a metaphor to say that an image is a sign, but this is, I believe, a fruitful metaphor. Also, as recent work in linguistics shows, it is perhaps no more metaphorical than to call language a sign system. For where does one locate the *sign* in language? At which level of formalization? Only the naive would see a sign in what dictionaries list as a word, and it would not be surprising if the Saussurian notion of *sign* were soon dropped entirely by linguistics. With this caveat in mind, one can see that my use of concepts such as denotative, connotative, and syntagmatic and paradigmatic axes are perhaps best to be taken as operative metaphors that in context are, as Wittgenstein would say, sufficiently delimited for the purposes of the critical language game we are playing.

To speak of a critical language game is not to speak pejoratively of my own critical endeavors. To talk of games is rather a way of recognizing that critical discourse derives from one of the most important aesthetic notions at our disposal today. That notion is quite simply that art is a form of play or, more precisely, a ludic construct. Indeed, one is tempted to trace our century's increasing distrust of what has been called the spirit of seriousness to our growing belief that ludic models lie behind the most varied manifestations of culture. The view that most cultural forms are forms of play then brings us back to the nature of mimesis and the recognition that if film is a form of mimesis—of mimicry, imitation, representation—then it is also a form of play. This recognition in turn suggests that one of film's primary functions is ludic.

The view that mimesis is a form of play is not a new one, but, with the disappearance of the belief that, as Susan Sontag puts it, substance or content is the essence of art, it is a view that is increasingly informing our perceptions of the nature of culture. Be it defined according to its origins as an instinct, a

4

drive, or a gratuitous manifestation of biological excess, the concept of play offers many keys for the understanding of the need for mimesis, repetition, organization, and form and chance, as well as perhaps the need to destroy cultural forms and to begin anew.

Although we may disagree with Roger Caillois's contradictory assessment of the value and function of play in culture in his *Les Jeux et les hommes*, we still might well turn to his classification of play instincts for a point of departure in understanding how, according to a modern theorist, play and ludic needs permeate nearly all cultural forms. Caillois says that there are essentially four forms of play: *mimicry, agon, alea,* and *ilynx* (or "disarray"). According to these categories, play forms appear to be based on the need (1) for mimesis or representation, (2) for competitive or agonistic confrontation, (3) to organize and master chance and aleatory forms, and (4) for bodily sensation and stimulation. While many kinds of play are based predominantly on one form or another, it would also appear that most kinds of play incorporate to some degree all four forms. To offer a familiar example, a football game provides an agonistic encounter, an aleatory outcome, and, for the participants at least, physical stimulation. The presence of the spectators transforms the game into a form of representation, since the spectators identify with the participants, thus creating a crude aleatory drama that also offers the spectators various physical sensations as well as vicarious stimulation. The leap from football to film is, then, not so great as it might appear, and their commonality is not merely the amount of popcorn consumed by the spectators.

High culture has distrusted play, both in the form of sports and in the form of movies, although it has separated mimesis from other aspects of play and attributed to it special values. Yet if we turn to one of the highest forms of play that our culture recognizes, Greek tragedy, we can readily see that the four ludic forms are present as the very ground of (the) play. The *agon* (or "conflict") is, for example, the heart of the tragedy. (The Greeks, it should be noted, regarded the production of these tragedies as something of a sporting event, for they were presented in an agonistic encounter at contests where the best plays received prizes.) Moreover, Aristotle's rationalization of tragedy in terms of catharsis—his seeking an ethical or utilitarian value for tragic play—should not blind us to the fact, as Nietzsche was well aware in *The Birth of Tragedy*, that the tragic play also forces us to confront *ilynx* (or "vertigo") while it portrays the aleatory forces that dominate human experience.

The ties between play and mimesis are recalled in Western languages every time we speak of theater and the theatrical side of film. A "play" is given a "performance" by a "player" (actor) who "plays" a role. In English, it is notable that the agonistic side of play is present when we speak of a player's performance or of the performance of the play, whereas the French use of *représentation* and the German use of *Vorstellung* emphasize how mimesis is a form of appearance, of mimicry made manifest. In French, *jeu* designates the notions of both play and acting (as well as games of chance), and the German verb *spielen* parallels the English verb in signifying both to play and to perform a play. It was in this same sense that English coined *photoplay* to designate early films, while the popular *moving pictures* or *movies* seems to reflect an intuition of mimesis as a form of sensation. *Lichtspiel*, literally a "light-play," remains today one German word for "cinema"; the Greek origins of the word *cinema* itself suggest the relationship between the concepts of motion and sensation and the concept of mimesis.

Looking beyond theatrical play, however, the contemporary mind is characterized precisely by its willingness to ask whether all mimetic forms do not arise in play. It questions in effect whether all representative and symbolic constructions, including language, are not forms of mimetic play. One knows what Wittgenstein's answer was with regard to language. Yet the notion of play continues to bear a strange stigma, for our traditional views of culture, buttressed by what one can conveniently call the spirit of seriousness, have often forced us to view play as a binary opposition to all that we must give highest value. According to this pervasive dichotomy, play must be viewed as the opposite of work, of productivity, of utilitarian activity, of ethical serious-ness. Protestants and Marxists alike find that play can be justified only in utilitarian terms, as the necessary complement to productivity or to some other activity whose purpose, in instrumental terms, transcends itself—all this as if it were not instrumental thought that must be justified, as if play were not the only self-justifying activity man knows.

This diffidence with regard to the value of play permeates the investiga-tions of even those who would attempt to chart how play lies at the heart of most if not all cultural forms. In his seminal work of historical anthropology, *Homo Ludens*, the Dutch historian Johan Huizinga defines the world of play as a world of voluntary activity, experienced with defined limits, that creates a perfect order. Though the possibility to play, according to Huizinga, is the basis for freedom, he still maintains a rigid distinction between the world of play and the world of ordinary experience, the latter being the domain where the need for productivity reigns unchallenged. Huizinga's work is undoubtedly the most important study to date of how play orders a world and how mimesis is grounded as a self-sufficient ludic construct. Yet it ultimately fails to challenge the boundaries that we accept when we relegate play to an inferior sphere of existence.

The notion of *inferior* and *superior* is of course a reflection of the dichotomy that has run throughout Western culture at least since Plato and that leads to the familiar distrust of all art and mimetic activity. By positing the existence of some substantial reality that exists prior to ludic activity, this Platonist viewpoint posits the artist's play as a derivative activity, and mimesis is regarded as the production of an impotent copy of something that has greater value than the representation itself.

One need not go back to Plato to find a *locus classicus* for such an attitude, for a similar view underlies such an exemplary modern mind as Freud's. Freud's view of child's play, for example, is that it is a way by which the helpless child compensates for his incapacity to deal with real situations. Mimicry is therefore interpreted as a symbolic enactment whose only value is that it allows the child a vicarious if unreal control over his environment, which in turn offers a mimed but hollow victory of the pleasure principle. In comparable fashion the artist seems to enact symbolic representations that procure compensation or offer gratification of wishes and desires that reality will not allow to be fulfilled. This view leads certain followers of Freud to the conclusion that, to paraphrase Norman O. Brown, in the world of play the representation of the gratified wish is accepted as real.

To say that the child, and presumedly the artist, is a dupe of his own play is a curious statement, one hardly borne out by daily experience. Such a point of view shows that those who see a substantial reality as somehow transcending and logically preceding play resort to bizarre arguments in order to grant primacy to whatever might precede mimesis. In this view, mimicry is so unsubstantial as to be possible only in conditions of delusion. Yet children know that play is not *real* in the sense that adults use the word, nor do artists think their acts of mimesis are to be taken as reality in that sense.

Viewing play as a form of compensation, or mimesis as a neurotic form of wish fulfillment, is one of several ways of alienating play from daily experience in order to salvage an ontology of substantial reality. It is a rather trite way of defending an epistemologically bankrupt notion of realism. Modern artists (and in this respect they are comparable to many contemporary scientists) are aware of this, and they have come to believe that our views of reality exist only in function of the representation of that reality. For the contemporary mind, no raw "reality" exists apart from the representation of that reality that the mind makes for itself. There are, in fact, multiple realities, existing at many levels of discourse, each one the function of the symbolic construct that allows us to perceive that reality. The notion of reality cannot therefore be separated from the mimetic act that brings it into a representational field. There are no limits therefore to the reality or realities that the creativity of play can produce through mimetic activity.

In this perspective, play and reality coexist, since "reality" comes to light through ludic activity. It exists only through the play that gives birth to symbolic enactment and mimesis. No reality can be known apart from the act of representing it. The history of twentieth-century art turns to a large extent on the growing awareness that the artist's task is, as Schiller already knew at the outset of the modern era, play in the fullest sense of the word. The artist's mimetic possibilities are limited only by his capacity to create works that are successful according to their own conventions or rules. In one sense, then, the artist faces each creative act as a game for which he must establish the rules that will allow him to create a given order of representation.

These considerations of the artistic and critical consciousnesses that have been developing during the twentieth century bring us to the historical axis underlying the order of this book, for in several senses this study of film is also a work of cultural history. Two of the key historical concepts behind my choice of films and the order of their presentation are the notions of *modernism* and *postmodernism*. Though I offer definitions of these terms at various points within the book, I shall explain them at the outset so that the reader has an overview of how the book is going to develop. My choice of a beginning for this work is dictated by a desire to study some key moments in the history of French film, starting with those works that reflect the first modernist influence on cinematic experimentation, especially the influence of surrealism. The idea of modernism, a literary-historical concept concerning the development of the central aesthetic canons of our time, is often seen as applying primarily to the avant-garde experimentation of the late nineteenth and early twentieth centuries. It can also be used in a larger sense, as indeed I use the term, to designate the development of that aesthetic doctrine that begins at the end of the eighteenth century, develops through German and English romanticism and through French symbolism, and culminates in the great works of those we tend to think of as *the* modernists: Joyce, Proust, Valéry, Rilke, to offer a few names. To be a useful historical concept, modernism must be sufficiently broad, perhaps dialectically flexible enough, to be able to show how what initially appear to be opposing phenomena—Flaubert's realism and Mallarmé's symbolism, for instance—are grounded ultimately in common aesthetic axioms and hence in a common historical development. As a wide body of scholarship demonstrates, modernism seems to be such a concept, for there is much agreement about what constitutes the basic goals and axioms of modernist aesthetics.

Modernism is, then, as I see it, a theologico-aesthetic development that begins approximately with the romantic movement and runs well into the twentieth century. The term *theological* is appropriate here, since modernism develops as something of a religious response to a crisis in our perception of temporality. The modernist is cursed by a sense of his fall into time and is possessed by a nostalgia for the plenitude of a present that can only exist as time past. From Hölderlin to Joyce, with many variations along the way, the development of modernism has been the development of strategies to overcome this belief that temporality is a form of fall (think of Joyce's "History is a nightmare"). These strategies have usually sought to use art to find privileged modes of revelation that can offer access to an ontologically superior realm that transcends time and history. Mallarmé's *Livre*, Flaubert's search for the perfect word, Proust's essences, Joyce's epiphanies, or Eliot's desire to make tradition a living presence are all ways of seeking a plenitude that exists as an atemporal presence. They are all ways, to paraphrase Rilke's Orphic bard, of making song into true existence. Modernism is, then, a quest for redemption in a universe cursed by time. It is, to quote Malcolm Bradbury and James McFarlane's introduction to their book *Modernism*, a form of art that gives itself "the task . . . to redeem, essentially or existentially, the formless universe of contingency."[1]

The tenets of modernism were first applied to film through the experimentation that the surrealists undertook. Surrealism is a central part of modernism insofar as its primary quest is for a locus of revelation that can transform existence. Frankly utopian in seeking a paradise on earth, in proclaiming the need to live poetry, surrealism's quest for what André Breton called the *merveilleux* is founded on a rejection of rationality, including the logic of temporality, and is in fact an exemplary modernist quest for a salvation

1. Malcolm Bradbury and James McFarlane, *Modernism*, p. 50.

grounded in the plenitude of the present. Probably the best translation of *merveilleux* that has been proposed is "revelation." Of course, surrealism was animated by a spirit of revolt that differentiates it considerably from other forms of modernism, especially insofar as its rebellion aimed at destroying what we might call, for want of better terms, the constraints of bourgeois rationalism. Surrealists proposed to abolish all that might limit human experience, and, curiously enough, attempted to do so by juxtaposing incongruous images that would offer a revelation of the "marvelous" that would destroy the restrictive categories of logic.

After a brief consideration of avant-garde experimentation undertaken by the Impressionists in Paris during the twenties, a subject of interest in its own right that also offers useful background for the subsequent works, I begin this study with what I take to be three of the most important modernist attempts to exploit film: Buñuel's *Un Chien andalou*, Ray's *Etoile de mer*, and Cocteau's *Le Sang d'un Poète*. Buñuel's film illustrates the surrealist revolt against rational categories of representation, whereas Ray's and Cocteau's works pose the problem faced by the modernist who would use film poetically, which is to say the problem faced by the filmmaker who attempts to endow film with semantic structures based on the creation of iconic figures and on myth. The essays on Vigo and Clair illustrate what might be taken to be the high point of modernist influence on film in France, especially insofar as the modernist exaltation of childhood has a determining role in the way these filmmakers have constructed their filmic vision. Modernism may, in a profound sense, have invented childhood, or at least our way of investing childhood with certain nearly magical properties, such as the capacity to live in an eternal present unsullied by a sense of temporality. Surrealists saw in childhood an exemplary state in which man is able to live the marvelous. Clair and Vigo were both associated with surrealism to varying degrees and reflect to varying degrees the surrealists' belief in the necessity for man to return to the child's capacity for spontaneous play.

The decline of modernism in the thirties can be attributed in part to the economic stagnation that afflicted Europe, to the growth of national fascisms (though the complicity of certain modernists with fascism is well known), and, in France, to the growing belief that the thirties was a period of historically decreed decadence. The decade's view of itself is singularly at odds with the extraordinary creativity that made the thirties one of the richest decades in the history of French culture. The same time span that saw Carné and Renoir make their greatest films saw Céline, Malraux, Sartre, Giraudoux, and others publish some of their most important works. It is certainly true, however, that the flamboyant modernist experimentation, that search for the surprise that Diaghilev had demanded from art, gave way in the thirties to works impregnated with a sense of malaise, if not of despair, about the possibility of triumphing over destiny, history, or the decline of an entire culture—or, more simply, of despair about simply surviving from day to day. The proletarian vision of a Carné and, for instance, a Céline share the same quietly homicidal assumption that society is bent on eradicating anyone who attempts to change his lot. The thirties' view that history had, in some fatalistic way, made such a shambles of social order may in fact be akin to Joyce's view that history is a nightmare, but for the artists and filmmakers of the time the thirties did not appear to be a nightmare from which one could easily awake. It is against this backdrop that I have written studies of Carné and Renoir and the mimesis of social and historical reality that one finds in their work of the thirties.

World War II, the Nazi occupation, and the Resistance marked French film as it did all other aspects of French culture, though perhaps in a more immediately negative manner. Even if one did not dare to publish, one could continue to write. In the case of cinema, however, the occupiers, following Goebbels's orders, refused to allow the production of any works that did not contribute directly to the cretinization of the French. The production of a work such as Carné's *Les Enfants du paradis* seems a minor miracle in such conditions.

In a broader sense, the climate created by the occupation was directly responsible for the rapid development of the existentialist thought—perhaps one might prefer the term *sensibility*—that dominated the French artistic and intellectual scene until the beginning of the sixties. The occupation had suddenly confronted Frenchmen with an absolute evil that could only be grasped as the absurd. The response to this confrontation brought about two seemingly opposing reactions. One was to take refuge in some religious response, the other was to embrace a philosophy of the absurd, such as the ones expounded by Sartre and Camus. Both responses sprang, however, from the same existential awareness. The works by Bresson and Truffaut that I study here seem to correspond to these two sides of the existentialist climate, for films by these directors illustrate the opposing, yet complementary aspects of an absurdist view. Bresson's film *Un condamné à mort*, moreover, illustrates magnificently the meaning of resistance and represents one of the most important works that Christian existentialism has ever produced. Truffaut's early films, on the other hand, show how the existentialist categories that permeated French intellectual life shaped the vision of one of the most representative filmmakers of the New Wave. The absurdist underpinnings of these films also represent a first step in the development of what is coming to be known as the aesthetics of postmodernism.

Postmodernism is another historical category, though one about which there is much dispute. This is hardly surprising, since postmodernism is a notion that springs from a sense of our own contemporaneity. The *post* of the expression would suggest that we have somehow moved beyond or broken with the modernist credo, while the *modernism* would suggest that we might still be living on the aesthetic capital that the great creators of the early twentieth century bequeathed to us. With regard to film, however, one point is clear. If we feel a bit uneasy in comparing the great literary works of modernism with the film works that modernists undertook, we have no need to hesitate at all when comparing the achievement of postmodern writers and filmmakers. Fellini, Resnais, Godard, Antonioni, Bergman, among others, have created a body of works that make of the fifties and especially the sixties a cinematic golden age. To a greater or lesser degree, these filmmakers are all postmodern artists.

In the concluding essays, on films by Robbe-Grillet and Resnais and by Godard, I offer fairly extensive reflections on what I believe to be the most important aspects of postmodernism. Bearing in mind our comments on modernism, one might easily guess that postmodernism would entail a refusal to believe in the possibility of finding atemporal essences or a privileged form of redeeming revelation. In this respect postmodernism and existentialism coincide in their rejection of the hope that one can overcome the absurd (read "temporality" for the modernist temperament) by finding refuge in aesthetic transcendence. Postmodern artists in this sense of the term would include such absurdists as Ionesco, Pinter, or Barthelme, or, in a slightly different register, certain works by such French directors as Malle, Chabrol, or Rivette.

This rejection of the search for a locus of revelation has seemingly entailed a change in attitude toward the nature of the artistic work, first with regard to what the work can tell us about the world, and second with regard to the ontological status of the work itself. Both of these changes are related, as we have already suggested, to art's increasing acknowledgment of its nature as a ludic construct. In the case of film and literature, this acknowledgment entails the recognition of fiction as a self-conscious form of play. Perhaps, rather than of self-consciousness, one should really speak of self-designating works, since it is certainly characteristic of the modernist work to carry within itself indices that reveal its consciousness of itself *qua* work. Postmodernists go beyond the often ironic self-consciousness of modernism and make the work itself or the creation of the work itself the object of mimesis. There is an almost programmatic side to this aspect of postmodernism, for, according to the latest French theorists, such as Jean Ricardou, it is necessary that every successful contemporary work designate its own functioning as a self-reflective or even as a self-generating work. Self-replication, it seems, has become an aesthetic ideal.

This questioning of the work by the work is of course a far more general feature of the contemporary artist's uncertainty than one might gather from listening only to Parisian theorists. One need only think of how Bergman, at the beginning of *Persona*, showing the camera and the burning celluloid, reveals his mimetic project to be, in part at least, a difficult quest for a film, or how Antonioni uses the photographer in *Blow-Up* as a double to signify the cinematic duplication that designates the work's automimesis. In this respect Fellini's *8 1/2* has already become a comic classic of the postmodern temperament.

Continental critics have often named the rejection of mimesis as one of the hallmarks of the postmodern work. In America, a persuasive spokesman for this viewpoint is the novelist-philosopher William Gass, whose essays, if not his creative work, argue at length against the naive acceptance of the work's representative function. But I think it more nearly accurate to say that the postmodern mind demands that the search for representation be accompanied by a self-representation dramatizing the quest of the mimetic task itself. Automimesis is often only a way of making the production of the work itself the central action of mimesis, as is the case in the films by Robbe-Grillet and Resnais and by Godard that I discuss. In representing the production of the work or in laying bare the way the work functions, postmodernism does not turn its back on the world. Rather, it lays bare the way we represent the world to ourselves in our fictions, our myths, and perhaps our dreams.

Thus the historical and conceptual axes of this study cross at that point where the development of film in France brings us to a confrontation with our contemporary dilemmas. Though a bit more than a decade has passed since the last films I discuss were made, I believe my critical commentary on Resnais, Robbe-Grillet, and Godard remains quite relevant for the cinema of today. In many respects they remain the filmmakers of today, as witness Resnais's recent *Providence*, Godard's work with television documentary, and Robbe-Grillet's continued experimentation with self-generating pop fantasies. As the seventies comes to an end, the postmodern uncertainties I discuss remain the defining forms of artistic expression for the doubts of our age.

The Avant-Garde

The Impressionist
Avant-Garde

It is surprising today to recall that French film producers once dominated the world film market; but this was during the period of primitive films before World War I. For the film historian it is a fascinating period. The diversity of these films is quite amazing, and they exercise an attraction on us that is undoubtedly out of proportion to their artistic worth (though Méliès, Durand, Feuillade, and others have their cults). As far as their influence on the elaboration of film discourse in France is concerned, they seem to belong to a remote epoch that has little in common with the silent films of the postwar period, not to mention with the classic narrative films of the thirties. World War I marked a rupture in French cinema, for during the war the French film industry nearly disappeared from the world market. It would appear that the early, primitive filmmakers were so nearly forgotten in the twenties that in 1924 René Clair could pay nostalgic homage to Méliès by putting the emblem of his Star Films on the rampaging hearse that stars in Clair's *Entr'acte*.

When companies like Pathé and Gaumont ceased to be the suppliers for the world's demand for film, Hollywood became the creator of the popular myths, of the vamps and sheiks, that soon became *the* modern form of popular myth. The disappearance of these companies' industrial power also meant, however, that in France it was possible for independent directors to step into the vacuum that the monopolies left behind them and to follow their individual creative bent. Thus a commercial avant-garde formed soon after the war in Paris. Influenced by the work of such theorists as Louis Delluc, this school, whose work should not be confused with surrealist, Dadaist, or cubist experiments in film, included such directors as Abel Gance, Germaine Dulac, Marcel L'Herbier, and the young Jean Epstein. Avant-garde in their zeal for experimentation and their desire to expand the mimetic range of cinema, these filmmakers were nonetheless also concerned with the commercial side of their work and wanted to reach a large audience, or at least the same public that serious literature spoke to. Cinema was no longer a product to be sent to circuses or music halls for a semiliterate, boisterous public of peasants, workers, and tipplers. For these directors, film was to become an art that could rival the stage and the printed page. Perhaps to differentiate them from the German expressionists of the early twenties, historians commonly call these filmmakers the Impressionist School, though there is nothing especially impressionistic about their work. In fact, one might even prefer *expressionist* as a more adequate term to describe their primary mimetic concerns, which went beyond the desire to explore the narrative techniques that American filmmakers such as Griffith and Von Stroheim were developing. Of course, the French Impressionists, like their Russian contemporaries, were quick to incorporate into their work the filmic conventions developed by the Americans that allowed filmmakers to transpose into film the narrative conventions of the Victorian and the naturalistic novel.

Griffith's role in developing narrative montage and the way in which this technique allowed him to represent the Victorian *Weltanschauung* in terms of a simplistic conflict of good and evil are well known. In Griffith's case, parallel montage is the structural principle that allows the episodic unfolding of ethical conflict. Equally interesting—though only belatedly recognized—is Von Stroheim's work in the transposition of naturalistic narrative structures. In his *Greed* (1923) it appeared that the logic of naturalistic narration could be completely transposed to the screen. The naturalistic novel's third-person point of view could be represented by the camera's exterior vision of the surface of objects and events. The seemingly objective nature of the photo-image could be accepted without question as a form of representation that was the equivalent of the naturalist's totally adequate descriptive language. For the naturalist, both image and word can exhaust, with often savage simplicity, the world through their expressivity. For this reason Von Stroheim had no need for the more complicated montage that Griffith developed. The image as Von Stroheim used it was adequate for mimesis, and the simple unfolding of episodic experience in terms of linear causality, with the sequence as the basic narrative unit, was adequate to express the relationships among events. Narrative structure and *Weltanschauung* again coincide, though here in the expression of a vision of man adrift in a world bereft of transcendental solace.

The French Impressionists quickly took over the American work on the development of narrative structures, but they were not as interested in the narration of episodic experience for its ethical or sentimental value. As might be expected of artists who were part of the generation that was reading symbolist poets, Bergson, and Gide while discovering Proust, Pirandello, and surrealism, these filmmakers were more interested in developing techniques that would allow film to explore more subjective modes of representation. By *subjective modes of representation*, one should understand a fairly wide scope of mimetic possibilities, including attempts to endow film with first-person narrative structures, the capacity to express what are generally called inner emotional states, and the attempt to represent hallucination and other idiosyncratically subjective images, as well as the effort to create poetic structures that could represent the director's emotional attitude toward the narrated experience (as in the case of Gance's experiments with rhythmic montage).

Exemplary in this respect (and important for an understanding of surrealist experimentation in film) was Pirandello's decision to allow Marcel L'Herbier to base a film on his *The Late Mattia Pascal*. L'Herbier's *Feu Mathias Pascal* (1926) is a key film for an understanding of the modes of mimesis that the Impressionist directors developed, for it attempts to combine linear narration of a naturalistic sort with exploration of subjective modes of representation. Pirandello's somewhat disjointed novel offered L'Herbier a first-person narration in which a middle-class protagonist has unintentionally and unhappily married a woman to whom he had proposed on the behalf of his best friend. He escapes from his prisonlike existence when he breaks the bank at Monte Carlo and then discovers that his friends and family erroneously believe he has committed suicide. Mathias has made a lifelong study of the nature of freedom. Suddenly rid of the burdensome identity that has denied him his own freedom, he goes to Rome, where he discovers that his lack of identity forces him to live outside civic norms. He is ensnared in a vacuous freedom that resembles a new form of imprisonment. It is worth noting that whereas Pirandello left his hero in his quandary, with no resolution at all, L'Herbier, perhaps for commercial reasons, appended a happy ending to his film by granting Mathias a new wife and a new identity.

This brief résumé indicates that such a film turns in large part on ideological and psychological questions such as the nature of freedom and identity. What is of interest, then, are the conventions L'Herbier used to represent the way in which his protagonist experiences the problems these questions pose. Though none of L'Herbier's choices are original, his work does bring together a series of solutions that are both typical of the Impressionist period and relatively successful within their own frame of reference. For instance, the sets that Cavalcanti designed for the film are initially its most striking feature.

Using multiple framing devices within the image frame—windows and columns or multiple arches within a hallway—Cavalcanti created rigid patterns that suggest boxes within boxes, confining walls within confining walls, abstractions limited by other abstractions. Though not as extreme in effect as the decor of *The Cabinet of Dr. Caligari*, this is nonetheless an expressionist use of decor in the sense that the decor exists as an extension or a representation by analogy of a character's inner state. It is an objective correlative that relates both a psychological state and an ideological problem to an exterior manifestation or symbol. This type of mimesis is hardly unique to film, though in various guises it continues to attract filmmakers, for it is what we might call one aspect of purely plastic representation.

L'Herbier's principles for montage follow the basic naturalistic order of sequential development, though here, too, he attempts to use editing for modes of subjective representation that neither Griffith nor Von Stroheim would have undertaken. L'Herbier attempts through montage to duplicate the sense of confessional intimacy that Pirandello's first-person narration offers. For example, during a village festival, the rapid cutting rate creates a series of collisions of images—dancing villagers, the city, fireworks, the carnival rides—that seem to express the inner passion and confusion that sweep up Mathias Pascal when, proposing for his friend, he instead allows himself to become engaged. The increasingly rapid juxtaposition of rows of frolicking dancers, a spinning merry-go-round, and the isolated couple produces a kaleidoscope of impressions that mimics the vertigo of new, if mistakenly placed, passion. L'Herbier breaks off this sequence with a dissolve in which the image of the dancing couple stays in focus. The couple then find themselves in the dismal kitchen that will be the scene of Mathias Pascal's newfound domesticity. The surprise that Mathias feels when he suddenly finds himself there underscores the jolt of awareness that shakes him as he awakes to his new condition. Here the ellipsis brought about by the montage is a correlative to a psychological transformation. In other scenes L'Herbier uses rapid dissolves and fast cutting not only to suggest his protagonist's flight from his family, but also to represent the very frenzy that seizes Mathias as he flees or, later, as he escapes from the luxurious hotel where a desk clerk demands to see the identity papers he no longer has. In these examples cinematic "punctuation" becomes a mimetic device that seeks to represent an inner state as well as to denote an event.

As we shall see, what undoubtedly most amused Luis Buñuel and his surrealist contemporaries in L'Herbier's attempt to find conventions that could signify psychic reality was his use of trick photography in order to offer images that would present mimesis of inner life. Again one must stress that L'Herbier was hardly original in this respect. One need only think of Dulac's *Smiling Madame Beudet* (1923), among numerous other examples, and her use of superimpositions to convey Madame Beudet's obsession with her miserable husband; or various irising and other bracketing techniques that American filmmakers developed to represent interiorized images of recall and memory. But L'Herbier is again exemplary, for he attempts by using various devices to combine several levels of representation in a single image.

To offer a key example, when Mathias is attempting to forge a new identity outside the confines of social recognition, he turns and is suddenly facing a smirking double of himself. This image of Mathias facing himself is intended, of course, to represent not only the conflict that tears at him psychologically but also a more philosophical view of the difficulty, if not the impossibility, of denying the past. In one sense L'Herbier has used trick photography to create something of a metaphor within the frame. If this kind of image succeeds as a philosophical metaphor, and this is doubtful, it is certainly literally naive as a mimetic device for representing psychological states. Another and even more dubious device is found when Mathias leaps forward in slow motion to strangle an adversary who, presented as if he were in the room with Mathias, threatens to disrupt his amorous life in Rome. Nearly all early directors attempted to utilize slow motion in various ways; most inevitably attempted to transform it into a sign of some kind of psychic representation, usually as a form of dream or fantasy. Here L'Herbier is true to what we might call the codification of a device, or its transformation into a conventional sign. Mathias's slow-motion attack on his enemy represents a form of projection or wish fulfillment that in a literary work would be narrated by either a first-person narrator or an omniscient author, or perhaps in the form of an interior monologue.

The most interesting aspect of these mimetic devices, especially the ones using various sorts of trick photography, is how quickly their status changed from that of arbitrary inventions to that of a codified series of conventional signs that audiences quickly learned to "read" as a form of psychological representation. On the other hand, the Impressionists also sought to create more original devices for mimesis, and in this quest they often turned away from narrative structures borrowed from the novel and from the representation of psychological states that one could attribute to a single character. They then sought to develop purely cinematic devices for the representation of various poetic states. This search for mimetic devices of a poetic rather than a narrative sort seems in general to derive from the nature and the manipulation of the camera. Such work is typified by Jean Epstein's *Fall of the House of Usher* (1928)—a film, we might add, for which Buñuel was the assistant, immediately before making *Un Chien andalou*. This film is typical in that it too attempts to rival literature, although Epstein, perhaps more influenced by Baudelaire and Mallarmé than by novelists, was as much interested in creating a Poe-like atmosphere as in retelling a Poe short story by cinematic means. Borrowing motifs liberally from "Ligeia" and "The Oval Portrait," as well as "The Fall of the House of Usher," Epstein used narration only insofar as it gave him a framework in which he could create images expressing various poetic states. By *poetic states* one might understand emotional states that are dissociated from any specific protagonist and exist as a form of communication that has no narrative function. Rather, all narrative functions in the film are subordinated to the communication of these various states.

To borrow from Poe's symbolist doctrine as he expressed it in "Ligeia," we might say that Epstein seeks to render the viewer sensible to a "circle of analogies" that exist "in the commonest objects of the universe." Poetic communication is achieved when these analogies are made evident. The principle of analogy is especially noticeable in Epstein's montage, in which he often juxtaposes somewhat disparate images so that by a kind of visual metaphor based on contiguity he might communicate the irrational associations that obtain in the world of the film. Usher, for example, sits in his cavernous salon and plays his guitar. The following images show trees as the wind buffets them about, suggesting both affective turbulence and a world permeated with the passion of music. The outer world of nature and its violence are set in analogy to the inner world of creation and the demonic imagination (which, as in "The Oval Portrait," is destructive of life). The juxtaposition of the outer and inner worlds creates foreboding and dread, though unlike the case of *Feu Mathias Pascal*, one should not necessarily attribute this state to any character within the film.

Another comparable example can be given: the scene in Epstein's version of "The Fall of the House of Usher" when Usher's wife dies (Epstein's changing the story's sister into a wife would appear to be his way of refusing the incest motif that fascinated Poe). Using a form of montage within the frame, Epstein superimposes rows of candles on the shot of the funeral procession as it proceeds slowly through a somber forest. Here the analogy is created by trick photography as Epstein, in an overly contrived bit of juxtaposition, uses his candles to suggest that grief permeates the world of nature. In the same sequence, however, Epstein reverts to the mimetic device of a supposedly subjective camera; the "subjective" camera represents the point of view of a character within the film. Epstein's creation of this type of subjective mimesis is ingenuous. As the bier is transported, he points his camera toward the sky, thus espousing the point of view of the corpse and at the same time representing her as a living being—which she is in one sense. Within a single sequence, then, Epstein runs the gamut from poetic analogy to subjective representation of a most peculiar sort.

Epstein also typifies development of the most varied use of camera movement and angles for types of mimesis that rely entirely on the mobile nature of the camera. In exploring the cursed house, for instance, the camera, shooting from an awkward, oblique angle, rushes down the hall of the mansion, skirting along the floor, as though fleeing some impending catastrophe. Here motion itself is a form of mimesis, and the camera's extremely rapid forward trajectory through space is an analogy for the fear-flight that permeates the film. This use of motion to create analogy is perhaps the film's most unique feature, and one that, after the Impressionists, does not appear to have been really exploited again until Resnais. Indeed, for many viewers the most memorable moment in the film is probably the sequence in which Usher, after he has killed his wife by incorporating her soul into his painting, is propelled across the room in another moment of anguish-flight. Here Epstein placed his actor on the camera dolly and sent it rolling across the floor. Usher's face thus remains at a fixed distance from the lens while the background flies by in a blurred rush. The effect of such a composition, as Usher's mad eyes remain fixed upon us, is not unlike Munch's *The Scream*, for the blurred background, isolating Usher's contorted face, acts again as an analogon to the dread that engulfs Usher's world.

The comparison with Munch, whose influence on expressionist painting can hardly be overestimated, is instructive, for it points to the affinities that the so-called Impressionists have with their German contemporaries. Perhaps this is one reason why French critics and historians have often been less than sympathetic to filmmakers like Epstein. Georges Sadoul, for example, considers the Impressionist School to be a deviation from the naturalist tradition that he sees as the most constant aspect of French cinema. This seems a rather strange way of viewing both Epstein and the Impressionists in general, for even if they were not entirely successful in their experimentation, they seem to us to be typical of an avant-garde tradition that is as constant an aspect of French cinema as naturalism. They were singularly important for making American and Russian developments known in France and for attempting to translate some of the narrative and poetic concerns of literary modernism into filmic expression. Moreover, they created the climate in which Dada and surrealism could come to grips with film. For example, it is only against the backdrop of the Impressionist School that one can fully understand Buñuel's first work in cinema.

Surrealism's Enduring Bite:
Un Chien andalou

Buñuel and Dali's *Un Chien andalou* is undoubtedly the best-known work of surrealist cinema, and it will probably remain so until the family of the Viscount Charles de Noailles decides that his soul will not roast in hell if *L'Age d'Or*, the film the Viscount financed, is ever released again. For those who cannot catch *L'Age d'Or* at a film festival or at the Cinémathèque in Paris, the film about a Spanish canine must remain the primary initiation to surrealistic cinema practice. Yet, widely known as it has been since its creation in 1928, *Un Chien andalou* remains a very much more misunderstood film than *L'Age d'Or*, that embodiment of what André Breton called *l'amour fou*. Buñuel's first film is commonly categorized either as an unadulterated bit of nonsense or as a symbol-laden exercise in hermeticism that only the initiated can understand. Although neither of these ideas is entirely false, neither is adequate for a full comprehension of one of the most important films of the avant-garde. We should, then, like to propose an interpretation that, if it will not elucidate every image in *Un Chien andalou*, will at least situate this example of surrealism so that its full stature as a film becomes clear. For this dog has hardly had its last bark.

The background against which *Un Chien andalou* and the surrealist incursion into cinema can best be viewed is that provided by looking at the development of filmic narrative conventions we saw take place in the twenties, as well as at the development of the avant-garde in both the plastic arts and film. By 1928 silent films appear to have reached the summit of their development insofar as they had found those narrative conventions that allowed them at times to rival novels as forms of narrative discourse. Film theorists have often discussed the various "syntactical" developments of silent film, but, in spite of Eisenstein's writings on film and novels, few have noted that these efforts to create film syntax were aiming largely at the transposition to the screen of narrative logic as defined by the nineteenth-century novel. Filmmakers wanted to cope with the problems of temporality and the mimesis of episodic experience as well as with character functions and point of view, not only in the same manner as a realistic novelist, but more especially *because* the realistic novelist had defined these concerns to be the central preoccupations of mimesis. From a surrealist's point of view, then, film, by 1928, was another repository of what we might call the bourgeois ideology of realistic mimesis. Film's pretensions to represent reality in terms of bourgeois realism or the psychologism of the Impressionists could only meet with scorn from a surrealist.

On the other hand, and one must distinguish here between surrealism *per se* and the more general avant-garde in painting, the twenties saw the first efforts to exploit the purely plastic properties of film through the creation of cinematic collages and abstract films. Buñuel's attitude toward these film experiments is quite clear, for in one of his more sweeping statements he declares that avant-garde filmmakers as diverse as Walther Ruttmann and Dziga Vertov, René Clair and Man Ray, are to be rejected for their aestheticism and their occasional "display of a perfectly conventional and reasonable mood."[1] Though one might well take Buñuel's polemic with a grain of salt, it is certain that there is little in, for instance, Eggeling's *Diagonal Symphony* or Richter's *Rhythm* series that could appeal to a young surrealist. Lines that move, squares that jump, abstractions that undergo transformations—none of these forms, any more than the conventional logic of realistic literature, could appear to be a way of placing cinema in the service of desire. What could a surrealist make of Richter's *Studienfilm* (1926), in which, in order to show the relation between pure form and natural objects, Richter sets in motion, like so many marbles, a series of rolling, disembodied eyes? Buñuel obviously felt that he had to teach the avant-garde that their eyes must be opened.

Our initial postulate for understanding *Un Chien andalou* is that surrealist practice is a ludic activity, a form of play that attempts systematically to subvert the rules of the game, whether it be in the realm of syntax, narration, or iconic representation. *Un Chien andalou* is, then, an antigame that, by the systematic way it proposes to destroy the rules of earlier cinematic games, transforms itself into a superior form of play. By systematic negation of the rules, the surrealist work develops a new set of ludic definitions at the same time that it acquires an ironic self-consciousness. Buñuel uses his film to parody, and through parody to destroy, the filmic conventions that two generations of filmmakers had evolved. From its very first sequence, in which Buñuel appears and slits an eye as tranquilly as one would slice a ripe melon,

1. Luis Buñuel, quoted in *Art in Cinema*, ed. Frank Stauffacher, p. 29.

the film sets forth an image of the destruction of vision, the vision that the spectator normally brings to film and that he normally expects to find in it. The film's opening images, which constitute a kind of prologue to the rest of the film, are thus an attack on the passivity with which the spectator accepts the conventional logic of representation—the rules of the game—as well as the passivity that this logic inflicts on the spectator.

The film's first title, "Once upon a time," opens this assault by making an ironic appeal to the conditioned response normally elicited by this kind of narrative signpost. "Once upon a time" notifies us that a certain narrative code is at work, a sequential narrative order in which events are subordinated to the simplest form of unfolding chronology. In short, the order to be followed is the linear chronology of epic, myth, and movies. Thus the spectator naturally supposes that there must be a logical connection between the title and the following image of a man sharpening a razor. Such a juxtaposition in cinema is conventionally based on causality, and so the viewer automatically assumes that the various shots of the man's face, his hands and the razor, the testing of the razor on his fingernail, are offered in function of some developing coherence. The shot of the moon and the sky that follows also seems motivated by conventional filmic syntax, for the man looks away, a sign that the following shot will offer a "subjective" image, the grammatical equivalent of "This is what I see."

Nor does the following shot of a woman's face disturb the logic of film narrative, for the dissolve Buñuel uses to introduce this image seems to state, according to conventional syntax, that an ellipsis has taken place. A hand, however, opens one of her eyes, and another hand holding the razor comes into the shot. The following shot, showing clouds crossing the moon, suddenly forces the spectator to realize that the coherence that has been developing is not one commanded by any form of narrative logic, though all the signs of that logic are present. Instead, he is confronting a parodistic "montage of attractions": the eye calls forth the razor with all the persuasiveness with which the moon attracts the clouds. The razor, with all the guileless violence that "Once upon a time" sanctions, slits the eye, and the filmic conventions that underlie this representation stand revealed in their arbitrariness.

In thematic terms this prologue to *Un Chien andalou* is a prologue to that part of Buñuel's work in which he frequently jeers those "who have eyes and will not see." Consider, for example, how in *L'Age d'Or* the surrealist hero,

Gaston Modot, is taken into custody by the police for having attempted to rape his lover in the mud while priests lay the foundation of Rome. Modot's first act after being released, however, is not to resume immediately his quest for *amour fou*, but, in a wild fury, to kick down a blind man who happens by. Or one might think of the lecherous, blind beggar in *Los Olvidados* who beats his small young helper, Ojitos—"Little Eyes"—or Buñuel's choice of a Christ for *Viridiana*'s mock Last Supper: another leering yet blind mendicant whose image is "fixed" by the *maquina* of a ribald whore. By constantly reversing the conventional connotations of the terms *blindness* and *sight*, Buñuel undermines our belief in the accepted power of sight.

The prologue also presents a parodistic sexual metaphor that prefigures the sexual motifs in the rest of the film. One might even say that the severing of the eye is a rape of the spectator's vision, an idea that Buñuel corroborates in a later film, *The Young One*, when he prefaces the girl's rape with the same image of clouds crossing that traditional symbol of virginity, the moon. By forcing us to view unwittingly the razor's penetration of the flesh, Buñuel commits a violent transgression against our desire to protect our privacy. With seeming impunity Buñuel forces upon the spectator a visual rape that affirms the violent freedom of desire and play beyond all categories of good and evil. Like the Marquis de Sade, whom the surrealists placed in their pantheon of revered heroes, Buñuel uses a razor that cuts in two directions, for his ironic celebration of the absolute freedom of desire also recognizes the primordial violence attached to that freedom. Closer to Georges Bataille than to such surrealists as Breton and Eluard in this respect, Buñuel has never had recourse to the Platonic myth of original unity to explain the fascination of desire. Rather, as Buñuel has consistently shown throughout his work, desire's power lies in its capacity to transgress against those repressive categories of reason and logic that would order our world or, perhaps more precisely, our representation of the world.

Buñuel's ironic destruction of the logic of filmic narration and his celebration of violent desire point to what is perhaps of ultimate importance in this prologue and in a good deal of Buñuel's subsequent work. This celebration of violence is a supreme example of black humor. André Breton underscored the importance of black humor for surrealism when, in the introduction to his *Anthologie de l'humour noir*, he described this form of humor as "a way of affirming, beyond the absolute revolt of adolescence and the inner revolt of the adult age, a superior revolt of the mind."[2] Breton sees black humor as a liberating form of narcissism by which the self refuses suffering in the exterior world by converting this suffering into a source of pleasure.

Pleasure and revolt combine when the poet, to paraphrase Breton, overcomes the temptation to solipsism (or the romantic temptation to be interested in only the "caprices of his own personality") by turning to the "accidents" of the exterior world and declaring the superiority of the self over these accidents. Black humor, as a form of revolt, brings about a dialectical reconciliation of the subjective world with the necessities of the objective world. This is also the goal of all surrealist activity: to abolish the distinction between the objective and the subjective, between the repressive working of the reality principle and the pleasure principle. According to Breton, it is by converting the pain that necessity inflicts upon the self into pleasure that black humor brings about the liberation of desire. Or, by shifting the focus slightly, one can see that black humor is another form of play that aims at subverting the imperious claims of the reality principle.

This is, of course, a very Hegelian argument and will probably strike even the most sympathetic Anglo-Saxon as a bit extravagant. Yet the severed eye is an example of the intolerable and the unacceptable, and it would seem that the spectator must react to it in one of two ways. Either the viewer must feel that he himself, as well as the girl, is the victim of utter dementia, or the viewer must force himself to see this mutilation with a certain distance and with this distance gain an ironic perspective. This perspective allows him to view the aggression as a willed affirmation by which Buñuel converts the unthinkable act into an object of contemplation and, by its humor, of pleasure. Buñuel's black humor—which many critics simply attribute to his Spanish heritage—is a sign of surrealist revolt throughout his work, and it seems emblematic that he should begin his first film by an act of pure rebellion. When, in *L'Age d'Or*, a gamekeeper uses a shotgun to put an end to his playful son's bothering him or the Duke of Blangis finishes an orgy by raping and murdering an innocent thirteen-year-old; when, in *Los Olvidados*, a group of adolescents assault a legless cripple and reduce him to a squirming insect; when, in these and many other examples, innocence must bear an aggression whose very gratuitous-ness seems intolerable, then we see that Buñuel has never given up the form of subversion that marks the beginning of *Un Chien andalou*.

2. André Breton, *Anthologie de l'humour noir*, p. 16. (All translations are mine, unless otherwise indicated.)

Having experienced this most direct initiation to black humor, what can the spectator who has opened his eyes now expect? Buñuel offered a key to the rules of the game he and Dali played in making the film when he, in a typically laconic fashion, remarked to François Truffaut, "Dali and I would select gags and objects that would happen to come to mind. And we rejected without mercy everything that might mean something. I have kept this taste for the irrational."[3] The systematic avoidance of meaning—which sets up the formal rules of the game—does not mean that there is no sense to the series of irrationally associated images that follow the prologue. For the destruction of logical meaning is, indeed, a form of sense, conveying Buñuel's contempt for the traditional constructs that purport to represent reality. Moreover, it allows Buñuel to play with typical surrealist themes while maintaining a critical distance from them that shows that no form of discourse, not even antidiscourse, is exempt from his critical scrutiny. Let us then turn to these images and offer some observations concerning what they present the awakened viewer.

After the prologue, a new title informs the spectator in search of meaning that it is suddenly eight year later; it is probably unlikely that the viewer, in spite of the parodistic context, will be entirely able to resist the temptation to impose a chronological framework on the following images: Pierre Batcheff, wearing white cuffs, a cap with white wings, a collar, and a skirt over his suit, with a striped box hanging from his neck, pedals a shaky bicycle up to a building. Inside sits the same woman whose eye has just (eight years ago) been cut in half. Buñuel uses an appropriate number of dissolves and superimpositions to pay pseudohomage to the Impressionist conventions used to represent movement and the passage of time. These techniques, moreover, endow the bizarre cyclist with the aura of a cinematic epic hero.

Sensing the presence of the Beguine-appearing rider, the woman—both eyes intact—goes to her window, looks down, and sees the cyclist come to a stop and topple over on his head for no apparent reason. The heroine descends and, finding the cyclist with his head on the curb, begins to kiss him passionately. In this brief sequence, Buñuel has succeeded in parodying the spectator's desire for continuity, motivation, and verisimilitude, as well as certain specifically cinematic mimetic devices such as cutting and the various motivations it presumes, both narrative and psychological. Indeed, the woman's rising and looking down in surprise is a parody of the type of cutting used in

3. François Truffaut, "Rencontre avec Luis Buñuel," p. 5.

L'Herbier's *Feu Mathias Pascal* when the young heroine looks down into the street from her window and is frightened by the appearance of the sinister medium, Caporale. The high-angle shot, linking the inner world with the outer world (as in the Vermeer paintings that the Buñuel heroine is looking at), is usually motivated by some form of revelation that the filmmaker wishes to dramatize. But Buñuel uses shooting angle and cutting so that they turn against themselves, serving only to underscore the absurd revelation of a cyclist who gratuitously falls on his head.

The next sequence, if use of a vocabulary dealing with dramatic units is permissible here, continues the film's erotic drama. The woman takes a striped tie from the enigmatic striped box and, replacing a plain tie that was lying on the bed with the cyclist's frilly cuffs and stiff collar, creates an ensemble that seemingly outlines an invisible man. The striped tie suddenly knots itself in place, which leaves the woman rather pensive. Perhaps she is wondering what Freudian critics are going to make of this scene, or why this type of trick photography, which amused the circus crowds that went to see the films by Méliès and Cohl before the war, is still being used in the cinema of the twenties. Perhaps Buñuel, thinking again about his Impressionist contemporaries, is showing the gratuitous nature of the various tricks they used in the name of subjective realism. By isolating the photographic trick *qua* trick, he lays bare the arbitrary nature of the attempt to assign a mimetic function to a cinematic device. Buñuel may also be recalling the surrealist contention that the true workings of the mind must be expressed by the "marvelous" inherent in the quotidian.

When the young woman discovers that the cyclist is present in the room, fixedly contemplating a busy stream of ants that are crawling from a hole in his hand, she becomes quite properly alarmed. Dali's obsession with ants and Buñuel's training as an entomologist have been offered as alternate explanations for this image. But this hardly explains the image's function, which is essentially to create what we might call a surrealist figure, one, moreover, that is quite parodistic. The figure is created by the juxtaposition of the incongruous and the verisimilar. Here, confronted with the astonishing image, the young woman reacts with alarm, which is portrayed in terms of the most banal conventions of psychological realism. One might also see an attempt to create another surrealist figure in the following images, where a close-up of a sunbathing woman's armpit dissolves into a close-up of a sea urchin. Such a juxtaposition could be likened to a surrealist simile, in which the bringing together of disparate images creates a dislocation of our normal way of viewing relations and reveals the marvelous. However, in the case of Buñuel, it seems more likely that this montage is really a negation of montage, a parody of the kind of poetic montage that dominated much filmmaking in the twenties.

Another dissolve, offering a pseudoassurance of continuity, brings the viewer back to the street, where a rather androgynous person is using a stick to poke a severed hand that lies on the pavement. The motif of mutilation, with all its sexual connotations, is thus picked up again, and the sexual reverberations seem to affect even the crowd that gathers. A policeman puts the hand in the ever-recurrent striped box and gives it to the androgyne who, now left alone, remains immobile in the street until he is struck by a large car and forced to drop the box. This final mutilation has so aroused our cyclist hero that he turns on the heroine, who retreats until she is cornered. As the amorous cyclist begins to fondle her breasts, Buñuel again parodies some standard mimetic devices of the times, for the camera suddenly reveals the woman's breasts as bare, and then they turn into nude buttocks, which the hero rubs with great relish. This revelation of the invisible, satirizing the "subjective" use of the cinematic image, is appropriately accompanied by an "objective" image of exteriorized desire, for a close-up reveals Batcheff's eyes convulsively rolled back in lust while blood trickles from the corner of his mouth. The attack is completed when he assaults the heroine with two dead-donkey-laden pianos that are further encumbered with symbolic, though rather surprised, priests.

After a return to the ant colony, Buñuel offers an even broader attack on the Impressionists' attempt to introduce ethical seriousness and psychological conflict into cinema. One model for this kind of subjective mimesis would again appear to be L'Herbier's *Feu Mathias Pascal*, especially the scene in which Mathias comes face to face with his old identity in the form of his double and, striving to rid himself of the past, attempts to shoot down his old, mocking identity. This trick photography, springing from an attempt to create a first-person narrative, is of course an effort to transpose directly the grammar of verbal narration into film. Drawing on this scene, Buñuel presents his solution to the problem of subjective narration by placing his cyclist hero in bed and then, with another pseudonarrative signpost, telling us that it is "Towards three in the morning." Another man appears, enters the room, and throws the cyclist's frills, including the striped box, out the window. The stranger, who is revealed to be the hero's double, forces the cyclist to stand against the wall as if for punishment, while another title offers a pseudo-flashback by announcing, "Sixteen years before." The double takes two books from a school desk and gives them to his seemingly penitent, less mature version. But the books turn into pistols, and the double is gunned down with all the flourish one would expect from a good Western.

Buñuel is parodying several modes of subjective mimesis here. In the flashback, the fiction of an image representing a past event is brought under attack, for a cinematic image, regardless of the conventions that designate it as a memory image, will always be an image in the here and now, in all its fullness as the present. The confrontation of the hero and his double, of course, is supposed to represent something akin to the statement "I am suffering a conflict"; Buñuel brings this convention to its pseudological conclusion by allowing one half to gun down the other. By opening the sequence with his hero in bed, Buñuel also plays with the cinematic dream convention in which images are designated as subjectively representing what a dreamer perceives. In these instances, the parody is not of devices used to represent a subjective point of view, or something supposedly seen from a protagonist's point of view. Rather, the parody aims at conventions that would designate an image as an entirely interiorized subjective image, one that only the protagonist who we see on the screen could take cognizance of. This point is worth stressing, since many critics have considered *Un Chien andalou* to be the representation of a dream. Yet the force of the film's attack is surely directed against any attempt to endow the image with some mimetic convention that says "here we are now in the head of a person undergoing ethical or psychological conflict" or "now we are in the head of someone who is dreaming." Images, Buñuel seems to imply, are in and of the world and are not to be found elsewhere.

By traditional association, death is related to eros, and Buñuel, still playing with the spectator's desire for some kind of coherence, next cuts to a meadow, where the dying double tries to grasp the back of a seminude beauty as he falls. She fades from the shot, and Wagner's *Liebestod* (played at the original showing and in the later sound version of the film) offers even more thematic coherence as it accompanies the funeral procession that gathers to carry away the corpse. The music is essential here, more so than the tango that accompanies the earlier attempted rape, for it is the music that endows the irrational images with a pseudomeaning. This use of music foreshadows

Buñuel's use of a Brahms symphony in *Las Hurdes*, in destructive counterpoint with the images presenting a world gone totally awry. In *Las Hurdes* the juxtaposition of the heroic melodic line and images of sickly dwarfs transforms that travelogue into another, more subtle display of black humor. In *Un Chien andalou* the use of rhapsodic Wagnerian motifs transforms the images by seemingly offering them a dimension of thematic coherence—until we realize that the music has meaning only in itself and that it is only because of convention that we attempt to force its meaning to adhere to the gratuitous image.

After a close-up of a death's-head moth—death permeates the world of eros—and more parody of trick photography, particularly of that used in recognition scenes, Buñuel offers his final assault on the logic of continuity by having the heroine leave the room where she has again found herself with the cyclist. Noting that he has taken the hair from her armpit and is now using it for a mouth, she angrily walks through the door onto a beach, where she joins another man. The newly formed couple walk together along the water's edge, passing by the dirty remains of the cyclist's frills, including the ubiquitous striped box. Buñuel appeals again to our conditioned reflexes by invoking the principle of genre that states that a romance always has a happy ending. The narration seems, therefore, to have a denouement, for the couple hold each other, and the title, "In the spring," seems to offer romance's promise of bliss. Buñuel's final exercise in cruelty, however, is to conclude the film with a shot of the couple buried up to their chests in sand while the sun burns them and swarms of insects devour them. This extraordinary image is another example of black humor, but even more, it is a final image of the narrative quest. In this respect, one inevitably thinks of Beckett, in whose work the search for structures of meaning can merely end up in the muck. There is, of course, a surrealist vitality in Buñuel that points to a belief in a realm of discourse beyond the conventional structures of representation. But that realm of discourse has perhaps yet to be invented.

The parodistic destruction of mimetic devices in *Un Chien andalou* points to the first level of interpretation of the film. It should be apparent, after this discussion, what skepticism one should grant the usual critical approach to the film, which labels it some kind of dream representation and then searches for a latent discourse to which various symbols give rise. Buñuel has perhaps encouraged such interpretations by making comments on cinema such as the following:

> Cinema is a magnificent and dangerous weapon if it is wielded by a free spirit. It is the best instrument for expressing the world of dreams, emotions, and instinct. By the very nature of the way it functions the mechanism that creates cinematic images is the one that, of all means of human expression, recalls best the work of the mind during sleep. Film seems to be an involuntary imitation of dream.[4]

By an "involuntary imitation" Buñuel does not mean, however, that he seeks to transcribe dream images in his films or to find mimetic devices that will allow him to represent dreams. Rather, he is stating that film can be a mimetic means for representing the world of repressed desire. In addition, the way in which one perceives a film has some features in common with the way in which one perceives a dream. Moreover, film can make use of the irrational associations and transformations that one finds in dreams. These are three distinct points, and if Buñuel chooses to abolish the principle of noncontradiction in his works, this does not mean that he is seeking to represent a dream world, the one realm of our normal experience where the principle of noncontradiction does not hold sway. It would seem more appropriate to say that he frequently borrows from the rhetoric of dream discourse in order to contest the more constrictive rhetoric of traditional narrative discourse.

The importance that surrealism gave to dreams as a privileged mode of experience should not be construed as an interest in dreams for their own sake. Dreams are of interest only insofar as they offer access to the world of repressed desire. Exemplary in this respect is the treatment Germaine Dulac gave to Artaud's scenario *La Coquille et le Clergyman*. Artaud had set forth in this scenario an irrational series of transformations that would, as he put it, create "a stream of images that would communicate with the soul."[5] Interested, like most Impressionists, in finding ways of reproducing subjective reality (compare her *Smiling Madame Beudet*, with its attempt to reproduce daily fantasies of an unhappy wife) and perhaps not knowing what to make of Artaud's images, Dulac decided to convert the scenario into a "dream by Antonin Artaud" in order to justify the script's irrational incongruities. But presenting a series of irrational associations is not sufficient to represent a dream, and so Dulac used certain conventions that purport to represent dream perception and designate the image as a dream image. In the film's first

4. Quoted in Freddy Buache, *Luis Buñuel*, special issue of *Premier Plan*, no. 13 (1960):77.
5. Antonin Artaud, *Oeuvres complètes*, 3:77. Compare p. 23, where Artaud states explicitly that his film is not a dream.

sequence, for example, the camera moves forward down a long, empty hall, which, one might suppose, represents the descent into the unconscious.

After passing through a door, the camera reveals Artaud's clergyman sitting in a dark, vaulted cellar, busily filling beakers with a substance contained in a large seashell and then breaking the glass containers. This image and its dark symbolism have in effect, however, been placed in parentheses by the initial camera movement, which has told the spectator that he need not be dismayed, for this is to be taken as only a dream. Dulac appears to have been afraid of presenting Artaud's images directly, without all the cinematic claptrap—prolonged dissolves, superimpositions, distortions, bizarre cutting—that the Impressionists used for the mimesis of the psychic and the subjective. Dulac, in a sense, reduced Artaud's struggle to overcome the limits of rational mimetic conventions to a mere dream. Not too surprisingly, Artaud, Breton, Desnos, and other surrealists tried to break up the first showing of the film.

Once one decides that *Un Chien andalou* is an imitation of dream reality, then it almost automatically follows that the proper critical approach is to apply the science of the irrational and to interpret the film in psychoanalytic terms. Psychoanalytic concepts offer a useful approach to the film, since they point to a level of symbolic discourse that is present in the film, though not in the latent manner that many critics would have it. For I should contend that Buñuel and Dali have, in a completely self-conscious fashion, used the symbolism of psychoanalytic discourse to create another level of discourse that they have, in turn, systematically subverted.

A typical psychoanalytic interpretation of *Un Chien andalou* might begin by positing a general principle of coherence in function of which the symbols are organized. This principle might be that of adolescent sexual development or of sexual frustration.[6] Using such a principle to explain the images in the film, the interpreter could then construe the film as beginning with an invocation of the castration complex or perhaps the sexual act. According to such an interpretation, it might appear that the main character has not overcome his castration complex, which explains his subsequent erratic behavior toward the girl. One might also see infantile narcissism at work. The

6. In the following résumé I have drawn mainly upon François Piazza, "Considérations psychanalytiques sur le 'chien andalou,' " pp. 147–56; and Mondragon, "Comment j'ai compris le chien andalou," p. 9.

hero's striped box is a feminine symbol that could be indicative of a mother fixation, another possible cause for his rather puerile behavior. Few critics would have trouble recognizing Dali's influence in the choice to portray mutilated hands, for these are masturbation symbols. Most critics would also recognize the character's homosexual tendencies, as evinced by his fascination with the androgyne.

In Batcheff's response when the androgyne is run over, for instance, one critic can see regression to an infantile stage: "Severed hands, the mutilated body, these are so many images that reinforce the sadico-anal eroticism of the character who, nonetheless, is trying to overcome his inhibitions"[7]—as his attack on the girl demonstrates. The donkey-laden pianos with their melons and priests are symbols of inhibitions in the super-ego that, with the castration complex, prevent the cyclist from finding normal expression of his sexuality. Hence the return of the ants. The scene with the pistols and the double again shows that the protagonist is "sexually disarmed," for the falling double fails to seize the nude woman. The displaced hair, leaving the woman's armpit to replace Batcheff's mouth, would portray the woman's dissatisfaction with her partner, for the suggested oral sex is inadequate—or perhaps this is another image of sadistic humiliation. Finally, the lovers buried in the sand, surrounded by insects, would show "the obsessive omnipotence of desire and its fundamental lack of satisfaction."[8]

This type of interpretation indicates the kinds of symbols that one can easily find in *Un Chien andalou*. However, the importance of these symbols is not that they express some latent psychic reality but rather that they are posited in a self-conscious way as the elements of a filmic discourse. This is, of course, a form of parody that aims again at a ludic subversion of this kind of discourse. It is this self-conscious dimension that marks *Un Chien andalou* as a privileged moment in this history of film. With this surrealist incursion into cinema filmic discourse becomes subject to the same kind of self-criticism and ironic subversion that the modernist notion of self-consciousness had already applied to literature and painting.

In modern terms, self-consciousness is a reflexive form of creation in which the work is endowed with indices that constantly point to the work as an artifact. The work thus contains a perspective on itself, and this perspective, superimposed on the naive perspective of normal vision that wishes to accept

7. Piazza, "Considérations psychanalytiques," p. 151.
8. Ibid., p. 154.

the work as an authentic form of representation, creates the double perspective or vision that is the basis for modern irony. Surely this is one of the marking features of modernism: ironic consciousness of mimesis is raised to the same level of importance as the act of mimesis itself. Surrealism, in its joyful subversion of all fixed forms of representation, perhaps goes one step further in this direction when it finally proposes that this ironic consciousness is the only worthy artistic act that the poet in quest of liberation can undertake.

Buñuel angrily declared that few had understood *Un Chien andalou*, for none had seen that it was a "desperate call for murder."[9] Reading this, we can perhaps understand the urgency Buñuel felt in attempting to destroy our naive acceptance that film has the capacity to order the world through some objective mode of mimesis. *Un Chien andalou* is an attempted assassination of that belief. Beyond this attack on discourse, we must also see the film as another manifestation of the surrealist terrorism that, they hoped, would lead to the purging of consciousness. The surrealist apocalypse would be the eruption of pure consciousness, undivided, rid of all categories, at one with itself as a self-sufficient form of experience. Maurice Blanchot has described this surrealist aim in the following terms:

> Surrealist *experience* (it seems to me) aims at the point of divergence from which all knowledge, as does every limited affirmation of life, escapes from itself in order to be exposed to the neutral force of disarrangement. Surrealist *experience* is the experience of experience, whether it be in a theoretical or a practical form: experience that disarranges and disarranges itself, as it develops and, in developing, interrupts itself. It is in this way that surrealism, poetry itself, is the experience of thought itself.[10]

One may well doubt the success of any attempt to arrive at such a form of self-posession, but there is little doubt that *Un Chien andalou* admirably demonstrates the power of disarrangement. For this reason it will remain a touchstone for testing the limits of filmic experience.

9. Luis Buñuel, Presentation of Scenario of *Un Chien andalou*, *La Révolution surréaliste*, no. 12 (1932).
10. Maurice Blanchot, "Le demain joueur," p. 882.

The Surrealist Film:
Man Ray and the Limits of Metaphor

Man Ray's first short films, *Retour à la raison* (1923) and *Emak Bakia* (1926), are essentially Dadaist negations, exercises in antiesthetics, that are a part of the destruction of forms that the avant-garde undertook in the first part of the 1920s. *Retour à la raison*, whose ironic title underscores its subversive intent, is perhaps most notable for having been shown at the Soirée of the Bearded Heart, a festivity that marked Dada's decision to put an end to itself. *Emak Bakia*, coming after Dada's ultimate nihilistic act, resembles other attempts of the time to create abstract films, especially in its use of juxtapositions and superimpositions suggesting collage. It was only in 1928, the same year in which Buñuel made *Un Chien andalou*, that Man Ray achieved what we might call a purely surrealist creation in making *L'Etoile de mer (The Starfish)*. As such, the film offers the film critic and theoretician one of the most fruitful examples of how surrealism, immediately before the advent of sound, tried to push filmic discourse to one extreme limit of its possibilities.

In his autobiography, *Self-Portrait*, as well as in the film's credits, Man Ray states that he "saw" his film after hearing the surrealist poet Robert Desnos read a poem, presumedly one called "L'Etoile de mer." This suggests that the film may be a work of collaboration, perhaps a collective work, that one can consider to be an illustration to the second degree of a primary surrealist text. The film does contain some motifs found in poems that Desnos was writing at the time (see *Les ténèbres* of 1927 or *Sirène-Anémone* of 1929). Yet the existence of such a poem in a finished form is doubtful. Man Ray's description of the poem in *Self-Portrait* reads more like a résumé of his own film, and one might well suspect that, rather than a completed poem, Desnos gave him a certain number of themes, images, and perhaps tropes that the photographer decided to transform into a film. The importance of the poet's contribution, whatever it may have been, is that it orients our viewing of *L'Etoile de mer* as a form of poetical activity. The film does not aim at the mimesis of episodic experience. In fact, it seeks to represent nothing at all in a referential sense. Rather, the film seeks to communicate a certain number of revelations that spring from the creation of filmic figures and from a series of dislocations of conventional cinematic discourse.

These revelations and dislocations are predicated on a thematic coherence that is not unlike what one might find in a musical composition. Before addressing the question of the creation of filmic figures, we should examine the specific motifs that make up the film. These motifs are created by the repetition of images, and one can say that in this type of film, much as in surrealist poetry, the initial level of meaning is generated almost exclusively by recurrence. The most obvious example is the star-starfish motif that the film presents as its opening images. This image recurs most frequently in the film and dominates the thematic modulations. A description of the film also shows that in spite of the great diversity of images, a rather small number of motifs are generated in it. Most images are associated with the themes of eros and anti-eros and with the theme of the void or desolation.

After opening the film with the image of the star, Man Ray seems to place his work between brackets by offering the image of a window opening laterally. This shot takes on its full significance at the end of the film when we see the window closing. This suggests that the filmic space lies in a realm of desire. It is a mythic space, for, in modernist terms, the locus of revelation must lie beyond our daily realm of ordinary time and causality. By *modernist* we mean the aesthetic canon that held that the revelation of privileged moments of one sort or another was the essential function of art. In this sense, surrealism shared many axioms with artists as diverse as Proust and Joyce, Rilke and Valéry. For a better understanding of this notion of revelation, one might compare this way of bracketing the film with the way that, in *Le Sang d'un Poète*, Cocteau uses the opening and closing shot of a falling smokestack to place the filmic space outside of time. In both Cocteau's and Ray's films, then, the filmmaker has clearly indicated that the film's revelation lies beyond the realm of realistic mimesis. The films thus aim at the communication of states that are not subject to the laws of ordinary reality. In *L'Etoile de mer*, one might well argue, the locus of revelation is the realm of the repressed, for the next shot presents a blurred image of a man and woman together—the archetypical couple of surrealist erotic mythology. The distortion that Ray achieved by blurring the image should not be considered an expressionist device for representing some form of subjective image, since narrative point of view is of no import here. It would appear that the image, as Man Ray suggested, is distorted for compositional effects, perhaps as a correlative to the force of eros and the theme of the pervasiveness of desire.[1]

In a rather humoristic fashion, the theme of anti-eros, more especially the fear of eros and of woman, finds expression in the title "Woman's teeth are such charming objects," which is followed by a shot of a very seductive pair of legs and then completed by the title "That one should only see them at the moment of love." The image of legs, coming after the title has announced teeth, is comic in its subversion of our expectations, and there is a double comic overlap when the viewer realizes that the association of teeth and eros is a primordial expression of man's fear of female sexuality. The ambiguous relation between man's desire and his ability to realize his erotic goal finds a humorous variant when the man, after accompanying the woman to a room, watches her undress and then, rather improbably, wishes her "Adieu." The following title, in an untranslatable pun, again stresses what fear is attached to desire: "Si belle! Cybèle?" ("So beautiful! Cybèle?") For Cybèle is not only the earth goddess who represents the sum of natural forces but also the Phrygian Aphrodite, an erotic deity associated with castration rites.

Theme and countertheme then find an associated motif in what we might call the expression of void or desolation, as when, in the following shot, Ray's camera offers a long high-angle shot of a smokestack that rises with phallic rigidity above a deserted street. The composition recalls, though in darker tonalities, Chirico's scenes of lyrical emptiness, in which stark exterior forms serve to connote a feeling of inner lack.

These three motifs dominate the rest of the film and are consistently generated by the recurrent images. For example, the woman is next seen selling newspapers; this seemingly "objective" image acquires erotic values when Ray juxtaposes it with an image that reveals only the woman's eyes (the beautiful eyes of Ray's mistress Kiki), for the rest of her face is covered by a newspaper. The newspaper image thus takes on associative values within the thematic network of erotic motifs. Something of the same process seems to be at work when we see the starfish in, for example, the images in which the couple contemplate the starfish in a jar and after which Ray uses an iris shot to set the enigmatic echinoderm in strange relief. If the starfish is to be taken as a correlative for desire, then Ray has worked a dislocation of normal filmic relations that appears to be a parody of cinematic narrative conventions. Since

1. Man Ray, *Self-Portrait*, p. 277.

the couple stare at the beast, this correlative appears within the field of vision of those whose inner desires might be somehow associated with the aquatic animal. In surrealist terms, this dislocation has allowed the marvelous to invade the couple's world. Subsequent shots of the starfish, including a close-up in which its arms gently undulate and the myriad ossicles pulsate rhythmically, also seem to endow it with erotic connotations.

The frenzy of desire is also reflected as the man pursues blowing newspapers. The frenetic camera movement emphasizes the erotic motif, as does the appearance of stars in the headline of a paper the man seizes by chance. The relation of movement and eros is also stressed in the next series of rapidly cut shots that, taken first from a moving train, offer images of a train, a ship, a city harbor, and finally, the image of a flower. Eros seems to permeate these shots of the exterior world, of industrial civilization, for in this sequence the forward movement mimes the quest that leads to the desired woman, who can be easily possessed in the form of a flower.

As Xavière Gautier has pointed out in her feminist indictment of surrealism, the *femme-fleur* (woman-flower) association, though hardly unique to surrealism, presents one surrealist view of the feminine ideal as a passive being who waits to be plucked.[2] In other variations on this motif, Ray also celebrates the woman as a "flower in glass" and a "flower in flesh." Through a series of associations, the wish to possess the desired as a crystalline presence leads to a split-screen collage, consisting of three parallel rows of four images each, which contain crystal objects that seem to shimmer as a projection of the desire to possess and to store away. This collage (which may also be a parody of Abel Gance's Polyvision and its multiple juxtapositions within a single screen image) contains two starfish and, in a conspicuous position, a sword whose recurrent movements in and out of a sheath leave little doubt as to its fantasy function.

After the collage segment, the starfish begins to appear at a more rapid rate, in a Cezanne-like still life, on a book in the woman's boudoir, in another close-up. It seems to draw together various shots setting forth erotic motifs, such as the woman wearing a mask, one of the surrealists' favorite *objets trouvés*, or the apparition of stripes on the man's hands, perhaps an image of solitary pleasure. Another verbal pun, "Il faut battre les morts quand ils sont froids" ("You must beat the dead when they are cold"), ironically foreshadows the eros-death motif. The woman climbs a staircase, a shining knife in hand;

2. Xavière Gautier, *Surréalisme et sexualité*, pp. 98–115.

the starfish is then superimposed on the knife. As the American filmmaker Maya Deren subsequently remembered in her *Meshes of the Afternoon*, the knife image combines suggestions of death and erotic symbolism, as well as implications of mutilation. A dark image of the Santé prison brings us back to the third theme, that of emptiness, and completes this series of modulations through a tonal contrast that sets forth a harsh image of restriction and confinement. Related to this dismal image of failure is the poet's cry:

> And if you find
> On this earth
> A woman
> With sincere love. . .

Fear and suggested impotence give way to a melancholy lament.

The camera moves from the prison to frame the sky and constellations of stars. These stars reintroduce the erotic motif; at the same time they are associated with the black void and seem to show how nature itself joins these themes. The following images of running water, trees, and flames rising above the woman's face are so many images that, not unlike those in Paul Eluard's poetry, generate the erotic themes and demonstrate the pervasiveness of desire.

This lyric development is broken off by another comic evocation of the fear motif, for suddenly a female warrior, perhaps a Valkyrie if not the Phrygian Cybèle, armed with an ambiguous spear, stands forth against an incongruous white backdrop. This Bacchante-like image of destruction can seemingly only lead back to the world of emptiness, of nonfulfillment, and so Ray's camera offers a final view of the deserted street in an industrial quarter, though he now reverses the terms of rigidity, and a low-angle shot is made by tilting the camera up the smokestack. The shot seems to call forth the funeral overtones of the surrealist title that follows: "The sun, one foot in the stirrup, perches a nightingale in a crepe veil."

The final series of modulations begins with a blurred shot of Kiki, quite voluptuously presented in the nude, while the accompanying title assures that "You aren't dreaming." The erotic quest takes a new twist, however, when a second man enters the scene and Kiki leaves with him. The first man can only watch, perhaps left with the thought of "How beautiful she was." The presence of the starfish, however, seems to force him to come to terms with his present desire, for starfish and the desired mistress are joined in a series of close-up shots in which the title states "How beautiful she *is*." Kiki is doubly removed, however, for we must view her through a glass pane that suddenly shatters. This ambivalent image of destruction seems to be the final correlative for eros and anti-eros conjoined. Desire and fear, want and impossibility, violent yearning and frustration, all seem to emerge from this fragmented image as Kiki turns away, leaving us to face the glass window as it closes off the filmic space, the mythic space of eternal desire, of repressed eros.

The thematic coherence that characterizes *L'Etoile de mer* undoubtedly accounts for critics' generally laudatory attitude toward the film. For all the arbitrary transitions and associations that one can find in the film, every element in the work does seem to enter into a thematic relationship and thus acquire a level of sense. In terms of filmic communication, there is a transmission of meaning that is interrupted only when the viewer fails to see how an image might be integrated into the patterns that are generated by thematic concerns. This break in communication will most probably occur in the case of the starfish image, for it is difficult at times to see how it enters into an associative relationship with the other elements in the film. In these moments the image usually appears as an incongruously juxtaposed element. Conceivably, of course, the image could be viewed in terms of its own denotation, in terms of its immanent meaning, but since this is not a documentary about aquatic life, this way of viewing the image would also be a break in communication.

This rupture in thematic coherence points, however, to what is the film's more profound ambition, namely, the creation of surrealist metaphors capable of conveying the kind of revelation the surrealists called the marvelous. The mere orchestration of themes has never been the goal of surrealist activity. Rather, surrealist practice aims at the dislocation of normal relationships so that traditional logical categories and modes of representation no longer hinder our seeing new realities or prevent us from receiving revelation. In the twenties it was the creation of metaphor that carried the major burden in this task.

To paraphrase a standard rhetorical definition, a metaphor effects a transference in which an unknown is clarified and described in terms of a known. This is, in one sense, a rational, binary operation. Such a rhetorical definition, of course, applies to verbal tropes, and one might well maintain that a notion derived from binary verbal transferences can only be applied metaphorically to iconic representations. Jean Mitry, for one, has constantly maintained that film can at best present only comparative associations, since film lacks the specific means to establish comparisons and transfers between images. In fact, according to Mitry, most of what we call cinematic metaphors are really metonymical relations that work through their substitution of one image for another in terms of their spatial contiguity along what one can call, using linguistic terminology, the film's syntagmatic axis. In particular, most filmic tropes are synecdoches (a part represents a whole).[3] (Think of the floating corpse that, at the end of Rossellini's *Paisan*, represents the desolation war has brought, or of the famous balloon that in Lang's *M* symbolizes the child's rape.)

Before considering the surrealist practice of metaphor, I should state that in my opinion Mitry's view of film figures is somewhat limited, if correct in the essentials. In our concrete viewing experience, however, we often do recognize metaphorical statements or, perhaps more precisely, similes, since it does seem true that there are no filmic syntactical structures that allow a viewer to differentiate between identification and comparison. Consider, for example, Chaplin's juxtaposition in *Modern Times* of a crowd rushing into a subway entrance with a herd of sheep; or, in *The Strike*, Eisenstein's showing first a shot of workers massed together and then an image of cattle being slaughtered. There seems to be scarcely any other way to describe these juxtapositions than to call them a form of analogy in which a transference of sense takes place, thus creating a kind of metaphorical statement. In semantic terms, however, it would appear that these juxtapositions have meanings only insofar as the metaphor is derived from a context. In fact, the narrative structure of the film often provides the context that endows the juxtaposition with metaphorical significance. Without the context provided by a narrative structure, the viewer might well be at a loss as to what to do with this kind of rupture in continuity.

These cinematic similes are, it must be said, rather limited in semantic depth, and that is perhaps indicative of the limits that the very nature of film discourse imposes on the creation of figures. In one sense these figures appear to be little more than *fioriture* for specific contextual situations. Even a more elaborate analogy, such as Pudovkin creates in *Mother* with parallel montage, juxtaposing shots of demonstrating workers and the springtime breakup of the ice in the Neva, is ultimately generated by a narrative context and could probably not stand as a trope without this contextual support. This is a distinguishing difference between verbal tropes and cinematic figures: Lan-

3. Jean Mitry, *Esthétique et psychologie du cinéma*, 2:381–83, 446–48.

guage can generate figures independent of narrative structures, whereas, given the indefinite meanings that the juxtaposition of iconic representations can have, a cinematic metaphor can be created only within the confines of a very specific contextualizing structure, usually a narrative structure that informs the viewer's perception and clearly points out the "reading" to be given to the juxtaposition.

L'Etoile de mer has virtually no narrative structure. It thus forces us to confront one of the limits of cinematic discourse insofar as it attempts to create a prolonged metaphorical discourse. In *L'Etoile de mer* Ray and Desnos have discarded the rational use of metaphor as a form of binary transference and have attempted to juxtapose the star image with all the images in the film in order to create what we see as a prolonged surrealist simile. The juxtaposition of the starfish and any other given image—woman, knife, book, and so forth—is, in effect, an attempt to dislocate normal associative relations and analogies, with the goal of revealing those new relations that defy restrictive forms of logical discourse and thus reveal the marvelous.

The skeptical viewer can find the archetype for the surrealist simile in the writings of the nineteenth-century French poet Lautréamont, whose *Chants de Maldoror* constituted the equivalent of a surrealist breviary. The surrealists especially favored his simile "as beautiful as the fortuitous encounter of a sewing machine and an umbrella on a dissecting table." This type of simile was taken as the model for the kind of arbitrary juxtaposition that could reveal the marvelous—though Breton saw a profound motivation for the comparison in the latent content or sexual symbolism the objects possess.[4] To pursue our contention with regard to Ray's effort to create a metaphorical discourse, we might note that Ray himself pointed out Lautréamont's influence on him: "When I read Lautréamont I was fascinated by the unusual juxtapositions of unusual objects and words. And today I am inventing objects and painting astonishing things without giving the public any choice."[5] This statement is a reflection of the surrealist ideas about simile that Breton gave in paraphrasing the poet Reverdy in the *First Surrealist Manifesto*: "The more distant and true are the relations between the two juxtaposed realities the stronger the image will be—the greater will be its emotive power and its poetic reality."[6] It seems

4. André Breton, *Les Vases communicants*, p. 65.
5. *Surréalisme et cinéma I*, special issue of *Etudes cinématographiques*, no. 38–39 (First trimester, 1965):46. (All translations are mine, unless otherwise indicated.)
6. André Breton, *Manifestos of Surrealism*, trans. Richard Seaver and Helen R. Lane (Ann Arbor: University of Michigan Press, 1969), p. 20.

clear, then, that one of the overriding concerns of surrealism, at least in the twenties, was the creation of irrational similes that could overcome those logical antinomies that prevented "the true functioning of thought."

One might well ask if the mere presence in a film of juxtaposed objects or images of objects that share no rationally analogous properties can communicate a significance that is not normally associated with either one but is produced by the mere proximity of the objects. What happens, for example, when a starfish is juxtaposed through montage with a couple or explicitly superimposed on Kiki's face? There is no doubt that the effect is surprising, often comically so, for we anticipate some form of semantic or narrative coherence to prevail either in the choice of the sequence of images or in the composition of a single image. An iconic juxtaposition that merely results in incongruity is a way of subverting our expectations, and Ray often succeeds in producing comic surprises that may cause us to question our received notions about film perception. This subversion of our expectations does not necessarily, however, give rise to the creation of figures that can bring about poetic revelation.

This relative failure is instructive, for it would appear that it stems from an attempt to create iconic figures that are nearly literal transpositions of verbal tropes. When viewing Ray's juxtapositions, the viewer finds himself compelled to translate them into verbal equivalents in order to give these incongruities some semantic function (such as "beautiful as the encounter of a starfish and a book in a boudoir"). Yet there is nothing intrinsic to the flow of images that justifies this kind of translation into a figure. When, to give an example of a well-known surrealist metaphor, André Breton writes, "Ma femme à la langue d'hostie poignardée" (roughly, "My woman/wife with a tongue like a stabbed Host"), the reader confronts a normal syntactical structure that allows the juxtaposition of three unassociated elements—a tongue, a Host, and, implicitly, a knife. The syntagmatic relation here imposed by language binds together the three elements, seemingly guarantees the semantic possibility of their being juxtaposed, and thus allows the poetic communication. In a film, however, the viewer finds no equivalent syntactic structures that can relate the starfish and the knife or the book. At best the simple fact of spatial proximity and sequential juxtaposition may offer some form of syntagmatic relation in a film. But without syntax, this syntagma can offer no particularizing relations; it can only generate the simple semantic functions that contiguity allows. In short, film is not conducive to the creation of metaphor, especially the surrealist type of metaphor that depends upon syntax to weld together its irrational juxtapositions.

The only way film can compensate for the lack of syntax is through the presence of a narrative context or some other "semanticizing" structure that limits the possible readings an image can offer. Of course, Man Ray has refused to attempt narration in this film, for narration represents a sum of conventions that surrealists considered to be essentially a repository of bourgeois, repressive categories. In another sense Ray's failure to create a successful metaphor is emblematic of the impasse that surrealism reached toward the end of the twenties when neither automatic writing nor other techniques—including cinema—had produced the liberation of discourse that the surrealists aimed for in every area of their activity. Thus Breton could, in 1929, angrily disavow the search for analogical forms of discourse (and perhaps the rationality that this implies) and claim that the image in itself was to be the source of the marvelous:

> It seems to me that it is absolutely necessary to state it: the time of Baudelairian "correspondences" is finished, for they have been transformed into an odious critical commonplace. For my part I refuse to see anything in them other than the expression of a transitional idea, a rather timid one at that, and which, as far as today's poetic and pictorial experiments are concerned, no longer gives an account of anything. Oneiric values have definitely won out over all others, and I demand that anyone who would still refuse, for instance, to *see* a horse galloping on a tomato be considered a cretin. A tomato is also a child's balloon, since surrealism, I repeat, has abolished the word "like" [*comme*].[7]

Dream images, then, and no longer figures—analogical correspondences— were to offer access to the realm where the omnipotence of desire could realize itself in a world of magic. The thirties was to be the decade of the painters, while the poets often left surrealism to find a more satisfactory form of practice in political militancy.

In conclusion, however, one should point out that *L'Etoile de mer* does open up another direction for exploration of cinematic mimesis by expanding the way in which film uses images for purposes of connotation. Taken in itself, with no specifying contextual elements, the cinematic image seems to denote a universal rather than a particular. The mere repetition of the image, in this case the starfish, can, however, endow the image with many associative values

7. André Breton, *Point du jour* (Paris: Gallimard, Collection Idées, 1970), pp. 57–58.

or secondary associations that have nothing to do with its primary meaning. Perhaps cinema can more easily through repetition than by juxtaposition strip an image of its denotative function and force it to enter into an associative network of connotative values. This is not a metaphorical function, since no transference or even comparison is involved. As Ray uses this kind of recurrence, it becomes a surrealist form of dislocation, since there is no analogical reason why a starfish should be associated with a still life, a boudoir, a beautiful woman, the quest for eros, or anything else in the film, for that matter.

Few surrealist films have been made, and we might suggest that, in spite of the many assertions that film is a natural medium for surrealist activity, cinema may not be the royal road to the marvelous. True, as Buñuel has consistently demonstrated, film can disorder narrative and logical relations with a sense of concreteness that no other art form possesses; for cinema is above all an art of permutations. But cinema is also a form of discourse whose concrete mimetic nature allows neither the simple oneirism of the painted image nor the subversion of semantic codes in the way that language does. *L'Etoile de mer* is exemplary in this respect, for it both demonstrates a limit of filmic discourse and shows how the function of recurrence might lead to what Breton called the "superior reality of certain forms of previously neglected associations."[8] In this sense *L'Etoile de mer* might yet point to new modes of filmic representation.

8. Breton, *Manifestos of Surrealism*, p. 26.

Le Sang d'un Poète:
Film as Orphism

When the Viscount Charles de Noailles financed the production of Luis Buñuel's *L'Age d'Or* and of Jean Cocteau's *Le Sang d'un Poète*, it is unlikely that he knew he was subsidizing those two opposing modes of sensibility that have tended to dominate France in the twentieth century, total revolt and tragic acceptance. Indeed, there appears to be something contradictory in his putting up money, on the one hand, for a surrealist work that provoked riots on its first showing, and on the other hand, for a film that was, as Cocteau later put it, an "attack on the all-powerful surrealistic politics of the era."[1] In retrospect, however, both films are seminal works of the modernist imagination. In terms of what we might call surface ideology, the films are quite opposed. Yet both films share the same modernist aesthetic premises in that both aim at forms of revelation. The surrealists called the goal of their art the revelation of the *merveilleux*, whereas Cocteau saw the end of his poetic practice to be *dévoilement* or "unveiling":

> Toute ma poésie est là: Je décalque
> L'invisible (invisible à vous).[2]
> [All my poetry is there: I trace out
> The invisible (what's invisible to you).]

It is little wonder that the public tends to confuse Cocteau with the surrealists, since their *merveilleux* and his *dévoilement* often offer the same kind of irrational imagery. Yet, in a broader scope, it is useful to see that both Cocteau and the surrealists had goals that were not unlike Joyce's search for epiphany or Proust's disclosure of privileged moments. All these modernist artists saw their art as a form of ecstatic knowledge. Buñuel's iconoclastic revelation may well be in the service of desire and may seek to lay bare the repressed, while Cocteau's unveiling aims at making visible our eternal tragic destiny. But both artists seek revelations that are removed from the rational categories of time and causality; this seeking is the essential modernist quest.

1. Jean Cocteau, *Entretiens autour du cinématographe*, p. 69. (All translations are mine, unless otherwise indicated.)
2. Jean Cocteau, "Par lui-même," in his *Opéra*, p. 13.

49

Though Cocteau and the surrealists were often opposed to each other—Cocteau's work sometimes provoked violent reactions from the surrealists—one must note that Cocteau greatly admired Buñuel's first film, *Un Chien andalou*. In his diary, *Opium*, Cocteau makes it clear that he considered Dali and Buñuel's parodistic film to be one of the few great works that cinema had produced by 1929. His enthusiastic comments show, moreover, that he interpreted it in terms of the modernist canon:

> Advance and fall, bicycle, horse for a bullfight, rotten donkeys, priests, Spanish dwarfs! Every time blood flows in families, in the street, it's hidden, it's covered up with linens, people arrive, they form a circle that keeps one from seeing. There is also the blood of the soul's body. It makes one drunk with atrocious wounds, it flows from the corner of the mouth, and neither families nor policemen nor curious bystanders think about hiding it.[3]

Cocteau interprets the film, on the one hand, as a form of disclosure, of unveiling that reveals the invisible. On the other hand, he sees the open flow of blood in what we can call Orphic terms. In fact, the open intoxication with blood is plain in the Orphic ritual at the end of *Le Sang d'un Poète*. Cocteau's way of seeing the violence of eros in Buñuel's work foreshadows his own filmic poet and his death.

In their Orphism, Cocteau and the surrealists are again quite comparable, for as modernists they derived much of their poetic practice from the same sources. They both accepted, with some modification, Mallarmé's Orphism as well as Rimbaud's view of poetry as an ecstatic exploration of the unconscious. In Cocteau's case, Mallarmé's Orphism furnished a justification of poetry as a hieratic activity in which the poet consecrates himself as a guardian of the mysteries or revelation that poetry can offer to the initiated. As William Spanos has stated, the "strategy of Symbolist modernism was one of religio-aesthetic withdrawal from existential time into the eternal simultaneity of essential art."[4] The poet, then, in Mallarmé's and Cocteau's views, subordinates himself to language that in its highest form becomes an iconic monument unto itself, at the same time that it is a funerary medallion granting the poet his vocation and his destiny. Cocteau readily accepted the ideas that a poet's destiny is his death and that through his death he is consecrated by his work.

3. Jean Cocteau, *Opium* (Paris: Le Livre de Poche, n.d.), p. 167.
4. William V. Spanos, "The Detective and the Boundary: Some Notes on the Postmodern Literary Imagination," p. 158.

The notion of the poet's subordinating himself to his destiny, to his work and to death, is closely tied to Cocteau's view of Rimbaud—the true angel, as Cocteau once called him in a discussion of angelism. Cocteau took from Rimbaud, much as the surrealists did, the idea that poetry is a practice involving the submission of the conscious mind to those undiscovered, largely unconscious forces that constitute what Rimbaud calls the "true life." "I is another" ("Je est un autre") is Rimbaud's most condensed cry of his refusal of the limits of the conscious self. The locus of revelation must lie beyond the limits of the rational mind. Central to this view of poetry as a quest for revelation that lies beyond consciousness and rational discourse is the metaphor of the descent or diving. Like Rimbaud's drunken boat, the poet must plunge into the sea in order to bring back those marvels that lie beneath the surface. The sea and its depths are another metaphor, of course, for the poet's self and the locus of revelation, for the poet is both the explorer and the region to be explored. It is this metaphor that lies behind Cocteau's comment that *Le Sang d'un Poète* is a descent. As we shall see, it also points beyond the modernist search for revelation to offer an insight into Cocteau's view that poetry is always an act that designates its own genesis and creation.

The poet's descent into night, to offer a romantic metaphor that also lies behind the modernist search for revelation, is thus an exploration of the irrational that finds its justification through the disclosure of a superior realm of being. This unveiling of a region of being having ontological priority over those regions that realistic art represents is the essential modernist task, a task undertaken by both Cocteau and the surrealists. But beyond this, it should be stressed, Cocteau and the surrealists had little in common. Cocteau could never accept the cry for liberation that animated surrealism. In fact, his entire work is a meditation on the nature of destiny, particularly on the destiny of the poet or the mortal whom the often unconscious forces of destiny elect so that destiny can be revealed. Cocteau is, like his contemporaries Giraudoux and Montherlant, an inheritor of the tragic tradition, and it is not the least of his feats to have combined a tragic vision reflecting Sophocles and Racine with an Orphic sense of poetry such as Mallarmé expressed in his "Tombeau d'Edgar Poe":

> Tel qu'en Lui-même enfin l'éternité le change,
> Le poète suscite avec un glaive nu
> Son siècle épouvanté de n'avoir pas connu
> Que la mort triomphait dans cette voix étrange!

[Such as into Himself at last eternity changes
him, the Poet stirs with a naked sword
his century dismayed to have ignored
that death still triumphed in this voice so strange!]

The poet, the tragic scapegoat that destiny picks for its enigmatic purposes, is he who surprises, startles, and even terrifies by revealing that he triumphs over death precisely because destiny has selected him and set him apart.

These preliminary remarks allow us, then, to situate Cocteau's *Le Sang d'un Poète* in terms of its aesthetic axioms and, in addition, permits us to see that in some respects Cocteau has in this film gone beyond the modernist assumptions that lie behind his poetic practice. Our first impression on viewing the film, however, is that it is essentially modernist in its attempt to negate what we have called the artist's fall into time. The shot of the collapsing industrial smokestack that opens and closes the film represents the passage of time, which means, of course, that the entire film unfolds in a locus that is outside of time and our mundane realm of causal determinism. This manner of placing a work outside a framework or normal temporal-spatial reference is not unique to *Le Sang d'un Poète*. In both the play and, later, in the film *Orphée*, Cocteau uses the repeated arrival of a mailman to suggest by the recurrence that the work's perceived duration has taken place outside of the normal temporal-spatial coordinates of everyday reality. This desire to transform mimesis into a nontemporal, iconic form of simultaneous revelation is also found in his play *La Machine infernale*. In this modernist version of Oedipus, the first and second acts take place at the same time: Laius' ghost appears on the ramparts while fate grants Oedipus the illusion of freedom. This simultaneity suggests that, from the gods' point of view, temporal succession is meaningless, for the beginning and the end of the action are contained simultaneously in the very notion of tragic destiny. Cocteau's desire to present a vision of inexorable destiny thus coincides with the modernist ambition to attain a static, epiphanic vision. Destiny and mimetic stasis are two aspects of the same representation.

The theme of the poet's election by the forces of destiny is evident from the beginning of *Le Sang d'un Poète*. The film's first episode is entitled "The Wounded Hand, or the Scars of the Poet," and by scars one might well understand the stigmata that are destiny's mark on those it picks to fulfill the poet's mission, to mediate between men and destiny by revealing destiny's presence. The first representational space we see is the poet's room, which might be taken as the inner space of the poem itself. In this sense, then, the locus of mimesis is the film itself, and the work can be seen as a form of self-representation of the poet's creation. The poet is, however, dressed in a Louis XV wig, and the author's voice informs us that the young man we see is there at the same time that "the cannons of Fontenoy thundered in the distance." Since the poet rids himself of the wig and appears shortly afterwards with his hair sleekly combed back in a very contemporary way, the initial effect of the film's pseudohistorical preciseness is a form of dislocation. One of Cocteau's strategies of revelation, however, is the way he often whimsically literalizes his themes. If the poet can enter a realm that is outside of normal temporal determinants, then he can quite literally be at all places at all times. As we see in *Le Testament d'Orphée*, he must also come back into normal time. The exploration of eternity can entail farcical mistakes, for in this later film Cocteau enters time at the wrong moments, first appearing to the professor too soon, when the professor is still a child, and then too late, when the professor is about to die, before Cocteau finally finds the professor at a mature age and can be sent back to "his century." By representing literally Mallarmé's description of the poet as a meteorite that appears by chance in his century, Cocteau turns the premises of Orphic modernism into a source of comic revelation. One might think of similar effects that could have been had, should Yeats have found himself really carried back to Byzantium.

The central theme of this first episode is not atemporality, however, but the poet's wound. When the mouth of a figure that the poet is drawing becomes alive, the poet rubs it, and the mouth implants itself, woundlike, in the poet's hand. A friend who knocks at the poet's door sees this aberration and runs away in fright. The friend is undoubtedly representative of the public in general, who attempt to enter into the inner space of revelation, but, when confronted with the poet's often monstrous destiny, retreat in confusion and astonishment. The poet's cultivation of his wound also recalls Rimbaud's description of the poet's task as being akin to planting warts on one's face. The poet seeking revelation must not hesitate to undergo the most horrible experiences. Also, we again find Rimbaud's idea that the locus for the quest is the poet himself. Cocteau often expressed this notion, saying that he was possessed by angels, by inner forces that commanded him to give them expression. In this sense the poet is a mere vehicle for impulses that spring from within him. If Cocteau's film *Orphée* is a critique of the poet who accepts impulses that are not his own, *Le Sang d'un Poète* sets forth the struggle of the poet who must cope with his own body, his own inner space, and explore the wounds that destiny forces upon him. Once the wound is planted within the flesh, he must nurture it, give it air, and finally accept it in an ambiguous gesture of autoeroticism, as a lover accepts a caress.

The image of autoeroticism or narcissism is another image by which the work designates its own genesis. The poet's exploration of himself is clearly designated as erotic when he presses the mouth against his own and then, enraptured by this discovery of himself existing as another, falls into a chair and caresses his nude chest with the living mouth. The poet is transfigured by the discovery that he can be the object of his own desire. His eyes are transformed, and his face takes on the look of a theatrical mask. By taking himself as an object of desire, he has in effect transformed himself into a work of art. The poet's autoeroticism is, too, another image of the film's mimetic project, for the film springs from an androgynous self-fertilization, in which the film gives birth to itself as the object of its own representation.

This discovery of eros seems to lead almost automatically to the film's second episode, for, having accepted his androgynous nature, the poet can explore his inner world and confront the demands of his destiny. He can go through the mirror, plunge into himself, and enter the underworld from which erotic drives emanate. The forces that possess the poet must be found in what Cocteau calls the poet's night. Though these forces are erotic in nature, Cocteau refused to identify this night with the Freudian unconscious. Avoiding the problem of repression, he preferred to designate the poet's night metaphorically as a treasure grotto from which art takes its riches.[5] This notion of a treasure grotto allows us to see that the second episode takes place in that space of revelation where the poet comes into contact with his own vision.

The second episode begins after the passage of night, for the poet awakens to find himself in his room, though it now has neither windows nor a door. Moreover, he seems to be locked into this closed room with a life-size statue of a woman. Images of statues appear obsessionally throughout Cocteau's work, and through this recurrence they acquire a good many connotative values. They are frequently related to death in that they kill or are killed in a number of instances. They also appear in relation to sleep and dreams. In this sense they are associated with the poet's night and with eros, as we see in the film *Les Enfants terribles* when the statue watches over Paul and his sister's incestuous caresses. Springing from the poet's night, statues are a form

5. Jean Cocteau, *Journal d'un inconnu*, pp. 39–40.

of creation and are thus emblematic of the poet's destiny. They are a stone embodiment of the funeral monument the poet creates for himself.

All of these values are associated with the statue in *Le Sang d'un Poète* as becomes even clearer in the film's fourth episode, when it appears that the statue is also Europa, the goddess Zeus seduced by changing himself into a bull. The statue is an erotic emissary from the gods. In the second episode, the poet awakens the statue from what the commentary calls the "sleep of centuries" when he forces his hand's mouth onto the statue's mouth. In effect he gives voice to his destiny, for the statue can now speak to him. The poet may sneer at the statue, thinking perhaps for a moment that he has rid himself of his grotesque wound, his mark of election. Yet we see again in quite literal terms that the poet is trapped with his destiny, one that must be realized by a struggle within the inner space of the work.

The only way out of the room is through its mirror or, more precisely, through overcoming the crystallized self-consciousness the mirror represents. Challenged by the statue to live up to what he has written about mirrors in his poetry, the poet dives into the mirror. As the play *Orphée* shows, in Cocteau's personal mythology mirrors serve as death's exits and entrances. For instance, in the film *Orphée*, death seizes Eurydice when Orpheus looks at her in the car's rearview mirror, and Orpheus' own death, embodied in the Princess, uses his bedroom mirror to come and go between the world of everyday reality and the "Zone." In the Zone we find another image of the poet's night, or that region that Heurtebise defines in the film as one "made of men's memories and ruins of their habits." All of these images point both to the importance of the mirror and to what we might call the central poetic equation in Cocteau's work. The poet's mission is to descend into a region that can be likened to both night and death, a no-man's-land and a dream, where he can find a past, a mythic form of time that lies outside of normal time. He must overcome the world of habit, law, and causality, for, in a Proustian sense, revelation can occur only when the habitual laws of perception are broken. For Cocteau's poet this means he must descend to those nocturnal forces that can seize him and use him as a vehicle for expression. The passage through the mirror stresses the narcissistic side of the poet's mission, for it shows that he must overcome mere fascination with consciousness of his own image. He must literally go beyond himself in the quest for revelation. The poet may unite with himself for a second as he touches the mirror, but the very act of union destroys the reflected image and leads him to another realm.

The passage through the mirror leads, surprisingly enough, to the Hôtel des Folies-Dramatiques. It is this sequence, with its irrationally associated imagery, that has caused some critics to call the film a dream, or rather a transcription of dream imagery. In a sense this explanation allows the critic to dismiss the film as a form of subjective mimesis for which no explanation can rationally be found. However, if we take the locus of mimesis to be the work itself or, perhaps more precisely, to be the genesis of Cocteau's work in general, we can see that the Hôtel is the region in which the work generates itself, a mysterious labyrinth in which the poet himself is an alien, searching for the images to which he must give expression. One might say that the images he encounters, as in a dream, often appear unmotivated; they possess significance only because they recur throughout Cocteau's work. Like much of the imagery in modernist poetry and painting, these images are arbitrary in terms of the relationship they establish between a signifier and a signified, yet significant in terms of the relationships they establish among themselves. In short, they are a language, or what the French call an *écriture*, that the poet founds in order to describe the forces that besiege him.

The self-referential aspect of the representational space is emphasized by the first image that the poet sees when he looks through a keyhole in the first door in the hotel's corridor. He sees a double of himself, dressed as a Mexican, shot down by a firing squad. His double is quickly resurrected, though only, it appears, to be shot down again. This image of the poet's multiple death expresses another of Cocteau's favored themes, for the poet is, as he puts it in *Le Testament d'Orphée*, an expert in "phoenixology." This triumph over death is another aspect of the modernist quest for a release from the imprisoning spatial and temporal limits of everyday reality; it is also a part of the Orphic view that the work abolishes temporality as it establishes the simultaneity of all events seen from destiny's perspective. This victory over death resurrects the past at the same time it releases the self from the limits of space. Hence the commentary that states that at night—within the confines of the poetic quest—Mexico, the trenches of Vincennes, the boulevard Arago, and a hotel room are all the same.

The poet laboriously moves down the corridor to a second door, where a placard reads "Flying Lessons." (The French title, "Leçons de vol," has an alternate meaning of "Lessons in Theft." This play on words points to Cocteau's ironic stance toward his modernist vision, and it can hardly be overemphasized how this irony informs Cocteau's entire film.) When the poet looks through the keyhole into the second room, he sees a girl in circus tights being forced to defy gravity by an old woman with a whip. In one respect, this image presents an ironic double of how the poet is forced to overcome the limits of everyday reality and find release through levitation. In soaring, the poet becomes a modernist angel who can prevail quite literally over the laws of habit. As Frederick Brown has pointed out, this image also recalls a comparable scene in Cocteau's *Parade*.[6] This recurrent image of levitation is, then, another constant in Cocteau's personal mythology as well as another form of autorepresentation in which the poet shows himself "breaking the laws" of habit.

The third room, which contains "The Mysteries of China" and a "Celestial Ceiling," is an opium den filled with shadows and darkness. This realm especially entices the poet, for he tries to get a better view through the crack above the door. The opium den is, of course, an image of Cocteau's self-celebration and also the very image of that nocturnal world where Cocteau spent much time before he cured himself of opium addiction. More importantly, opium for Cocteau, as for Coleridge, is directly related to the poet's night, for it can suspend the diurnal laws of light and reason and place the poet directly in contact with obscurity and death, with the poetic underworld. Opium is a dangerous means of exploration, for its narcosis can lead to forms of narcissism that paralyze the poet in euphoric self-consciousness. Thus the poet flees when he finds that another eye is peering back at his own through the keyhole. This autocontemplation would drown revelation in self-fixation.

The poet's final vision brings him to another encounter with narcissism, for the last room's Hermaphrodite presents another double of his androgynous nature and of the temptation of autoeroticism. Even more than the opium den, this image of eros seems to tempt the poet and draw him toward an encounter with himself. As drums beat and the Hermaphrodite reveals its various guises, the poet arches his back and presses against the door until the self-fertilizing creature lifts up its robe to reveal a sign proclaiming "Danger of Death." This is, of course, another whimsically literal "unveiling" in which Cocteau, offering a concrete representation of his metaphor for poetic activity, again shows the poet confronting eros and death conjoined. Cocteau's originality here, as a later generation of New York filmmakers would testify, is not in exploiting the metaphor, something of a cliché in itself, but in literalizing the cliché in all the tacky splendor that a white-faced hermaphrodite can possess.

6. Frederick Brown, *An Impersonation of Angels*, p. 298.

Cocteau's ironic stance toward this Orphic quest is also clear at the end of this sequence, when the poet takes a pistol proffered to him and shoots himself. His gushing blood becomes his laurels and, in mock celebration of another poetic cliché, he appears to accede to immortality. The poet, however, has had enough of it all and, after muttering a few oaths, returns to smash the statue who has set him on his quest. This is a literal act of iconoclasm, for after traversing the iconic space of revelation, the poet revolts against the icon that embodies his destiny. One might be tempted to see another critical attitude here, for the destruction of the icon is a destruction of the privileged mode of modernist revelation. The revolt against the space of revelation leads, in turn, to the exploration of the spatialization of time. The next episode is situated in the poet's past, though the poet appears both as a child and as one of his future incarnations: he has transformed himself into a statue that presides over the children's games. The simultaneous spatial presence of the poet as child and as an immortal annuls temporal relationships and again suggests the spatial omnipresence of all moments as they are revealed in the poet's work.

The third episode, "The Snowball Fight," centers on a privileged moment of the poet's past life, for it presents the revelation of beauty that occurs during a snowball fight in the Cité Monthier. This street recurs throughout Cocteau's work, and especially in his novel *Les Enfants terribles*, as the privileged space where Dargelos, the child-angel, throws the snowball whose force is that of an epiphany when it strikes the poet down. In the novel as in the film the street becomes a stage for the enactment of the childhood scene. This theatricalization of memory indicates that the recalled event is both an eternally reenacted ritual and a revelation that can take place only within the confines of the work of art. The principal difference between the snowball fight in Cocteau's novel (and film of the same title) and the one in *Le Sang d'un Poète* is that the boys in the film find the poet's statue pensively looking at them, but, in another act of iconoclasm, they quickly tear it apart and use it as ammunition in their battle. This doubling of the iconoclastic acts again stresses the simultaneity of all events when seen in the light of revelation. It is worth stressing how in the novel *Les Enfants terribles* the blow that Dargelos gives Paul is also related to a statue, for as Paul falls he feels "a dark blow. A blow of a fist of marble. A blow of a statue's fist." In both instances, then, the blow is associated with the statue, though in the film the child-poet is felled with a piece of stone that comes from his own future *tombeau*. For the Paul of *Les Enfants terribles*, the blow is the revelation of beauty that will determine all his amorous quests for the rest of his life. This revelation is, however, only another double of the same election that determines the child-poet's quest.

The blow Dargelos strikes is thus another form of election or sacrament by which the poet recognizes his fate. Cocteau again stresses the hieratic aspect, for the fourth episode is called "The Profanation of the Host." Cocteau does not change the decor for this episode, however; he retains the theatrical decor that transforms the past into the eternal present of dramatic enactment. Moreover, this decor stands as a metaphor for the mimetic space, designating again how the work represents itself. In this episode the work, through the profanation that occurs, becomes a locus of atonement in which mimesis itself can be seen as a sacrificial act.

The profanation is quick to happen. The child-poet now lies alone on the snow, before the pedestal that is now empty, awaiting his future enshrinement as a statue. While the child-poet's blood flows, perhaps in anticipation of the Orphic atonement that will be his lot, a crowd arrives to witness the fourth episode. The theatrical metaphors of the novel *Les Enfants terribles* are concretely realized as the windows of the buildings on the street turn into theatrical loges. The crowd, an elegant group, have gathered to watch the mature poet, who is now playing cards with the feminine statue while the bleeding child-poet's body lies at their feet. The poet's election has been turned into a mere spectacle for the entertainment of the wealthy and idle. Yet it would appear that this profanation is inevitable, for it is always in the theater that the rituals of destiny are celebrated. The theater's essential ambiguity is then that it is the locus of both profanation and hieratic atonement.

The ritual of chance is thus enacted for an indifferent public in the fourth episode. The motif of gambling and cards is another familiar one in Cocteau's work and can be associated in general terms with the broader constellation of destiny's various guises. In a literal sense the poet is gambling for his death, which lies already at his feet. In an ironic gesture, the poet attempts to cheat at the game. He removes the needed ace of hearts from the child's jacket, but his slow-motion movement is utterly obvious. The ace of hearts in turn calls forth the child-poet's guardian angel, a black angel who appears to be an emissary of death or perhaps a representative of the underworld forces of the poet's night. The angel's limp grants him a specificity that endows his literal appearance with a dowdy credibility. This limping angel, with his bric-a-brac wings, is another literalization of the kind of poetic motifs that occur throughout Cocteau's work. The encounter between the mature poet and the angel, as a game

of chance takes place, recalls, for instance, the poet's bedroom struggle with
the recurrent angel Heurtebise in his poem "L'Ange Heurtebise":

> L'ange Heurtebise, d'une brutalité
> Incroyable saute sur moi. De grâce
> Ne saute pas si fort,
> Garçon bestial, fleur de haute
> Stature.
> Je m'en suis alité. En voilà
> Des façons. J'ai l'as; constate.
> L'as-tu?[7]
> [The angel Heurtebise, with unbelievable
> Brutality jumps on me. Please
> Don't jump so hard,
> Bestial boy, flower of great
> Stature.
> You've put me in bed. Those are
> Strange manners. I have the ace. Look.
> Do you have it?]

The recurrent ace is emblematic of a struggle in which the poet must accept
chance as destiny. The poet's struggle is, somewhat ambiguously, an attempt
both to overcome the chance cutting of the cards and, at the same time, to
accept the hand that is dealt to him. Cheating in this struggle is of no avail, for
Cocteau's angels are there to insure that the mysterious decrees of a
haphazard destiny are carried out.

The child is literally absorbed by the angel, and the poet is left to face his
implacable opponent. In Orphic terms, one might say that eternal chance now
proclaims its victory in a way that recalls Mallarmé's struggle against chance in
Un coup de dès or, even more specifically, in his *Igitur*, a work first published
in 1925 that undoubtedly attracted Cocteau's attention. In fact, *Le Sang d'un
Poète* often appears to be an ironic transposition of this unfinished series of
prose notes, in which Mallarmé sought to present a vision of the theatricalization of chance. In *Igitur* it would seem that Mallarmé desired to present a
five-act drama in which the poet's destiny and the destiny that theater celebrates would be united as a theatrical ritual exposing the poet's exemplary
struggle.

Cocteau's poet ends his struggle against chance with another self-
assassination, though this defeat, as a form of theatricality, is a form of victory.
The crowd applauds his demise, and as the poet's blood flows we see that the

7. Cocteau, *Opéra*, p. 47.

poet has become another Orpheus who has taken on the crowd's death through his own. By assuming their death, he attains Orphic immortality, and it is this victory over time that represents his greatest triumph. The poet is thus a universal scapegoat who takes upon himself man's fate in the ritualized self-murder that fate inflicts upon him.

Mallarmé's Igitur finds himself "expelled from his race," much like Cocteau's poet who, in his immortality, must leave the realm of his "tribe."[8] The woman cardplayer resumes her role as a statue who can lead the Orphic bard into the realm of universal allegory. She leads him from the chance realm of particularized existence, or the rue d'Amsterdam where the poet first underwent revelation, and takes him to the realm of myth lying beyond the space of revelation, to meet the bull Zeus. The poet, like Mallarmé's Igitur, is now "outside of time," having left the accidental place in which chance caused him to intersect with history.

The lyre lying between the bull's horns marks the momentary displacement of the film's mimetic space. The film points beyond the poet's self-representation or, to compare again Cocteau's poet with Igitur, beyond the crisis of self-consciousness in which the poet can only reflect on his own work, and offers a representation of the universal archetype. The archetypal realm of myth would be the realm of the absolute, or what Mallarmé describes, in his presentation of *Igitur's* fourth act (called "le coup de dès" or "The Throw of the Dice"), as the realization of the infinite:

> In short, in an act where chance is in question, it is always chance that accomplished its own Idea by affirming or denying itself. In the presence of its existence both affirmation and negation fail. It contains the Absurd—implies it, but in a latent state and prevents the absurd from existing. Which also allows the infinite to exist.[9]

The poet thus overcomes the existence of absurd destiny by hypostatizing the realm of myth, the realm of the infinite that lies beyond history, time, and accidental existence. This is his final victory over chance.

Yet Cocteau, perhaps like Mallarmé himself, could never give up his ironic stance toward this Orphic triumph, for he could never fully suppress his acute consciousness that it is only the work of art that grants this victory. The film thus retreats from this archetypal representation to return to a represen-

8. Stéphane Mallarmé, *Oeuvres complètes* (Paris: Bibliothèque de la Pléiade, 1965), pp. 440–41.
9. Ibid., p. 441.

tation of itself as a mimetic act. The film again designates itself as the self-contained locus of salvation through the various devices that Cocteau uses at the end to call attention to the film as film: the presence of the technicians, the obvious falsity of the final statue, and what a later generation of film viewers would call the "camp" nature of the film's ending. Here again Cocteau appears to have ironically transposed Mallarmé in certain respects. Just as Mallarmé's Igitur is threatened by the "torture of being eternal," Cocteau's poet must face what he calls in his final commentary the "mortal tedium of immortality" ("l'ennui mortel de l'immortalité"). This ironic deflation seems to lay bare the archetypal triviality of the infinite itself.

In conclusion, we can see that Cocteau's ironic stance toward both his Orphism and the modernist quest for aesthetic salvation points directly to a postmodern sense of the necessity for the work to justify itself. On the one hand, *Le Sang d'un Poète* is typically modernist in its celebration of what one critic has called, in speaking of the modernist epiphany, "the most radical manifestation of the contingent existence of things."[10] In Cocteau's case this celebration is concerned with the poet's victory over the very contingency of his existence. On the other hand, Cocteau's recognition of the fortuitous nature of the work itself leads to the creation of a self-designating work that attempts to justify mimesis by grounding the work in itself. This self-designation foreshadows the crisis of postmodernism and the questioning of the very possibility of mimesis, the questioning that we see in the work of directors as diverse as Antonioni, Bergman, and Fellini. In fact, in *Le Sang d'un Poète* we see how the axioms of modernism gave rise to their own demise, for the very logic of transforming the work into a self-justifying and thus self-contained discourse would seem to lead inevitably to the questioning of mimesis that characterizes much of postmodern literature, art, and film. It is not by accident that Cocteau was a patron saint of the New Wave.

10. Renato Barilli, "Aboutissement du roman phénoménologique ou nouvelle aventure romanesque," in *Nouveau Roman: hier, aujourd'hui*, 1:110.

In the Wake
of Surrealism

From *Entr'acte* to
A Nous la Liberté:
René Clair and the Order of Farce

Today it may seem a little puzzling that René Clair, joining such silent-film makers as Chaplin and Eisenstein, was opposed to the use of sound in films. In light of subsequent developments in film, it might appear that the attitude of Clair and his cinematic confreres was somewhat quixotic. Yet before one becomes too laudatory about a change in technique that changed the nature of an art form, one would do well to recall that the advent of sound meant the decline, if not the total demise, of great comic cinema. This rather astounding fact—and any theory of film must take account of its astounding nature—should force us to look at Clair's work, as well as the work of the other silent comics, and to consider why a comic-film maker felt no need for sound and even suspected that it would be inimical to his art.

One might take as a point of departure for this inquiry the way Clair himself, at the outset of his career, defined the nature of cinema. In 1924, well before the coming of sound posed a threat to silent-film makers, Clair rejected the cinema's attempt to rival literature or theater as a form of mimesis (precisely what the coming of sound would allow it to do) and called on filmmakers to return to the comic tradition of those primitive filmmakers who worked in France before World War I:

> That cinema was created in order to register movement can hardly be
> denied, and yet this is what seems to be too often forgotten. The principal
> task of the current generation should be to bring cinema back to its origins,
> and, to accomplish this, get rid of all the pseudoart that is stifling it. . . . If
> there is an aesthetics of film, it was discovered at the same time as the
> camera and film by the Lumière Brothers in France. One can give a résumé
> of it in a word: movement. Exterior movement of objects perceived by the
> eye and to which we can add the interior movement of the action. From the
> union of these two movements can arise what people talk about so much
> and which we see so infrequently, namely, rhythm.[1]

1. René Clair, *Cinéma d'hier, cinéma d'aujourd'hui*, pp. 62–63. (All translations are mine, unless otherwise indicated.)

Dramatic action or mimesis of an action is necessary, then, only insofar as it serves as a support for the plausible orchestration of movement. This subordination of mimesis to movement explains why Clair felt no desire to introduce sound into his works. Sound, as he correctly perceived, could only enhance film's realistic mimetic capacities and lead to a neglect of those visual rhythms that are the basis of film farce.[2]

The creation of rhythm, understood as a form of serial repetition that is perceived as having a temporal regularity, is at the heart of the work of the great silent comics. Serial repetition, or the creation of an ordered series, is the basis for the perception of the order that farce always presupposes. For film farce is essentially the destruction or the subversion of a given order. This destruction is usually brought about when the film reveals this order to be nothing more than a mechanistic series. The revelation of order as merely a kind of repeating mechanism is, as Henri Bergson showed, one of the fundamental sources of the comic.[3] Though the subversion of order can be accomplished in a number of ways, film farce usually entails the use of a mimicry that, by offering an exaggerated imitation of order, lays bare the comic rigidity inherent in order. Film farce thus demands the creation of a visual rhythm for its destructive mimicry. It demands the creation of an antiorder that is derived from a preexisting ordered series. Rhythm is, therefore, the basis for the controlled but joyous aggression that farce unleashes against order.

These remarks on film farce point in turn to an understanding of farce as a supreme form of play that uses mimesis only in order to subvert it, as Clair's films amply demonstrate. Play is, in a generic sense, gratuitous; players, having no goal other than the intensity of pleasure that play brings, attempt to institute an ordered series of events. Farce is, then, a gratuitous, ludic activity that creates a self-sufficient order through its destructive mimicry of an ordered state of affairs. The perfect order that play seeks to found is achieved in farce by derivative rhythms, whereas the ludic pleasure that farce offers seems to find its source in the absolute freedom of destruction that farce demonstrates. Clair's film world, as many critics have noted, is close to a child's vision, but this is not because his characters are blissfully innocent. Rather, his farce allows us to participate in the play-fantasies of childhood with

2. An interesting confirmation of this idea is offered by the work of Jacques Tati, one of the few contemporary filmmakers who attempt to make pure farce. Tati deliberately minimizes the role of sound except as a rhythmic element or a perturbing element in the creation of gags.

3. Much of my commentary is taken from considerations that Bergson developed in *Le Rire* (1901), still one of the essential books for an understanding of comedy, farce, and the comic.

magical impunity, at the same time that it mirrors our desire for anarchistic aggression in a world of restraints and order.

With these brief theoretical comments in mind, one can turn to Clair's most successful silent farce and examine how in 1924 he combined theory and practice in the creation of *Entr'acte*. In one sense this farce is a film manifesto in favor of the ludic spirit. It is also a surrealist assault on the spirit of high mimetic seriousness. Based on a sketchy scenario by Francis Picabia, the surrealist painter and general impresario of the avant-garde in Paris, and accompanied by a score by Eric Satie, *Entr'acte* was an interlude for Picabia's ballet *Relâche*, which was performed by the Ballets Suédois at the Théâtre des Champs-Elysées. The conditions of its first showing are of more than a little interest, since this joyous little film filled the entr'acte of a ballet whose title means "No performance." Both titles thus suggest that the work is part of a surrealist attack on performance conventions. The order that gives rise to farce is here the order of representation itself.

Entr'acte is, however, far more than a simple Dadaist act of destruction and mockery such as Man Ray's *Retour à la Raison* of the same year. Clair, in his manifestolike description of his film, presented it as a work that, in harking back to such comic films as Lumière's *L'Arroseur arrosé*, Méliès's *Voyage dans la lune*, and the Keystone Kops comedies, aimed only at the orchestration of movement:

> Here now is *Entr'acte*, which claims to give a new value to the image. It was up to Francis Picabia, who has done so much for the liberation of the word, to liberate the image. In *Entr'acte* the image, "having been diverted from its obligation to mean something," is born to a concrete existence. Nothing seems to me to be more respectful of film's future than these visual stammerings whose harmony is orchestrated here.[4]

By invoking André Breton's declaration that images must be diverted from an obligation to mean something, Clair places *Entr'acte* under the banner of the surrealist crusade against the symbolic nature of meaning. From a traditionally rationalist point of view, meaning is found in the establishment of a relation that subordinates the image to a signified that transcends it. In a ludic perspective the image is self-justifying, deriving its sense from the farcical order in which it is presented. In short, the image has no other goal than the pleasure of play.

Entr'acte is both a surrealist exploration of the marvelous and a tribute to

4. Quoted in Jean Mitry, *René Clair*, p. 18.

the early film comics who pursued the fantastic with no inhibitions. *Entr'acte* is an homage to film, a film that is consistently about film and its self-justifying play forms. In this sense it is a play form to the second degree, deriving its order from other films. Consider in this respect the opening sequence, in which a rolling seventy-five-millimeter cannon seems to stroll onto the roof of a Parisian building. Rolling from one side of the building to the other, then turning its barrel toward the camera and the spectators, this mobile artillery-piece recalls the animation Zecca and Cohl used to set objects free from the restraints of rational causality and grant them the comic sovereignty of free agents that play at mimicking human activity. Play and destruction of received order, these are the interrelated axes of Clair's filmic universe, in which play establishes the order of motion and rhythm while, in Bergsonian terms, the film reproduces the very essence of the comic through mechanical objects that conduct themselves like human players.

Clair's use of animation is a self-conscious homage to the ludic order that earlier films created as well as a destruction of many of the standard conventions of cinematic representation. The spectator who might think that Clair's cannon is merely another if rather late example of naive cinematic fantasy is quickly disabused when Satie and Picabia come bounding in slow motion onto the roof from opposite sides of the screen and shoot the cannon at the audience. The slow-motion shell they send at the audience acts as a reminder that the destruction of the audience would be a logical outgrowth of this systematic subversion of cinematic order. *Entr'acte* thus presents itself from its beginning as a surrealist provocation that uses the ludic freedom of early cinema to subvert joyously the order of filmic mimesis and transform it into a self-conscious form of playful aggression.

Animated boxing gloves, matches that dance on a head of hair that catches on fire, the superimposition of the Place de la Concorde on Marcel Duchamp's chessboard, a self-propelled, sausage-ornamented hearse that leads its mourners on a mad chase, all these images are at once disruptions of received mimetic order and celebrations of the naive ludic values of early films. Perhaps most revealing in this respect is Clair's placing on the camel-drawn hearse the emblem of Star Films, Méliès's firm, or his placing a conjurer in the coffin that rolls off the hearse. This magician not only repeats Méliès's stop-action photography in order to make his pursuers vanish but, in a final provocation, leaps through the word "End" in a comic subversion of the cinematic convention that would confine the work to the closed space of the screen. This aggression against the screen's limits is of course presented within the limits of the screen itself, but this irony is ultimately an even greater assault against our sense of the order of filmic discourse and the conventions of representation.

In more specific terms, Clair's work uses those two essential filmic devices for the subversion of order, the gag and the chase sequence. The best example of the gag in *Entr'acte* is the famous "ballerina" who recurs throughout the first part of the film. Shot from beneath a glass plate, the dancer appears to leap gracefully upward. The spectator sees the usual graceful legs and tutu that suggest both the conventional beauty and the cultural seriousness that is attributed to ballet. Moreover, the repetition of the shot creates an assumption of thematic regularity in the film, for recurrence here seems to designate a building pattern of order. After a series of these shots, the camera pans down as though to reveal the dancer from another perspective that might complete the creation of thematic significance. The spectator does indeed find another perspective, for the dancer is a very hirsute male, with beard, mustache, and spectacles. The perturbation brought about by this surprise converts the entire recurrent series of shots into a ludic series that lays bare the mechanical nature of the repetition used to create significance in cinematic discourse.

Clair's use of gags is consistent throughout the first part of his career; he builds a pattern or series that is then converted into a farcical order by a sudden dislocation. The chase sequence, on the other hand, relies on a gathering momentum in which a perturbing agent sets up what we might call a magnetic field that transforms received order into farce as the field irresistibly draws legions of followers in its wake. In Bergsonian terms, the pursued object transforms the pursuers into robots who are, by the logic of the chase itself, forced to follow in mechanical and serial fashion. The American silent farces of Buster Keaton offer good example of "magnetic fields." As the beleaguered hero runs through city streets in *Cops* or through a mountain valley in *Seven Brides*, he draws behind him an army of cops, thousands of frustrated brides, or a sea of boulders that threaten to crush him at the same time they automatically follow his magnetic presence.

The chase sequence is based on pure rhythm that uses acceleration to underscore mechanical repetition. Clair uses the chase in *Entr'acte* both for its comic value and as another form of homage to his primitive precursors, who set everything from gendarmes to pumpkins in ever-more-rapid pursuit.

Entr'acte's irrepressible hearse sets the pattern for the creation of rhythm that recurs throughout Clair's best work. First drawn by a camel, then setting itself free to roar along country byways and, presumedly, up and down a roller coaster, this extravagant vehicle draws behind it, first in slow motion and then at breakneck speed, the crowd of pompous dignitaries who seem to be representatives of the spirit of seriousness itself. Trick photography, rapid motion shots, and various gags augment the perturbation, underlining that this hearse has become a free agent capable of mobilizing a farcical ordering that in serial fashion transforms these followers into scurrying marionettes.

Entr'acte presents the fundamental traits we find in Clair's later silent films, such as *Les Deux Timides* or *Un Chapeau de Paille d'Italie*, and in his best early sound films, such as *A Nous la Liberté* or *The Last Millionaire*. These films in their best moments present a rejection of any realistic mode of mimesis in favor of an autocelebration of film and its power of fantasy subversion. Gags are constantly used to undermine received mimetic conventions and to create farcical orders of aggression, which in turn call forth the chase sequence in order to create purely ludic rhythms and movements. Clair's best work is essentially a mechanical ballet that combines both a surrealist rejection of codified systems of representation and a classical understanding of farce. Labiche and André Breton are strange bedfellows when one speaks of influences, but it is the joining of these two sources that gives Clair's work its powerful originality.

A Nous la Liberté (1931) is the most interesting test case for seeing how Clair, attempting to retain his artistic integrity, sought to reconcile the use of sound with his own understanding of film as the modern medium for the creation of farce. This work, which influenced Chaplin in his creation of *Modern Times*, is a paradigm of the film that is self-consciously ludic in its premises. It is also a work that has received little sympathetic commentary. Part of the misunderstanding of the film undoubtedly comes from critics' desire to evaluate the film in terms of its themes and the way in which it deals with social problems, with the historical crisis of capitalism and industrial society that in the early thirties was giving rise to depression and fascism. *A Nous la Liberté* certainly has all the social themes that a committed critic could ask for: the repressive state, labor versus capital, utopian socialism, and so on. The representation of social reality informs the film's action, and in this sense *A Nous la Liberté*, unlike Clair's silent works, undertakes a form of mimesis. Yet a complete understanding of *A Nous la Liberté* demands that the viewer recognize that mimesis is subordinated to the creation of rhythm and that any interpretation of the film that neglects its ludic principles must miss what is most important in the film. The Hungarian Board of Censors was unwittingly right to ban the film as subversisve, but it is not subversive in terms of traditional thematic concerns, satire, or the simple violation of taboo. The film's indictment of society lies at a different level of subversion, at that level where the ludic spirit calls for liberation.

From the outset of the film, Clair seems, in fact, to mix contradictory themes. First he presents the film's musical leitmotiv, "A Nous la Liberté," a jovial ditty that seems to undermine whatever seriousness the dramatic situation or the film's decor might impose. The decor in the first scenes seems grim indeed—a stark prison that might be construed as having the prophetic overtones of the decor of Lang's *Metropolis* and its vision of industrial civilization's ultimate development. In a sense the prison setting is offered as a synecdoche for capitalism, for we see an assembly line on which the prisoners construct toy horses. These toy horses are, however, the antithesis of the world of forced labor. They are a sign, in fact, of the ludic possibilities within the repressive order that constructs these toys seriatim.

The prison where we first see the film's two protagonists, Emile and Louis, has a thematic as well as a metaphorical value in the vision of industrial order that Clair sets forth. In simple terms, a prison equals a factory. This metaphor is quickly established by a series of shots after Louis's escape from prison. Emile helps Louis to escape by hindering the guards while Louis, after climbing over the walls, knocks over a passing bicycle racer and, in another demonstration of play's freedom, pedals simultaneously to a victory in the race and to freedom. The next sequence quickly traces Louis's rapid rise as a capitalist, as he re-creates about him the prison order from which he escaped. After using a ruse to rob a used-clothing dealer, Louis has sufficient capital to go into the secondhand phonograph-record business; the metaphorical equation is thus enriched through the association of capital and theft. Louis's success leads to his owning a record store, then to the creation of "Louis Records," and then, as the shot of a prisonlike factory attests, to the creation of a phonograph empire. The metaphor is given a final twist when we see that Louis has become an industrialist Louis XIV, a sovereign of absolute order who imposes his initial, "L," on all his possessions, to mark his dominion.

The chronicling of the rapid rise of Louis and the creation of his industrial order is followed by images of Emile, stretched out in a field as he listens to a bird and then to a flower singing, all of which sets forth a striking antithesis. The images portray a child's vision of freedom, one that reinforces the opposition of work and play, or the world of the factory and the world of song. Clair underscores the childlike freedom that Emile is now enjoying by cutting to a classroom where a teacher is busy inculcating his charges with the rudiments of the reality principle, teaching them that "work is obligation, for work is freedom."

Having no inclination toward work, Emile is jailed, which in terms of thematic antitheses would seem to suggest that the reality principle has defeated the pleasure principle. A series of gags, however, quickly subverts this reestablishment of order. When Emile attempts to hang himself, the prison bars fall out. He leaps out to freedom, only to fall on a huge, armless beggar who, in good Méliès fashion, suddenly reveals that he has only concealed his arms and lays hold of the hapless Emile. And the pretty girl who Emile thought was singing on her balcony walks out into the street while the song continues to come through the window, projected by a Louis phonograph—a gag that reveals Clair's attitude toward the use of sound in film while it also subverts the order of romance.

More gags and a chase sequence lead Emile to the inevitable encounter with Louis's factory. Pursuing the pretty secretary—the image of happiness that this mock romance proposes—he gets a job in Louis's factory, where the girl happens to work. It is, of course, impossible to introduce a free agent into a mechanical order without total disruption following. Although Emile and Louis, the childlike vagabond and the phonograph magnate, become reconciled in a new fraternity, Emile's presence in Louis's world initiates the reversal of the order that led to Louis's rise. Emile institutes the antiorder that forces Louis out of his capitalist empire. Quite simply, he brings chaos to the factory system as he pursues his image of happiness. Louis, on the other hand, must suddenly deal with his former gangster associates, who have recognized him. Blackmailed by gangsters, those anticapitalists (or supercapitalists) whose order is the converse of accepted social order, and then sought by the police, those "agents of order," Louis must flee his empire and take up the vagabond life of freedom that Emile proposes to him.

The final dissolution of received order results in a grand finale of chases whose multiple rhythms combine to create an enormous ballet. Pursued by the police, Emile arrives in the factory and unwittingly releases the locked-up gangsters, who are determined to find Louis's money. The satchel of bank notes Louis has collected for his flight ends up on the factory roof; a violent wind then distributes the notes among the bourgeois notables who have gathered for the inauguration of Louis's new, completely automated factory. The ceremony is transformed into a ritual dance in which representatives of officialdom mime the destruction of social order in a comic ballet of top-hatted marionettes. They charge back and forth across the screen, scrambling after the bank notes, while the wind, in a final demolishing of social rites, blows down the orator and the tribunes.

The film's ending stands as another ludic contrast with its beginning, for we see the workers liberated from all constraints by the factory that Louis has given them. This new, miraculous factory takes in nuts and bolts and spews forth rows of assembled phonographs. The importance of this ending is not in some Marcusian affirmation of automation's possibility to liberate man from all alienating labor. It lies rather in the ending's contrast with the film's beginning, since we see the workers at play, fishing, dancing, playing games, freely giving vent to their ludic desires. This affirmation of the ludic impulse does point to some form of liberation, but not to a literal freeing through science-fiction gadgetry. Rather, Clair is stressing the tension between these two forms of order, the order demanded by work and the antiorder of play and farce. This seems especially evident in the final contrast between the geometrically perfect rows of phonographs the factory produces and the images of the workers themselves, finally released from the geometrical order that has previously regulated their existence. In this contrast we see a complete reversal of terms between the film's beginning and its end, for the order of rationality is now in the service of play.

Clair has in effect translated the social tensions of the early thirties into a representation of formal orders. The two films we have discussed are alike, then, in that *Entr'acte* directs its aggression against the ordering of filmic discourse and ceremonial order, while *A Nous la Liberté* extrapolates order from the contemporary social context only to submit it to comic subversion. In *A Nous la Liberté* the formal properties of order are conveyed largely by the decor's stark patterns and geometrical rigor, and by the manipulation of groups and objects so that they conform to the same geometrical patterns that characterize the prison and the factory. These patterns are developed in terms of the rhythmic values, and these values in turn create a temporal order that is the basis for the creation of farce.

The prison, for example, a place of confinement, is shown as an order closed in upon itself. With its absolute linearity and geometrical sharpness, its mechanized routines and rhythmic periodicity that govern the flow of life, the prison stands as an iconic metonym for order itself. The moving line of toy horses, an incongruous image of play subjected to industrial rationalization, thus becomes associated with the lines of prisoners marching to their cells and with the lines of prisoners eating in silent rows, under constant surveillance, at the long tables that recall the work tables of the assembly line. Through these various associations the very notion of linearity and regularity acquires an antiludic value, associated with confinement, repression, regimentation, and work.

Louis's rise to power is portrayed visually by his ability to impose more and more geometric shapes on his world. When he is a secondhand-record dealer, all is irregularity, as exemplified by the rather baroque amplifying horn of the phonograph on which he plays his wares. As the head of "Louis Records," he owns a modern office building constructed as a series of glass and concrete squares, and in front of it sit row after neatly ordered row of delivery tricars. Finally, as the owner of an industrial empire, he is able to force workers to conform to one geometrical pattern after another, all in the name of efficiency, to be sure, but more especially as a sign of the order that he has the power to impose upon the world.

The factory reproduces an insectlike order that seems to function autonomously. From this very orderliness originates the comic antiorder that lies implicitly within any mechanized system in which men are reduced to automatons. This comic potential is explictly realized when Clair shows us the factory dining hall where, as in the prison, lines of workers sat seated in regular rows. Here, the mechanical rationality of the factory has obviously been applied, for the workers' food passes before them on a rolling belt, just as the partially assembled phonographs pass before them on the assembly line. The transference of this work order to what should be the realm of pleasure is a form of comic perturbation that again subverts the received notion of order. Chaplin, in his *Modern Times*, greatly amplified Clair's brief visual gag by creating the sequence in which he is strapped into the extravagant feeding machine. Chaplin, however, portrays himself as the victim of the machine, as the little man who cannot adjust to this absurd application of industrial order yet nonetheless mimics it in his gestures and reactions as he is beaten into submission. Clair's workers, on the other hand, are more dehumanized, mere elements in the patterns of mechanical order that Clair orchestrates so as to be able to create forms of antiorder.

The primary subverting force in *A Nous la Liberté* is Emile, the childlike vagabond who seems impervious to the demands of order as he pursues happiness. Unlike Chaplin, he is never forced to mimic the aberrant order that surrounds him but remains the free spirit, the leader of the chase, the child who is a permanent perturbing agent. As such, Emile functions in the creation of the two different devices for farce we saw in *Entr'acte*. First, by his refusal to adapt to order, he creates the serial gags implicit in such an order. His inadaptation presents something of a reversal of Bergsonian terms, for his comic function is not a result of a mechanical rigidity in his character. Rather, farce results from his spontaneity and from his unpredictable behavior, which erupts in the midst of a repeating series and converts that series into a comic order.

A good example of this type of serial gag occurs when Emile, attempting to keep an eye on the jealous foreman, lets a phonograph pass by on the assembly line without screwing his bolt into it. He pursues it, runs into the worker next to him, and while tightening that bolt, lets a second phonograph get by. In his effort to catch up with the first one, he prevents his fellow worker from adding his piece to the errant phonograph and fails to add his own. The two then rush after the phonograph, only to run into a third worker, and so on, until eight workers are grouped at one position, frantically trying to keep pace with the inexorable flow of phonographs. Emile's inadaptation has converted this mechanical flow into an absurd repeating series that reveals the other workers to be marionettes or automatons, comic extensions of the work series that would order their gestures. To use a Brechtian notion, Emile's collision with the machine's rhythm strips its order of its inconspicuousness and reveals how human beings have been transformed by a destructive rationality.

Emile's second role is to inaugurate the conversions of order that lead to the chase sequence. In the assembly-line sequence, for example, Emile picks up the handkerchief of Jeanne, the pretty secretary whom he is courting, and inadvertently places it on the moving line. Emile again refuses to adjust to an order that menaces his happiness and, in a spontaneous gesture that is emblematic of his refusal, throws himself into pursuit of the beauty's handkerchief. The handkerchief flies into the air and ends up in the factory courtyard. Emile knocks down the burly foreman, slaps a guard, and, as all give chase, sets up the pattern that draws these hostile marionettes behind him. This sequence is especially typical of the way in which Clair sets up a confrontation between order and the ludic rhythms, for Emile draws his cortege into the courtyard, where they crash through the absurdly long lines of workers marching there. This disruption of what should be a human order is transformed into an abstract relation as we see one pattern disrupting another, as ludic seriality disorganizes the geometry of work order.

These two comic devices, the gag and the chase sequence, point to the central ludic structure that lies at the heart of Clair's filmic world: the systematic transformation of ceremony into comic play. It has often been observed how easily ceremony and ritual lend themselves to the creation of the comic, because mechanical repetition is the basis for all ceremonial activity. Yet, it should be recalled, ceremony in its origins is also a ludic function, an attempt to create a perfect order within a delimited ritual space. Ceremony, however, is serious play that satisfies our need for order and solemnity through the creation of sanctified forms. Comic aggression against ceremony is, then, the creation of anticeremonies that affirm the need to transform cultural forms and to allow free impulses to undo ossified structures. Artaud understood the importance of this function of cinematic comedy. In *The Theater and Its Double* he praised the Marx Brothers for their creation of an "objective poetry based on humor" that was a form of revelation. For the comic, to use one of Artaud's favorite metaphors, is a way of burning cultural forms, of bringing about the disclosure of the unforeseen, the dangerous, and the unpredictable.

Entr'acte's funeral ceremony, with its capricious hearse and surprising cadaver, is emblematic of the kind of destruction of sanctified forms that Clair undertakes throughout his best early work. In this respect, one can think of the marriage ceremony that gives *Un Chapeau de Paille d'Italie* its ritual framework. Though the entire film is a long chase sequence, the marriage ceremony lends itself to the best serial gags. For example, after the assembled guests misinterpret an awkward gesture, the fear of impropriety leads the ceremony's participants to grope furtively at their throats to see if their ties are still in place—with the exception of the comically blind participant whose tie has come undone and who has made shambles of the ceremony. In *Les Deux Timides* it is legal ceremony that is comically transformed when mice run through the tribunal and the judges' seats collapse in the resulting havoc. Again, in the last film Clair made before going to Hollywood, *The Last Millionaire*, the court ceremony of royalty is the basis for the creation of antiorder. A blow on the head of the financier who has become a dictator changes him into a berserk prankster who forces his ministers to crawl about on their knees. But the best example of this kind of ceremonial destruction in Clair's work is provided perhaps by the finale of *A Nous la Liberté*. Here Clair transforms the celebration of social order and progress into a farcical antiritual as the notables pursue the bank notes until finally nothing is left of them on the screen except their top hats, which the wind blows about. Clair's final metonymy for social order reduces these bourgeois to their essence, beings who exist only in function of social ceremonies, rigid "top hats" whose existence is ludicrous when not integrated into the social ritual that supposedly justifies their existence.

This destruction of sanctified forms is thus a joyous aggression that channels our anarchistic impulses into a new order, a comic ludic order, the order of farce. When at the end of a dinner party—that ritual of bourgeois private life—Emile and Louis bombard Louis's pompous portrait with apples, we see a concrete representation of the way in which pure play can give rise to a joyous, destructive aggression. The destruction of the portrait and of the social order it represents are contained within the limits of the ludic order that Clair has created, yet the aggression is plainly there. For farce must be understood as an expression of destructive yet liberating impulses within the ordering framework of play.

It was this understanding of farce as springing from our darkest impulses that Clair himself pointed to when, in commenting on *Un Chapeau de Paille d'Italie*, he noted that the chase sequence holds the potential for becoming a form of carnage. For the hero the pursuit is, as Clair said,

> the worst of dreams. The search for the hat is a form of torture by experience in which the victim escapes from a double peril only to run toward a more serious one while fleeing in a groom's suit those monsters that have set upon his destruction: an irascible father-in-law, a former mistress, an enraged officer, and a deceived husband. This insane pursuit, in which the pursuer is himself pursued, could end only by a final explosion or slaughter if Labiche, that clever magician, did not pull a happy ending out of a hat.[5]

Ludic order, then, turns aggression into play and pleasure by limiting it to the closed space of the work. The happy ending is a kind of closure of the play

5. In Presentation of Labiche, Eugène Marin Labiche, *Oeuvres complètes* (Paris: Au Club de l'Honnête Homme, 1966), 3:viii.

space, an essential game rule that insures that farce, like all ludic activities, operates within its own limitations, its own closed sphere. Within this closed sphere, however, farce is the continually renewed, magically prolonged representation of gratuitous violence.

Happy endings notwithstanding, one might well wonder if the world of silent comedy and farce were not doomed to disappear precisely because it makes our aggressiveness too manifest and forces us to confront our desire to destroy sanctified forms. For, in a sense, every silent-film farce was a surrealist act. The introduction of sound was surely inimical to the continued creation of silent farces. But one can also see that in the France of the thirties, with the economic crisis, the spread of Marxist and fascist ideologies, and the growing obsession with French decadence, there was little energy to be devoted to ludic experimentation in film. And so René Clair left France for Hollywood, leaving behind him a body of work that, with all its childlike, boisterous vitality, we might call a monument to the era of surrealist innocence.

Vigo's *Zéro de conduite:*
Surrealism and the
Myth of Childhood

The modernist quest for a locus of grace, for an ecstatic form of consciousness in which the self exists withdrawn from the vicissitudes of time, goes back at least as far as Rousseau's "Fifth Revery" and the dissolution of the time-bound self that it portrays. But this quest, which runs through romanticism before becoming the essential modernist theme, took many other forms throughout the nineteenth century. One of the most important is the quest for a time past in which the self knew neither the anguish inflicted by its perception of temporality nor the constraints of causality, habit, and destructive rationality. In one sense this turning toward the past caused the premodernist writers to transform the classical myth of a golden age, or the childhood of the race, into the myth of childhood, or the golden age of the individual before his fall into time. After Rousseau, then, Hölderlin could proclaim the divinity of childhood ("ein göttlich Wesen ist das Kind"), for the child, who is not immersed in temporality, knows that immediate realm of being that the Greeks knew before their fall into History.[1] This vision is transposed in Mallarmé, who finds that the poet's task is to confront the absurd chance that comes into man's life after "the child abdicates his ecstasy" ("l'enfant abdique son extase").[2] For Proust, childhood is, in one sense, the ontologically privileged realm where the child knows an atemporal paradise before he comes to know that he is condemned to be governed by the mechanical laws of society, biology, and, finally, time. This ecstatic paradise can perhaps be recovered by art, but it is also a source of anguish for a man haunted by the memory of plenitude, as one sees in the final lines of Rilke's poem "Childhood":

1. Friedrich Hölderlin, *Hyperion*, in his *Hölderlins Werke* (1797, 1799; reprint, Salzburg: Die Bergland Buch Klassiker, n.d.), p. 441.
2. Stéphane Mallarmé, "Prose (pour des Esseintes)," in his *Oeuvres complètes* (Paris: Bibliothèque de la Pléiade, 1965), p. 57.

O Kindheit, o entgleitende Vergleiche.
Wohin? Wohin?
(O childhood, o images slipping from us.
Whither? Whither?)[3]

André Breton's belief that childhood offers one of the closest approximations to the marvelous is perhaps one of the last variations in this history of the myth of childhood. The goal of all surrealist activity is the disclosure or revelation of the marvelous, or that transrational state in which the antinomies of subjectivity and objectivity, irrational and rational, dreaming and waking, are overcome. Such a revelation of an ontologically privileged state can be given by dreams, but, as Breton states in the *First Surrealist Manifesto*, childhood also allows man to remember a lost paradise:

Man, that definitive dreamer, every day more unhappy with his fate, has great difficulty assessing the objects that he has been led to make use of, and that his nonchalance or his effort has given to him. . . . If he retains some lucidity, all he can do is turn back toward his childhood, which, however much it may have been butchered by his trainers, seems to him nonetheless to be full of magic. There the absence of all forms of restriction offers him the perspective of several lives that one can lead at the same time.[4]

Childhood, then, is not only a locus of revelation but also, as Breton's comments show, the moment when the power of the imagination can lead to that simultaneity of perception that modernists like Apollinaire saw as a triumph over time. Moreover, from a surrealist perspective, a return to childhood is a return to one of the sources from whence springs the adult's need to revolt against all forms of restraint that would make of life anything less than a continuous plenitude.

These opening comments will, it is hoped, offer the perspective that endows Jean Vigo's *Zéro de conduite* (1933) with its fullest significance, since it seems to us that this extraordinary film draws on the modernist myth of childhood as it conveys an often surrealist vision of the insurrection to which a vision of childhood grace can lead. Vigo seems to be at one with Breton in that *Zéro de conduite* portrays children as being surrealists by their very nature,

3. Rainer Maria Rilke, "Kindheit," in *Translations from the Poetry of Rainer Maria Rilke*, trans. M. D. Herter Norton (New York: W. W. Norton, 1962), p. 49.
4. André Breton, *Manifestes du surréalisme*, p. 11. (All translations are mine, unless otherwise indicated.)

quite ready to use the full powers of their imaginations to transform the world and then to participate magically in whatever realm their fantasy can create. In *Zéro de conduite* we see in fact a vision of childhood as a form of paradise whose essential characteristic is the free pursuit of the pleasure principle, and not the least of Vigo's achievements in this film is to have shown the omnipotence of desire in the child's world.

Nearly every sequence in *Zéro de conduite* turns on the polarity that exists between, on the one hand, the children's world of free invention and joyous eroticism and, on the other hand, the adult "trainers'" world of repressive discipline, order, and degraded eroticism. Consider the film's first sequence: The opening title, "Vacation is over. The semester begins." ("Finies les vacances. La rentrée."), shows that the children are obliged initially to leave that conflict-free time of freedom, of life as pure play, to return to the repressive realm of school and socialization. The return from vacation to school stands, of course, as a synecdoche for the fall from childhood, the loss of paradise, that the school is instrumental in bringing about.

This passage from ludic time to social time acquires something of a demonic dimension when we see the night train that carries the boys from vacation to the confines of their scholastic prison. The lighting, weak and intermittently setting the rather sinister smoke in relief, suggests a descent into an inferno. Moreover, the first shots of Caussat give him an aura of isolation; the boy sits alone, a child who has been torn from the summer's ludic freedom and now sits like a small adult in the "real" world of travel and train schedules. But the camera then reveals that an adult is sleeping on the seat across from him. This adult body, like a huge, slumping marionette, is a strange apparition that stresses the incongruity of this night passage. It is also the first of the seemingly inescapable adults that we find throughout *Zéro de conduite*. Adults are incongruous presences throughout the film, yet they manage to intrude in nearly every scene; the inert body on the train seat foreshadows the disruptive way in which adults suddenly appear in the children's realm as grotesque or sinister beings, incomprehensible in their very absurd bulk.

The atmosphere is changed by the sudden arrival of Bruel. Together Caussat and Bruel can seemingly find the courage to confront the return to their drab *lycée*. They begin a series of games that are so many signs that the boys' imagination has not yet given in to the restraints of adult logic. Bruel magically separates a knuckle from his finger, while Caussat puts a small trumpet in his nose and plays it. Two balloons are transformed by the boys' imagination into female breasts, a feat matched only by Caussat's sticking a feather in his rear and metamorphosing himself into a bird. Their final trick, which is a satirical comment on both boys and adults, is to simultaneously pull cigars from their pockets, light them, and convert themselves into mock adults. Vigo here uses very low angle shots to underline how the boys have undergone satirical metamorphosis, for throughout the film low-angle shots offer a child's perspective on the adults the children must face. At the same time, this angle facilitates the framing that Vigo uses to decapitate most of the adults.

Filling the compartment with smoke in much the same way that the locomotive fills the night with mysterious vapors, these pseudoadults seem to create a fantasy world of which they are the only proprietors. Caussat, however, suddenly becomes aware of the adult presence in their midst and cries out, "He's dead!" ("Il est mort!"). The slumping body puts an end, almost symbolically it would appear, to the boys' frolic. The adult presence now imposes a limit to their play. The fantasy voyage, though remaining on one level a descent into an inferno, gives way to a rather provincial railroad station where the *surveillant* Parrain is waiting for his charges. It should be noted here that Parrain (Pète-Sec), Huguet, and the silent *surveillant général* (Bec de Gaz or "The Creep") are not teachers, as most criticism in English would have it. They are all *surveillants* or "adult monitors"; they have only a repressive or disciplinary function. They are the guards of the prison order.

The first sequence thus ends in a railroad station, with the sound of a real locomotive replacing the joyous music that we have heard until now. This scene, in which Vigo presents Huguet, Tabard, Parrain, and the others, is virtually the only one that he shoots in semirealistic terms, and even in this scene lighting and, more especially, the characters' gestures—who can take seriously Parrain's glaring refusal to tip his hat?—undermine any belief in a pure representation of social reality.

After this scene Vigo continues to shoot sequences that bear much resemblance to either a fantasy or a dream in order to set forth the quality of the imaginative world that the children would oppose to the adult world that surrounds them. The dream and the fantasy modes are, in effect, the mimetic modes that Vigo uses in an attempt to convey the sense of the marvelous that permeates a child's experience. In this respect, we might see here an essentially surrealist attempt to offer a vision unmediated by the categories of rational or "realist" representation. For surrealists, dream and fantasy are two primary modes of exploration that can reveal how truncated is a rationalist view of what constitutes the limits of representation. Dream offers a rhetoric of representation in which both the law of noncontradiction and causality are suspended; it also offers demonstration of how desire informs one's way of representing to oneself the psyche's deepest concerns. Fantasy, on the other hand, asserts the right of the imagination to live all imagined possibilities in the face of restrictions that reason might impose. Vigo's use of oneiric and fantasy modes is thus at once a way of revealing the children's desire to live an imaginative paradise and also a surrealist indictment against the repressive rationality that would interdict this paradise.

The dream mode is used in the film's next sequence, when the boys find themselves in the dormitory for the night. First, a very high angle shot offers a view of the foot of each bed, but no children can be seen, and it almost seems as if their ordered little universe were not meant for inhabitation. The only human presence is an enigmatic figure wearing dark glasses who stands at the end of the corridor that separates the beds. Yet one can hardly speak of human presence, since the machinelike night watchman is merely an extension of the order that the school seeks to impose. Even after we hear Parrain announce that Tabard will not spend the night there, we must still intuit, as in a dream, that this emptiness can be a place of human animation.

The first moving figure in the scene scarcely adds a human presence, for the mute *surveillant général* glides into the room silently, as in a dream. His ubiquitous presence permeates the school like the repressive principle he seems to embody. The oneiric quality is enhanced by the destruction of narrative logic. The boys begin to create a disturbance, so Parrain calls, quite arbitrarily, for Dupont to come forward. Then for no evident reason Bruel, Caussat, and Colin come to the foot of his bed. One arbitrary decision is countered by another, which suggests the associative quality of a dream development at the same time that, in this case, it maintains the tension between the adult and child worlds. The dormitory is ordered by adult logic, but we see it as it might exist in the oneiric realm of a child's imagination.

Thus, later, when the children finally enact their revolt against the school, it begins in this dreamlike setting. *Zéro de conduite*'s most famous sequence is its most oneiric. It is the slow-motion revolt in which the boys, rallying around Tabard, declare war on the teachers, on the school, on all that would confine them. The visual beauty of this sequence is stunning, for it unites a call to revolt and the means for that revolt—the recovery of dream and desire—in the same series of images. After Tabard has attached the black flag of anarchy to the school's roof, the boys in their jubilation engage in a pillow fight, so the entire sequence is bathed in a billowing snow of feathers. The ethereal quality of the scene is reinforced by Jaubert's music, which is played backwards on the sound track; it endows the scene with an otherworldliness that lifts it into the realm of the victorious imagination. Dream, magic, and joy have joined with desire to create a revolt that can destroy all constraints; even the *surveillant général* must for the first time beat a hasty retreat when he tries to enter the dormitory and transgress against the power of children's dream.

The boys' nocturnal procession unites dream and revolt on a plateau beyond mere rejection of bourgeois institutions, though they are certainly targets of this revolt. Dream leads to the ritual of pure revolt, of revolt that refuses all limits to desire. Even critics who fail to see that Vigo and the surrealists are one on this point usually are forced to recognize how total Vigo's revolt is. As John M. Smith, for example, remarks at the end of his essay on *Zéro de conduite*:

> What is seen feels like a ritual re-enactment of what is permanently the case. Though this is true in the comparatively boring sense that the film conveys 'the essence of childhood,' I mean rather that the narrative is handled in such a way that individual events don't have only a literal existence (even where that is most arguable) but rather refer to a continuous state of being and to a spiritual process. The revolt is permanent and not an event: the triumph of instinct over insensitive officiousness refers to the permanent superiority of the imagination and physical sensation over attempts to deny them.[5]

The procession's dream mode gives way the next day to the massacre of the puppets, of the town's notables, which is of course a self-conscious fantasy. For both dream and fantasy are forms of the "ritual re-enactment" of permanent revolt. And the film's final image, in which the boys climb the roof and reach for the sky, opens up on the limitless horizon of Vigo's total rebellion. Their hands raised in joy, the boys begin an ascension for which there can be no boundaries. Quite properly, there is no concern shown for where the revolt might lead, since such a question can only be the product of an adult, instrumentalist mind concerned with the rationality of ends and means. Rather, we see here an enactment of a child's revolt, which, though it may be

5. John M. Smith, *Jean Vigo*, p. 105.

the origin of the adult's later refusal of limits, can be quite satisfied with a permanent refusal that, ignorant of time, glories in the perpetual presence of its own freedom.

Grotesqueries are perhaps more obvious in *Zéro de conduite* than is praise of eros, since all the adults, with the exception of Huguet, the sympathetic *surveillant*, are ludicrous in their very physical presence. The principal is especially emblematic in this respect, for he is a fantasylike dwarf with a huge beard. He seems to incarnate the very contradiction that Vigo discerns between adult pretense and capacity. A deformed puppet, the principal also embodies antieroticism, especially in his efforts to destroy the relationships that the boys have established among themselves. Bruel and Tabard, Caussat and Colin form couples in which eros plays a major role, and the principal tries to interdict the bonds that unite them. He calls in Tabard, for example, and warns him of the "psychological" risks he runs in his friendship with Bruel. The scene turns into a comic nightmare as the principal leaps up and, his arms spread wide apart, seems to spring from the depths of some inferno. In this brief but explosive image Vigo conveys a feeling for the neurosis underlying adult punitive measures that could be compared with the description of hell that Stephen must endure in Joyce's *Portrait of the Artist*.

Tabard, first presented as a sheltered and rather feminine creature, the sissy who has been overly protected by his mother and must prove himself to his comrades, ultimately leads the boys' revolt because he cannot tolerate the adults' perverted eroticism, especially that of the grotesque chemistry teacher. The only teacher seen in the film, the chemistry teacher is one of Vigo's most extraordinary creations, for in this one character Vigo sets forth all he finds detestable in adult degradation of the body. A high-angle shot, taken from the point of view of a student sitting high in the tiers of seats, at the back of the classroom, first shows the chemistry teacher in a position of inferiority as he ambles into the room like some lumbering animal. Immediately following him, suspended on a wire and manipulated by some unseen wag, is the classroom skeleton. These bare bones set off the teacher's body in all its massive obesity. The contrast turns his corpulence into an obscene mass, for, to use Sartrian terms, the flesh is revealed as flesh and hence as obscene. As he enters, this overly friendly teacher gives the first sign of his perverted eroticism, for his fleshy hand caresses Tabard's head as he passes by. This ambiguous gesture is followed by a series of repugnant gestures that even further undermine the possibility of adult flesh being anything other than grotesque.

The teacher begins to put on his lab jacket, but then pauses, sticks his fingers into his armpit, and sniffs them to see how much stench is there. This image of the body's debasement is followed by the teacher's placing a tube in each nostril and sniffing in. Then, as the camera pans and shows his young charges, we hear him gather spittle in his throat in preparation for a long expectoration. These images conveying an extraordinary sense of disgust thus prepare the spectator for the symbolic rape to which the teacher forces Tabard to submit when he places his hand on the boy again.

In *Zéro de conduite* adults' hands play the same role that the dancers' thighs played in *A Propos de Nice*; both are images of degraded eroticism. For example, earlier in *Zéro de conduite*, when Tabard and Bruel return together from the outing in the town, the principal tells the *surveillant général* that this couple must be watched. The "Creep's" reaction is to rub his hands together in a lascivious gesture that seems almost like an act of autoeroticism in the film's context. His hands express what seems to be either a form of envy or perhaps his designs on the happy and innocent couple. In the classroom sequence with Tabard described above, the chemistry teacher expresses his desire first by running his hand again through Tabard's hair. Then, seemingly solicitous of Tabard's welfare, the fat lecher asks him why he is taking no notes—and then places his hand on Tabard's. A close-up shot again reveals flesh as flesh, flesh as a form of aggression, as the teacher's obese fingers caress Tabard. The close-up seems to transform them into a grotesque sexual organ. It is to this menace that Tabard finds his comic cry of rebellion, "Monsieur le professeur, je vous dis merde!" (roughly, "Sir, shit on you!"). In the face of debased desire Tabard finds the scatological expression that serves as a springboard to the entire school's revolt.

This revolt against adult degradation of eros should not, however, cause one to lose sight of the joyful expression of desire that runs throughout the film. For the solidarity that unites the boys, both as couples and as a group, is grounded in the polymorphous forms of eros that the children enjoy. In the very first scene, the boys delight in each other's presence while they play erotic games that spring from the free play of their imaginations, such as their transformation of balloons into female breasts. The couples—examples of what the French call *amitiés particulières*—are bound by erotic ties, but in no exclusive manner, for the children's eros is the basis for the bonds that create their fraternal solidarity. Other examples of this solidarity abound throughout the film. One need only recall that the boys become quiet in order to prevent a sleepwalker from waking up and meeting a sudden death or that the revolt against beans comes to a sudden end when Caussat realizes Colin is suffering from this attack upon his mother, the cook. The most striking images of this solidarity grounded in eros are found in the dormitory, when the boys grasp hands as they circle around Tabard in celebration of their revolt, and when, during the procession, a boy does a double backward somersault and lands in a chair the others are carrying. His nude body turns slowly in the air, adding a strange, almost hieratic quality to the fantasy procession; at the same time, it is the very image of the children's free enjoyment of their bodies and their solidarity in revolt.

Foreshadowing *L'Atalante* in this respect, Vigo also sets forth an image of the male–female couple as the perfect realization of desire and poetry. In what is one of his least-transposed personal memories he shows the nascent couple when Caussat goes to see the daughter of his *correspondant* (adult sponsor) on a Sunday afternoon. In this scene there reigns an innocent sensuality born of the freedom the boy and the girl know as they play together. She covers his eyes and then shows him a goldfish bowl suspended from the ceiling. This simple image reveals the world of the marvelous that the children can know as a couple. From a surrealist point of view, of course, the couple is the privileged unit, for in the couple desire can overcome the limits of subjectivity and become waking dream. Vigo's sense of composition and lighting is all-important in this scene, for he bathes the couple in a light that suggests the world of the child's plentitude, of pure desire and wonder. Flesh is revealed as being in the service of joyous pleasure. Yet Vigo does not allow his idyll to remain free from the menace of adult authority. The *correspondant* is always there, ambiguously hiding behind his newspaper, a faceless adult who seems to be lost in his world of print and logic, but who nonetheless acts as a censor of the children's freedom.

Huguet, the surrealist *surveillant* who has not lost his sense of the marvelous, also illustrates the quest for eros. The sequence in which he leads the boys on an outing in the town turns into a madcap race for freedom that culminates in an erotic chase. Vigo's editing in this sequence also creates a series of puns that reflect a surrealist sense of humor. Vigo cuts between shots showing the boys and Huguet as they walk and shots showing the principal in his office making reproving comments on Bruel's, Tabard's, and Huguet's conduct. At one point Tabard and Bruel, who have been separated by Parrain, rejoin each other and, through Vigo's use of a quick cut, appear to look into the principal's office as if to mock him and the deferential *surveillant général*, who is with him. However, in the outing sequence Huguet is the central figure. He is a *rêveur*, a waking dreamer who soon lets the boys go their own way while he pursues his revery. The boys lose him, but find him again; his revery has led him to a lovely lady. Huguet, pursued by all his protégés, quickens his pace and throws himself into chasing the elusive beauty. She suddenly turns a corner, though a flash close-up shows a hem of a skirt disappearing around the building. The next shot shows that this skirt belongs to an angry priest whom Huguet has nearly pounced on. Not only does this visual pun dislocate the narrative logic in a manner worthy of Buñuel, but it caps off the chase with its own commentary on the limits of desire in a world of institutionalized repression. In good surrealist fashion Vigo gives both the church and the state, the priest and the schoolmaster, credit for hobbling man's imagination.

If Huguet can pursue eros freely, it is because he is the only adult in the film who can still play. Vigo first presents Huguet on the train, for it turns out that he was the enigmatic "dead" man. His identity is revealed on the station platform when, tipping his hat in a friendly fashion, he meets the icy stare of the desiccated Parrain. This comic encounter foreshadows the plotting threesome's pronouncement that Huguet is "a good guy," for not only does he protect them as they plot in the courtyard, but he also joins the children in their games. Huguet participates in their gratuitous exercise of the body and the imagination. For example, he imitates Charlie Chaplin, which, in context, is both Vigo's homage to the American comedian's gentle anarchy and a metaphor for Huguet's refusal to accept the school's repressive order. But it is especially in the dreamlike scene in which Huguet, after leaving the toilet, prances about surrounded by laughing children that we see him as an agent of joyous liberation. Shot from a distance with a telephoto lens that makes him stand out in all his fantasy, Huguet dances in a magic world that continues to exist even when the children leave the play space of the courtyard and enter the classroom where for a chaotic moment Huguet is in charge.[6]

6. With regard to this scene, Barthélemy Amengual has very perceptively noted, "The telephoto lens surrounds the detail it has isolated at a far distance with what might be likened to a virtual circular matting or to an iris that nonetheless remains imperceptible. Everything the lens shows, it shows as so many islands. And since these islands (shot through the telephoto lens) are put together without discrimination with "normal" shots of average focal distance, since what was far away, eccentric, and untouchable is successfully mixed with what is near, immediate, and palpable, the reality created by the montage is affected and charged with an aura of unreality. This plurality of spatial "monads," *this Brownian movement of space-time* as the surrealist Ribemont-Dessaintes would say . . . is typical of both the child's psyche and the destruction of

The fantastic and the farcical dominate when the children return to the study hall, where pandemonium reigns. Huguet's classroom, in one sense, is an anarchistic symphony conducted by Huguet. Fantasy abounds as Caussat, through trick photography reminiscent of Méliès, engages in magic feats and Huguet walks on his hands in order to show a child how better to accomplish this bit of wonder. Standing on one hand, he then draws a satirical caricature of the *surveillant général*, an example perhaps of how farce is always on the side of those who would destroy a repressive order. The children pursue the pleasure principle with great gusto—until the silent *surveillant général*, his sinister presence setting off this spectacle in all its exultation, enters and reimposes adult discipline. Meaningfully enough, his caricature converts itself into a sketch of Napoleon! Yet the *surveillant général* and the slavery of the imagination he represents have been effectively disarmed by the joyous farce. As Huguet seems to know when he shrugs his shoulders under the *surveillant général*'s disapproving stare, the free play of the imagination can make a mockery of the most stringent repression.

Behind this exuberant farce lies, however, the paradisiac vision of the omnipotence of the child's imagination, unfettered by the neurotic constraints of adult reason, capable of subverting all order in the name of a magic plenitude. The importance of *Zéro de conduite* lies, then, in what we take to be its nearly unique attempt to express the modernist myth of childhood in a film. If there is some truth in the much-repeated idea that Vigo was cinema's Rimbaud, it is not because he was a young filmmaker who left us a small opus of a few somewhat mutilated films, or because he was an anarchist with feelings of revolt akin to those of the young Rimbaud. Rather, the similarity lies in the way Vigo attempted in *Zéro de conduite* to portray the ecstatic openness of childhood and the child's desire to live in a realm of perpetual revelation, the realm that we glimpse at times in the fulgurations of Rimbaud's *Illuminations*. If Rimbaud recognized in his "The Drunken Boat" that he had failed in communicating his vision, that his quest was too demanding for the child-poet, his realization did not stop his work and his life from becoming one of the main sources for the modernist myth of childhood and the poetic quest. Vigo's relative success, on the other hand, seems to have contributed little to the creation of cinematic myths. Perhaps this is not merely due to the way in

reality brought about by collages. We find a perfect coincidence between a child's mind and surrealism." "Monde et vision dans l'oeuvre de Vigo," *Jean Vigo*, special number of *Etudes cinématographiques*, no. 51–52 (1966):78.

which *Zéro de conduite* was censured, partially truncated, and held from the commercial market until after 1945.[7] Perhaps it is really due to the fact that *Zéro de conduite* comes at the end of the development of a myth and, as extraordinary as the film is, marks the end of a myth and an ideology.

7. These problems are well documented in P. E. Salès-Gomès's *Jean Vigo*, in his chapters on *Zéro de conduite* and on the vicissitudes that Vigo's work has suffered.

Film and Society

Jean Renoir
and the Mimesis of History

Two directors dominate French cinema of the 1930s: Marcel Carné and Jean Renoir. Though Carné is rarely given the same recognition as Renoir, it is instructive to note that both, in their best films, seek to ground their work in a vision of history and to come to grips with the historical crisis that had brought about depression, fascism, and the threat of another war. In Carné's *Quai des Brumes* or *Le Jour se lève*, for example, we find an essentially metaphysical vision that accounts for the historically decreed moment of decadence in which a malign destiny condemns Carné's dispossessed heroes to failure and self-destruction. Tragic destiny and historical determinism overlap in a representation of history that is essentially theatrical. For history has become a tragic fate that decrees the fall of its hapless victims. One inevitably thinks of Malraux when one sees that Carné has implicitly identified the determining forces of history with some form of tragic destiny, since through this metaphor he relates individual fate to that of an entire class and a nation.

In *La Grande Illusion* and *La Règle du jeu* Renoir also seeks to represent history through a series of theatrical metaphors. Like Carné's work, Renoir's reflects his time's view of history, which held that the thirties was a time of impasse, a period of decadence and immobility that one could explain only in terms of some form of historical determinism. Artists on both the right and left saw their most imperative task to be the representation of historical forces, and neither Carné nor Renoir is unique in his recourse to theatrical metaphors to confront this task. However, Renoir, among filmmakers, is perhaps unique in the scope of his undertakings, for one can see in the films he made before World War II nothing less than an attempt to rival the great novelists and historians of the nineteenth century who had charted the succession of social classes that had taken power in France. This attempt is visible not only in his adaptations of literary works such as *Madame Bovary*, *La Bête humaine*, and *Une partie de campagne*, but also in his political documentary *La Vie est à nous*, made for the youth movement of the Popular Front, and, more especially, in *La Marseillaise*.

La Marseillaise, financed by subscriptions from the C.G.T. labor union, is not only, in its portrayal of the French Revolution, a committed film in the sense that it is an attempt to create proletarian art. It is also a very direct expression of the historicism Renoir held at the time. Explaining why in this film the Royalists and the Marseillais revolutionaries could not be reconciled, Renoir offered a succinct résumé of his view of historical change:

> Aside from their misunderstanding they are separated by something most obvious and which is essential in world history: by whether or not they are in harmony with dates. It happens that excellent principles, that are indisputable and absolutely worthy of defense, disappear or even become dangerous and homicidal simply because they are no longer applicable to their era. And it happens that much less developed principles . . . function admirably because they are in harmony with their time. . . . Louis XVI is a loser because he no longer had any purpose at that time.[1]

This kind of vague determinism is hardly Marxist or revolutionary, though it does suggest how Renoir's idealism could lead him to become, at the end of the thirties, a "man of the left." It also points to the necessity of understanding Renoir's much-discussed use of theatrical metaphors in relation to history and historical evolution. Theater provides models for understanding social evolution at the same time that it provides an explanatory metaphor for the comprehension of individual behavior and fate. Theatrical metaphors are, in short, the key to Renoir's mimesis of history.

La Marseillaise presents, in a rather summary form, Renoir's central metaphor, in which history is identified with a theatrical decor and individual adaptation to this decor with successful role playing. Society is thus conceived as akin to a theatrical backdrop, and against this backdrop historical personae play out roles embodying principles that may or may not be in accord with their setting. By extension of this play metaphor, history is the unfolding of a series of game situations that dictate certain rules for performance. The players who survive are those who master the rules and play in accord with the necessities that history has decreed. The "rules of the game" are never fixed once and for all, but depend on the transformations that history works from one generation to the next.

La Marseillaise thus provides a key for an understanding of more complex works like *La Grande Illusion* and *La Règle du jeu*. Considered together,

1. Quoted in Jacques Rivette and François Truffaut, "Nouvel entretien avec Jean Renoir," p. 42. (All translations are mine, unless otherwise indicated.)

these works seem to indicate that Renoir was working toward the creation of a historical saga extending from the French Revolution to his own time. This seems true not only of the general historical outlines that the works present but also of the presentation of certain details. Central to this project is the aristocrat of *La Marseillaise*, La Chesnaye. This nobleman is the proprietor of those domains that are later purchased by the Rosenthal family of *La Grande Illusion*. It is this rich, Jewish, bourgeois family that, having assumed the aristocratic name La Chesnaye, appears in *La Règle du jeu*. The name *La Chesnaye* is a historical token revealing various roles that appear in the course of the evolution of French society. The original La Chesnaye as we see him in *La Marseillaise* is a blind player, for he still believes that he can choose, in aristocratic terms, to "conquer or die." But, giving voice to Renoir's historicism, Louis XVI reminds this artistocrat that the "comedy" in which the royalists find themselves engaged cannot be brought to a quick ending by an act of volition. La Chesnaye must play out a role that ultimately condemns him to the guillotine and then pass on his name, like a mask, to new players in the historical pageant.

One should not exaggerate the continuity that ties *La Marseillaise* to the other films, but it is of fundamental importance to see how this film presents Renoir's kind of historical determinism and suggests his view of theater as a model for understanding societal organization. It is, of course, in *La Grande Illusion* and *La Règle du jeu* that his work finds its richest expression as Renoir, orchestrating theatrical and ludic motifs, seeks to create adequate filmic modes of representation of contemporary history.

An introduction to *La Grande Illusion* might well begin by recalling that "illusion," coming from the Latin *illudere*, means to enter into play. This film deals with both the delusions that men entertain at a given historical moment and the forms of play and theatrical artifice they enter into as they conduct their daily lives. Of course, the historical moment is of central importance. *La Grande Illusion* takes place during World War I, though it is not a war film in any ordinary sense. Rather, it deals with the various roles men assume within a very specific historical configuration. Concrete details of the war are, in fact, curiously absent from the film. When reference is made to the war, it seems a rather abstract phenomenon, an event such as one might know about by reading a newspaper or an official report—the latter the only contact that the film's prisoners of war have with the fighting on the front. The war serves as a historical frame of reference, perhaps as a causal force in terms of dramatic motivation, but it has no physical presence, unlike the war in Losey's *King and Country* or Milestone's *All Quiet on the Western Front*. These films attempt to represent war by using concrete synecdoches, by showing its mud, rats, and individual death, whereas in *La Grande Illusion* war is more a term of comparison in the metaphorical relation that equates society and a theatrical backdrop.

La Grande Illusion is a fairly straightforward film so far as the narration of episodic experience is concerned. It is divided into four principal tableaux, following a simple linear chronology that traces a continuous present-tense narration. Each tableau is set in a different decor, which allows Renoir to develop specific role-playing relations before each specific backdrop: first in the French, and then in the analogous German officers' canteen in which we meet the principal characters; next in the German prisoner camp to which the French aviators are sent; afterwards in the castle-prison to which the aviators are sent after their numerous escape attempts; and, finally, in the German countryside, with its idyllic peasant farm.

The first tableau comprises two scenes whose decors are essentially the same. Renoir's insistence on the similarity between the French and German canteens parallels the quick fraternity that arises between the French aviators who have been taken prisoners and their German captors. This fraternity, however, establishes itself on class lines, between the aristocrat Boeldieu (Pierre Fresnay) and his German peer Rauffenstein (Erich von Stroheim), and between the working-class officer Maréchal (Jean Gabin) and a German officer who has worked as a mechanic in Lyon and thus speaks French. The officers' canteen is one of the last bastions of aristocratic role playing, for Rauffenstein receives his "guests" much as if they had merely finished a joust or some other ludic activity in which sportsmanship is the highest ethical quality.

Illusion in its meanings both of play and of masquerade is, of course, the essence of an aristocratic attitude. The aristocrat, in the face of the demands of reality, wills play and its rules as his defining activity. Illusion in its meaning of delusion and error is also present in this tableau, as Renoir underscores in several ways,. First, the presence of proletarian officers points up the incongruity of the play ceremonies that Rauffenstein attempts to enact. The German aristocrat scarcely deigns to recognize the presence of Maréchal, who, if he can hardly engage in noble role playing, is nonetheless an officer. Second, the arrival of a funeral wreath for a French pilot the Germans have shot down seems to point both to the sporting illusions these aristocrats entertain and to another incongruity between their attitude and historical reality. Mechanized death hardly seems compatible with chivalrous homages. Third, the arrival of a military policeman who has come to take the prisoners marks the intrusion of bureaucratic order into this world of play and illusion. This intrusion of the military's bureaucratic order sets forth an ironic juxtaposition between the rationalized routine of war and the aristocratic order that finds its expression, as we see in the image of the soldiers seated together, in the portrayal of enemies gathered in warrior fraternity around the Round Table.

The film's second tableau deals primarily with the French prisoners' efforts to escape from the prison camp to which they have been sent, though it also presents their attempts to create an evening of theatrical entertainment. These two activities are related by an implicit metaphor, as we see from the tableau's outset. The tunnel the prisoners are digging is constructed with wood taken from the prison theater, and the dangers of this form of play are revealed when, after the arrival of Boeldieu and Maréchal, the Parisian actor nearly suffocates in the hole they hope will lead them to freedom. The film's title again ironically illuminates the soldiers' activity. Illusion means a form of theatrical play as well as a form of blindness, and the two forms are linked here in the game of make-believe the prisoners willingly play. In fact, the men's belief that they can escape from the war "theater" is much like the frankly theatrical illusion that offers them a transvestite vision of women. In both cases the men want very badly to believe in a saving illusion.

Boeldieu's attitude toward the other officers emphasizes again the ambiguities of class differentiation. As an aristocrat he, too, is a player in the game of escape, for it is his very essence to play. Boeldieu, however, is quite conscious of the gratuitous nature of this ludic activity, as he makes clear when he explains that he accepts the rules of war in the same way he accepts the rules of tennis or golf. One plays golf on a golf course, and one tries to escape from a prison camp. Yet the rules of war have changed, and Boeldieu is contemptuous of a game whose rules require that he laugh at the actor's slapstick or demand that he participate in a war that has brought about an inversion of values. For he sees German children "playing at being soldiers" while his own soldiers "play at being children." Moreover, Boeldieu's ludic vision of war is hardly in harmony with the nationalisms that have brought about the combat he plays in. In this respect, too, Boeldieu shows himself to be a self-conscious anachronism.

Ironic ambiguities also permeate the frankly theatrical scenes of this tableau. The box of feminine clothes that Rosenthal's wealthy family sends the prisoners allows the men to indulge in imaginative speculation about women and to play erotic make-believe. After a young soldier has dressed as a woman, Renoir's slow pan shot, showing the prisoners' pangs of desire as they stare at the all too convincing illusion, is a masterpiece of derisive revelation. The image of the alluring transvestite denotes illusion in the strictest sense. Yet it also connotes a derisive awareness of the human frailty that demands the creation of such illusions, as well as Renoir's compassionate understanding of the need for illusion and belief. These connotative ambiguities, demanding from the spectator the capacity to empathize with an image and at the same time to maintain an ironic distance, account for what we might call the semantic density of much of Renoir's imagery. As in this example, his images are charged with connotative values that often appear, when considered individually, to be in contradiction. Such ambiguity or, more precisely, polysemantic richness, must be accepted, however, if the viewer is to enter into the full play of meanings that Renoir's images generate.

This same sort of ambiguity is present throughout much of the evening of theatrical acts that the prisoners present to entertain themselves. Renoir's use of his camera is essential in the creation of other ironic metaphors here. He first shows us the stage, where the actor sings a Parisian ditty, from the audience's point of view. A reverse angle-shot, showing the audience as seen from the stage, framed by the same row of footlights, establishes a metaphorical identity between audience and stage, between avowed illusion and unconsciously held roles. The derisive side of this metaphorical equation is most evident in the reaction set off by the news of a French victory at Douaumont, for the audience rises to sing the "Marseillaise." Renoir's camera comes to rest then on a young Englishman who, having removed his wig much as one would remove one's hat, is singing with great intensity. The singing of the French national anthem by a half-revealed transvestite is another image having equivocal connotations. It is derisively comic for, to paraphrase Bergson, the presence of physical incongruity can only deflate any pretense to spirituality or, in this case, to patriotism. At the same time, the image seems to connote something akin to reckless heroism and bravery—the Germans are not pleased by the singing—so that Renoir has again endowed the image with an ambiguous richness, making it both an expression of ironic lucidity about historical fate and a statement of sympathetic compassion for brave men.

The second tableau underscores the various forms of illusion that these soldiers—actor, worker, schoolteacher, engineer, aristocrat—entertain, while it also serves to establish the various theatrical metaphors that orient our perception of the rest of the film's representation of historical forces. Moreover, it presents new variations on the themes of fraternity and communication, as we see when Maréchal cannot understand his well-meaning German jailer or when the newly arrived British soldiers cannot grasp Maréchal's gesticulations as he tries to tell them about the tunnel in the quarters they are to inhabit. The notions of fraternity and mutual understanding that the first tableau presents are set in opposition with the impossibility of their realization. In Renoir's presentation of history every theme generates its countertheme, which in turn gives rise to the systematic ambiguity that is a structural part of *La Grande Illusion*.

The third tableau's decor is overtly symbolic, for it is a medieval castle, now converted into a prison for difficult prisoners. Representing medieval, heroic, and aristocratic order, this symbol of the glory of feudal times now has a degraded function in a war in which its stone battlements have become an anachronism. It is here that the two aristocratic officers, Boeldieu and Rauffenstein, confront each other in a requiem for a class that history has condemned to disappear. To the extent that the castle's fate is analogous to that of the two aristocrats, we can speak of the decor as the first term in another derisive metaphor, though one that again expresses a great feeling of compassion. The castle's degradation stands in analogy to the kind of futile role playing to which Rauffenstein is condemned. As he points out with bitter awareness, the soldiers who man these crenellated fortifications are only old men "playing at being soldiers." Rauffenstein himself has suffered severe burns and fractures and, held up by a brace, knows that he has come to play a despicable role as a mere prison functionary. To play his role as an aristocrat, to engage in the superior forms of play that define an aristocratic essence, he must attempt to create the illusion that he is continuing to serve. Hence the elaborate *mise en scène* he creates in order to offer himself a suitable decor: the medieval chapel that is his chamber, the uniform and white gloves, the single geranium that grows in a pot.

Rauffenstein's attempt to create illusions is marred by his lucidity. If he refuses to consort with Maréchal and Rosenthal, with the French worker and the wealthy bourgeois, he recognizes that they are, as he says, "gifts of the French Revolution" and that their presence here as officers is the result of historical processes that have also brought about his class's demise. Renoir shows another side of his historical determinism in the reaction of Russian prisoners when they receive a gift from the Tzarina, an aristocrat who would be Rauffenstein's opposite number. Comically blind to the prisoners' needs and hence to the historical realities of the war, she sends them a crate of edifying books that the disappointed prisoners burn in anger. Thus, lack of lucidity on the part of the Russian aristocracy gives rise to an incident that in symbolic terms undoubtedly foreshadows the revolution to come. The aristocracy's lack of adaptation gives rise here to a comic form of blindness. The violent consequences of this blindness point to Renoir's vision of history as a series of successive destructions of the unadaptable, be they lucid or not.

The third tableau seems, in fact, to give a résumé of the two options that remain for the aristocracy. For the blind, there remains destruction in the violent conflagration of revolution. For the lucid, suicide is the ultimate solution. Boeldieu chooses suicide when he organizes the escape for Rosenthal and Maréchal. Filmic action is again based on a theatrical metaphor, for the escape is organized as another performance, this one suggested, as Boeldieu puts it, by the rehearsal the Russians gave with their spectacle. Much like an actor readying himself for an important role, Boeldieu insists that his costume be perfect, as we see when, in a gesture that ties his fate to Rauffenstein's, he meticulously cleans his white gloves. The suicidal role Boeldieu accepts in disorganizing the prison with an absurd fife concert is, of course, his final gratuitous act of play, that is, an aristocratic act that brings Boeldieu to his end. In the prison context it is an incongruous performance that marks how little Boeldieu is in harmony with his era; yet it is also a willed act that is essentially ludic. By forcing his peer Rauffenstein to shoot him, Boeldieu in effect enacts a suicide for their entire class. Rauffenstein understands Boeldieu's gesture and can only wistfully pay homage to it. This is the meaning of Rauffenstein's final gesture, cutting the lone geranium, a *fleur* that has a double meaning, not only a flower but also the superior quality that has passed on.

The theatrical metaphor of the escape performance creates the context for the interpretation of the film's final tableau. Here we see Maréchal and Rosenthal, seemingly bound by a fraternity born of necessity, seek their freedom by crossing cold expanses of German countryside. One's first impression might well be that they have escaped the world of theater and artifice to enter nature, a nature that some critics have taken as the antithesis of what is artificial and illusory. But one must remember that the escape, having become a performance, a form of theater, cannot so easily be divested of its metaphorical side, and it might well appear that Renoir, indulging in not-the-least interesting of his ambiguities, conceives of nature here as another backdrop against which men act out their historically determined roles. In this sense, then, the final tableau would be an ironic critique of that romantic attitude that sees nature as some locus of salvation in which man might escape from society, history, and role playing.

This interpretation seems to be confirmed by the romantic idyll that takes place on the German farm where Maréchal and the young peasant widow fall in love in spite of the language barrier that separates them. The triumph of class solidarity over national antagonisms is obvious in the couple's relationship. Yet it is a triumph that takes place in an entirely theatricalized space. Renoir constantly frames his shots through windows and doors to create a series of proscenium-type arches that convert the house's inner space into a theatrical space set in the heart of nature. The shots of nature, taken from within the house, seem to frame this outer, natural space in the same manner. By projecting onto the German countryside the theatrical space in which these actors pursue their illusions, Renoir has in effect transformed nature into another decor.

The final tableau is thus as systematically ambiguous as any of the ones preceding it. The theatricalization of space creates a theatrical metaphor that labels as illusory all the roles we see. Yet there can be no doubt that the relationships among the three characters at the end of the film are presented with great sympathy. Not only does the love affair between the French worker and the German peasant suggest a form of triumph over nationalism, but also the friendship between the worker and the Jewish bourgeois presents a victory over class and racial antagonisms. Perhaps we should speak here, as does André Bazin, of beneficent illusions in which men continue to believe in spite of all obstacles.[2] Certain roles, certain illusions, Renoir seems to suggest, are founded upon a lack of lucidity, upon a certain blindness that is necessary in order to make these roles work. Lucidity is perhaps the prerogative of those who know, like Renoir's Louis XVI, that their role is no longer in harmony with their decor. It is the bitter appanage of condemned aristocrats.

On the other hand, the film's final scene, when Maréchal and Rosenthal flee into the snowy mountains and it is "every man for himself," bring the viewer back to the ambiguity that lies at the heart of the notion of illusion. As

2. André Bazin, *Jean Renoir*, p. 59.

the spectator watches the two men struggling separately in the white wastes, he must feel that perhaps the emotion elicited by the earlier scenes of fraternity and warmth is a delusion. Renoir's final extreme long shot, which crushes his protagonists against the panorama of the deserted, snowy expanses, might even suggest that outside of theater and illusion there is nothing, only an inhuman wasteland. History condemns us all to be players, to be makers of illusions, even in the heart of nature.

Renoir did not abandon his actors Gabin and Dalio following *La Grande Illusion*. After *La Marseillaise* he used Gabin for the role of Jacques Lantier in his adaptation of Zola's *La Bête humaine*. Setting Zola's novel in contemporary times, Renoir gave Gabin the task of playing the train engineer whose heredity weighs upon him like a curse; under the stress of desire, he can turn into a homicidal maniac. This film again shows Renoir's desire to be a social historian, and if the film is not entirely successful, it is probably because Zola's physiological determinism is incompatible with Renoir's view of conduct as role playing. Lantier's outbursts, for which Zola offers a multitude of causal antecedents, appear insufficiently motivated in the film. This failure to adapt the causal integration that lies at the heart of the nineteenth-century novel also explains the failure of Renoir's *Madame Bovary*, an adaptation that at best can be called a series of illustrative tableaux based on Flaubert's work. However much Renoir admired these novelists' approach to the mimesis of social reality, he could not force himself to use the causal underpinning that endows their representations with an inner necessity.

This rejection of nineteenth-century mimetic causality becomes even more apparent in Renoir's greatest work, *La Règle du jeu*. In returning to his actor-character Dalio-Rosenthal, Renoir created a film based entirely on a web of theatrical and ludic analogies that aim to represent a vision of immediately contemporary history: the situation of the ruling class in France approximately one generation after the war portrayed in *La Grande Illusion*. As the film's title, *The Rules of the Game*, suggests, ludic metaphors are as important for an understanding of the film as are theatrical analogies in *La Grande Illusion*, though in *La Règle du jeu* Renoir has made use of a number of more self-conscious references to theater; these references are exterior to the film's represented reality. For after portraying the demise of the former ruling class, Renoir decided, in the cruelest of all his works, to show how the current elite demands certain roles and certain forms of play in order to maintain the integrity of its class identity.

Episodic experience in *La Règle du jeu* is subordinated to defining the roles that the main characters play with regard to each other. For this reason it is also subordinated to creating certain theatrical structures that have metaphorical relationships with a number of classical French plays. At the beginning of the film we see that the current La Chesnaye has married an Austrian woman, Christine. In order to be worthy of his wife's confidence, he decides to break off with his Parisian mistress, Geneviève de Marrast. Christine, for her part, has had a "friendship" with André Jurieu, the aviator who, in the film's first sequence, has just set an aviation record. Jurieu loves Christine and, aided by Octave, a friend of Christine's since childhood, the aviator succeeds in being invited to the country estate in Sologne to which La Chesnaye has invited a number of friends. The invitation comes, however, only after Jurieu has driven himself and Octave into a tree out of spite over Christine's not coming to see him at the airport.

The country estate is the dramatic locus where the various actors pursue their passions. For, once the various relationships are established, the film sets in motion a series of chases of pursued by pursuer, a series that finds parallels in the famous hunting sequence and its slaughter of the innocent as well as in the servants' imitation of the masters. Christine's chambermaid, Lisette, is pursued by Marceau, the poacher turned domestic, who in turn is chased by Lisette's trigger-happy husband, Schumacher. Each parallel pursuit finds its resolution when the perturbing agent is expelled from the game. Marceau is sent away for bringing about disorder; Jurieu, mistaken for Octave, is shot down by Schumacher. Once the intruders are removed, La Chesnaye can conclude the evening of theatrical entertainments that has been the high point of the sojourn at La Colinière. Theatrical order and social order, the two sides of the metaphorical equation, are reaffirmed in their inviolability.

Parallel structures setting in relation the world of masters and of servants are, of course, a common device in French classical theater and suggest Renoir's use of theater to establish metaphorical analogies. In fact, Renoir first considered naming his film after Musset's *Les Caprices de Marianne*. This desire to link his film explicity with Musset's romantic comedy offers the point of departure for understanding Renoir's dramatic structure. In this nineteenth-century play, the carefree Octave acts as a go-between so that his friend Cœlio can court Marianne, the young wife of the aging podesta, Claudio. This pseudo-Renaissance play conforms to the patterns of traditional romance, except that the play's resolution entails a case of mistaken identity in which Cœlio takes Octave's place for a rendezvous with Marianne and is then murdered by spadassins that Claudio has posted. As he dies, Cœlio hears Marianne cry out Octave's name.

Les Caprices de Marianne thus stands in a metaphorical analogy with the film that adds several new meanings to the resolution of the dramatic conflict. It also offers theatrical doubles for the characters Octave and Jurieu. In both the film and the play, taking on the wrong role brings about catastrophic results. Changing roles within a given social order can only subject the hero to danger, for the protean hero is always a menace in the social game that ordains and limits what role playing can be. Perhaps we might see in the destruction that role changing causes another variant of the historical determinism we saw in La Marseillaise. In contemporary society, as in any other society, the role one chooses must be in harmony with the decor, for if the freedom that allows one to change roles leads to inadaptation, then it also leads to catastrophe. The mobility of modern times, as we see it in La Règle du jeu, is a rather hollow form of freedom, since it encourages a spontaneity that deep-lying social forces will not abide. In this sense, then, freedom is an illusion, and any hero who, like Musset's Cœlio, mistakes his role is doubly deluded.

Renoir has, of course, considerably enriched the dramatic structure he found in Musset's play, and Musset's is not the only play he has used as the second term in an analogical relationship that endows La Règle du jeu with its web of theatrical metaphors. The film's opening title quotes Beaumarchais's Le Mariage de Figaro, and the film's opening music is taken from Mozart's operatic version of the play. The parallel structure of masters' and servants' pursuits finds its classic expression in Marivaux's Le Jeu de l'amour et du hasard, although it is true that Beaumarchais's work also evokes the play world of masters and servants. In Figaro parallel imbroglios suggest that the social classes mirror each other in their pursuit of desire. Moreover, the opening quotation, in its approval of inconstancy in love, stands as an ironic commentary on the rules of role changing:

> Sensitive hearts, faithful hearts,
> Who condemn inconstant love,
> Complain no more so bitterly—
> For is it a crime to change?

Musset, Marivaux, Beaumarchais, and Mozart offer a number of theatrical configurations and motifs that illuminate La Règle du jeu with ironic foreshadowings and metaphorical equivalencies. Indeed, Renoir is as self-consciously modernist as Joyce, at least in his use of mythical references that illuminate the world of the work through ironic contrasts and metaphorical identifications.

As in *La Grande Illusion*, these theatrical associations are closely related to another series of metaphors, for as the film's title makes clear, Renoir's representation of society uses ludic or game analogies to explain how this social class functions. In *La Grande Illusion* Renoir uses the notion of *illusion* in its several senses of play, artifice, theatrical representation, as well as delusion and error; in *La Règle du jeu* he exploits the related notion of *play* in its several senses. *Jeu* (or "play") has in French, much as in English, the various meanings of theater, game, spectacle, acting, chance, as well as the purely ludic meaning of play, from which the other meanings seem to derive. The characters in the film are thus actors in a play at the same time they are, by analogy, players in a game that imposes rules that cannot be questioned if the game is to be played. For, as Valéry pointed out, play allows no skepticism about the rules of the game. Any player who questions the rules immediately renders play impossible, for it is the nature of play that all players must accept the arbitrary coherence of the rules as an absolute. However, it is important to note that a player can cheat without calling the game into question, for cheating implicitly recognizes the existence of the rules. In a sense, then, *La Règle du jeu* shows the conflict between those who cheat and yet, by cheating, affirm the rules and those who do not abide by the rules and thus must be expelled from the game.

This ludic aspect of the film is made clearest in physical terms by Renoir's transformation of space into the delimited area that all play—in both the ludic and the theatrical sense—demands. As in *La Grande Illusion* Renoir carefully marks out the limited region that can serve as ludic space. For instance, in *La Règle du jeu* nature is much more clearly subjected to his vision of play, for the principal natural space we see is the forest through which the animals are harried to their slaughter. Nature is clearly a maze here, a delimited labyrinth that stands in a metaphorical relationship with the other spaces in the film. It is, moreover, the limited region in which the upper class gives itself over to the senseless play of killing for sporting reasons. This maze finds an analogy in the decor of the chateau La Colinière, whose floor's black and white squares suggest a kind of chessboard on which the players move as they pursue their passions.

Renoir appears to manipulate his actors consciously in order to make explicit how they are much like pieces moving in a limited play space. This is, of course, most obvious during the pursuit scenes and in the various spectacles that La Chesnaye presents during the evening of theatrical entertainments. But such manipulation is present in less easily noticed forms, in shots such as the ones of the guests at La Colinière frolicking in the hall, jumping about on the black and white squares like animated chess pieces, or, to offer another striking example, of Jurieu first seeing Christine. In this shot Renoir uses deep focus and lines his characters up like pawns on a board, so that they face each other across the rows of squares they must traverse if they are to come in contact. This metaphorical image is reinforced by the following reverse angle shot that shows the arrival of La Chesnaye. He runs forward along a line of black squares, like a chess piece held in its row by the "rules of the game." The chessboard, the maze, the theatrical space, these are all iconically presented metaphors that grant Renoir's representation of social order a semantic density. This density in turn endows nearly every image with a plurality of overlapping meanings illuminating what it means to "perform" in society.

In *La Grande Illusion* each character exists in function of his class identity and as such is a representative of various forms of illusion. In *La Règle du jeu* Renoir has delineated individual characters in greater detail, since the film's central focus is precisely on the way individual players perform within the historical context of the social game. Thus it seems appropriate to analyze the principal characters in terms of the metaphorical relationships we have set forth. In this respect, Octave, played by Renoir himself, appears to be the pivotal figure. As this name taken from Musset indicates, Octave is an intermediary, both between the exterior world of theater and the world of the film, and between various players within the film itself. Octave has an ambiguous status that allows him to consort as easily with the chambermaid as with the mistress. For he is an artist manqué, the familial parasite who is at once an equal and a déclassé, a friend and a tolerated amuser.

In this sense Octave resembles the newphew of Rameau whom Diderot portrays as the reverse image of the society whose largesse supports him. Yet Octave is also an artist, capable of disturbing societal roles, and La Chesnaye recognizes this when he call Octave, a bit nervously, a "dangerous poet." Renoir undoubtedly saw in Octave a degraded reflection of himself and thus chose to act this role in order to endow the film with another dimension of self-consciousness. Octave is something of a surrogate *metteur en scène*, albeit an impotent one who in the context of this society is only capable of mimicking the gestures of creativity. This is the sense of the scene where we see Octave standing on the porch, like a clown or a mime on an empty stage, as he shows Christine how her father, the great orchestra conductor, was once acclaimed for his genius.

It is, finally, Octave who brings about the catastrophe that destroys Jurieu. When Octave steps out of his role as intermediary and attempts to enter into the game itself, when he ceases to be an orchestrator of events and attempts to play an active role, he sets up the series of misunderstandings that lead to Schumacher's gunning down Jurieu. The series of mistaken identities that turn on Christine's and Jurieu's wearing the wrong coats are so many signs that the wrong roles, the wrong masks, have been taken on and that the rules of the game have been flouted. Once Octave has unwittingly brought about the transgressor's punishment, no role remains for him among the survivors. He can only return to Paris, the alienated artist who is more defeated than ever. And if Octave is to be taken as a surrogate for Renoir the artist, perhaps we must see in this defeat a metaphor for Renoir's own failure, in ideological terms, to do more than portray the machinations of the ruling class. Octave's defeat might be taken as a sign of Renoir's own awareness that *La Règle du jeu* has in no way compromised the social order that it depicts.

André Jurieu, Renoir's Cœlio and the film's sacrificial victim, must pay the price for Octave's failure in handling roles. As an aviator, as a modern hero who is free to set new records, Jurieu is also an emblematic figure. By his very nature he is an outsider who can understand only with great difficulty the true rules and rituals of La Chesnaye's milieu. His great illusion is, of course, thinking that he is free to enter into this milieu. At the film's outset, Renoir's montage establishes the opposition between Jurieu's world of modern technology and the ossified social structure he must cope with. The cut from the airport with its crowd and radio announcer, and all the contemporary values of technology they seem to represent, takes us to Christine's rococo bedroom, whose eighteenth-century ornateness seems to embody the theatrical values and class ideology that separate Jurieu from her world. Christine's chamber, moreover, seems to weigh down upon her, capturing her in a fixed, rigid decor that is emblematic of her class's refusal to recognize historical change. The impossibility of joining this world with Jurieu's is ironically underscored by the first shot of the room. Renoir first shoots a close-up of the back of the wireless receiver that is broadcasting Jurieu's exploits. He then employs one of his typical pan-shots to reveal the sumptuous decor. The incongruity of this electrical apparatus appearing in a decor meant for Marie Antoinette emphasizes the abyss that separates the modern hero from a class that bases its rules of conduct on modes inherited from another era.

Jurieu, however, does attempt to play according to the rules of La Chesnaye's game, though there is little chance that he can be a successful player. As an agent of pure passion, he is the perturbing force who menaces the order of the game at the same time he attempts to be a gentleman. This inner contradiction points both to Jurieu's fundamental disequilibrium and to the destruction he must undergo so that the game can go on. The inability to adapt transforms Jurieu into a comic figure as he attempts to embrace a social norm to which he cannot conform. As an agent of pure desire he should flee with Christine, but his attempt to play by "certain rules" paralyzes him in comic immobility. This comic contradiction culminates during the farcical theatrical evening when Jurieu, because he tries to respect this society's convenances, finds himself playing a buffoon's role as he gives his rival, Saint-Aubin, rather guignolesque kicks in the rear.

Renoir's mixing of genres has perturbed more than one critic, for, as in *La Grande Illusion*, he has again used forms of ambiguity that will not allow us to reduce any episode to a single point of view. Jurieu is eliminated from the social order in a tragic manner; yet he is a comic figure, one who introduces the antiorder that converts the theatrical rituals into farce. Moreover, the society whose order Jurieu menaces is one that Renoir appears to condemn through a fairly mordant satire, especially insofar as we identify this society with La Chesnaye and his manias. At the same time, however, Renoir uses the norms or game rules of La Chesnaye's society to define, at least in part, the norm from which Jurieu deviates, the norm that makes of him a comic figure. Renoir thus appears to condemn a class, yet he accepts its rules as the norm for defining comic deviation.

These same ambiguities lie, in different proportions, behind Renoir's portrayal of Christine, the only other character among the masters who questions her role. She is an emblematic figure for Renoir; as a foreigner and, more especially, as a woman, she is a double victim of the rules that condemn her to a life of sterile inactivity. A woman, as Renoir eloquently expresses it in a first version of the film's scenario, can find only two roles in the upper class. She can either be a mother and devote all her time to her children, a choice seemingly precluded by the sterile nature of the film's society, or she can be a socialite, pursuing a role consisting of equal parts of vacuity and boredom, living a life of discreet affairs consummated from five to seven in the evening.[3] As a foreigner, however, Christine is an outsider who does not comprehend her possible roles; La Chesnaye's mistress, Geneviève, disdainfully reminds him of this when she notes that a Parisian woman "would understand."

In his presentation of Christine, Renoir again plays with the ambiguous notions attached to the idea of illusion. When we first see her in her chamber, we quickly realize that she entertains illusions about the nature of the game, for she has not yet grasped the necessity of role playing, of creating illusions, of living the lies that assure social order. Her fundamental naiveté is revealed when she states that, although she knows nothing is "natural" in her milieu, "lies must be a very heavy garment to wear." She does not understand that mendacity is an accepted part of role playing and that theatrical artifice and prevarication are two sides of the same social need for illusion.

Unlike Jurieu, however, Christine is not a comic figure. She evolves throughout the film and, in one respect, the film turns on her coming to an awareness of the necessity for illusions. At first, she gives the impression that she might be capable of liberating herself from the game and finding a nontheatrical mode of being, a self-determined identity that is not a form of the role playing demanded by her class. At La Colinière, before the assembled guests, she succeeds in imposing her version of her relationship with Jurieu. She claims that they are friends, which means that she has defined a relationship with a man that this society, as Lisette makes clear, does not believe possible. Another significant step in her evolution seems to come when she announces after the hunt that she no longer cares for this sport. In a sense, she is rejecting this ferocious form of play, in which the upper class gives itself the illusion of undertaking aristocratic pursuits. This impression is strengthened a few shots later when Christine can see no reason for shooting the squirrel that Saint-Aubin would kill, had he kept his gun with him.

Renoir uses the image of the squirrel as a central image in the process of Christine's losing her illusions. Looking through a pocket telescope, Christine turns her vision from the squirrel, seemingly an image of innocence in nature, to the sight of her husband embracing Geneviève. This linking of images creates, by antithesis, a feeling of the fall, of the loss of innocence that sends Christine in pursuit of a role that will allow her to cope with her sudden realization. In those ensuing scenes in which Christine goes from man to man, it is useless to speculate whether she really desires Saint-Aubin, Jurieu,

3. Ibid., p. 184.

Octave, or perhaps even her husband, Robert. Her loss of illusions plunges her into a void in which she rapidly espouses a series of roles, and yet, if she is to survive, she is free ultimately only to accept the role that this class has assigned to her. Renoir's historical determinism and his vision of role playing are concretely illustrated in Christine's conduct, for they coincide in the ultimate determination of how she behaves.

The final image of Christine shows that she has been integrated into the game. After Jurieu's death, a high-angle shot sets off Lisette, Jackie, La Chesnaye, Schumacher, and Christine as they cross the bridge that leads them back into the chateau and, in a symbolic sense, into the game space. Robert and Christine are reunited as they parade in front of the now-awakened guests. Only Jackie, the student who pursued Jurieu, shows grief, and for this violation of the rules, Christine now knows the reprimand: "Jackie, you're being watched." These words reveal how she has come to accept the theatricalization of her conduct, how she accepts that henceforth she will play her role in front of the other members of her class. Or, if one prefers Sartrian terminology, she knows that it is the *regard d'autrui* that will now define her identity and that she exists only as a role perceived on a public stage.

As the film's final image thus makes clear, the survivors in this game are those who know how to pass off illusions that are publicly acceptable in terms of the game rules. They are those actors who know how to adjust their roles to their decor's exigencies. In spite of their conflict, the best players are Robert and Geneviève, and, as we see at the film's outset, they are united in greater complicity than are any of the other characters. Renoir first presents them together with a long shot that shows the Trocadéro through her apartment window—the very emblem of Paris's most wealthy neighborhood. He then frames them separately with a series of reverse angle shots that seemingly set the two lovers in opposition. But he undermines this apparent opposition by showing their metaphorical identity: In each shot he juxtaposes a Buddhalike statue with the character. This juxtaposition of living actor and oriental statue creates an ironic metaphor that shows how alike these lovers are in their acceptance of a fixed role, of a theatrical mask. With bulging jowls and gentle but rigid smiles, these statues set forth the self-sufficiency of these plutocrats who live in the shadow of the Palais de Chaillot.

If in *La Grande Illusion* Renoir compels us to recognize that his aristocrats, Boeldieu and Rauffenstein, are simultaneously condemned by history and worthy of our respect, in *La Règle du jeu* he forces us to view La Chesnaye simultaneously as a maniac and as a consummate performer. The millionaire spends his time collecting mechanical dolls, animals, and other gadgets in the same way that the family of his ancestor Rosenthal collected estates, portraits, and false titles. But he also knows, as his cook points out in reply to the servants' anti-Semitic remarks, when his potato salad has not been properly prepared. La Chesnaye's gastronomic abilities are part of the role-playing expertise by which the upper class publicly affirms its rights. The culinary ritual is only one of the many that must be mastered if one is to be a leader in the social rites that depend on theatricalized behavior. Robert La Chesnaye is, moreover, the supreme *metteur en scène*, or director of social dramatics. Renoir stresses La Chesnaye's expertise as a director in many ways. One might think, for instance, of the scene in which the guests assemble after Christine has made the speech that supposedly reveals her relations with Jurieu. The importance of Renoir's using a prosceniumlike arch within the frame in order to create a ludic space becomes all the more evident when we note that he has placed La Chesnaye in the center of this space. From this position he can orchestrate the characters as they move about him. La Chesnaye is the game director here, as he is in the later sequence where he attempts to direct a theater within a theater, a comedy within a comedy, and at the same time tries to control the farce that his own weaknesses have unleashed.

In this boisterous, comic sequence Renoir reduces all his protagonists to scurrying marionettes who, caught up in their pursuit of passion, become mechanized automatons that we can view as doubles of the mechanical dolls La Chesnaye collects. The collector is but another puppet in this mechanical ballet as he flees Geneviève, takes advice from his servant, and engages in a farcical fight with Jurieu. The mad chase in which he pursues Christine while she pursues Saint-Aubin and is, in her turn, pursued by Jurieu establishes, of course, the metaphorical relationships that qualify everything as theater. Farce within a farce, parallel chases between masters and servants, the presence of the stage and the mechanical toys, as well as the explicit references to theater, all these multiply the various metaphorical identifications that endow this sequence with its wealth of theatrical and ludic connotations. They also underscore the ambiguity of La Chesnaye's situation, for he is both the victim of theatricalization and the director of a society based on theatrical values.

This central ambiguity points to Renoir's impasse in *La Règle du jeu*. There can be no doubt that in this film he is trying to overcome the all-pervading classical humanism that gave rise to theatrical values and ultimately to the theatricalization of society itself. Yet it is also quite clear that Renoir's mimetic project depends upon this humanism and its theatrical values for its very existence. The values that La Chesnaye's class recognizes turn essentially on the classical dichotomy of passion and reason, or of freedom and order, which finds its highest form of expression in a theatrical vision of conflict. In fact, La Chesnaye's class owes its existence to a binary system of values whose classic oppositions of instinct and restraint, blindness and lucidity, excess and moderation, are the foundation for the games they play. This ruling class accepts the necessity of public performance, as opposed to private authenticity, as the model that assures verifiable gamesmanship. The theatricalization of social behavior is demanded as a mimetic means that allows society to perceive the honoring of its basic codes.

In this representation of conflict, Renoir has inevitably had recourse to those mimetic conventions that not only allow this society to represent itself but also underlie its most basic values. Renoir's satire of La Chesnaye and the imbroglios that arise from his conduct seem to point to a denial of the legitimacy of a humanism based on these values. But Renoir's very film depends upon these theatrical values as the basis for its mimesis of social reality. Theatrical models are the only ones that Renoir trusts for his own representation of history. Thus his film guarantees the legitimacy of the very society that it seems to attack. In the face of this dilemma Renoir's only recourse is an ironic self-consciousness in his use of theatrical metaphors; this awareness itself also shows that he can find no other mode of discourse with which to undertake social mimesis.

Renoir's acceptance of theatrical modes of representation underlies the ambiguity of the film's final images. With the elimination of Jurieu, who is shot down like one of the rabbits in the hunt, La Chesnaye can gain control of the comedy and assert himself as the supreme showman. He can gain control of the comedy and keep it within the limits of role playing that his class accepts. Renoir again uses a stagelike space to create his theatrical metaphor and show that the play has come to a successful end. With the guests gathered together like an audience, La Chesnaye appears on the porch, much like a director appearing on stage at the end of a performance. The framing again creates a proscenium, for after allowing the cast to cross the bridge and enter the theatrical space, Renoir shoots from behind the guests, setting La Chesnaye off in complete symmetry with them. The lights around the porch appear to be footlights as they illuminate La Chesnaye's enigmatic face while he wearily explains the version of the murder that will be made public. Intolerable as it may be, the play's end is a triumph of theatrical order, and thus of an entire class.

The final image of La Chesnaye's face as theatrical mask is perhaps comparable to the final image in *La Grande Illusion* in its equivocal nature. The image of Rosenthal and Maréchal struggling through the snowy expanse portrays their escape, but it also carries with it the suggestion that their hopes are illusory. The final image of *La Règle du jeu* affirms theatrical order at the same time that it points to its bankruptcy. In both films, then, theatrical modes of mimesis are offered as the only viable means of representation of society, while the values that underlie these modes are designated as inadequate or destructive. This final ambiguity reflects most directly the impasse that Renoir and many other French artists felt to be theirs at the end of the thirties: They were revolutionaries who did not really believe that history would allow the rules of the game to be changed. Destined to use modes of representation—brilliantly, to be sure—that were not adequate to the expression of a new system of values, Renoir could only produce masterpieces of ambiguity that led him finally to the brink of a nihilism he could never accept. His career after World War II is, in fact, a continuous reaffirmation of those theatrical and humanistic values that *La Règle du jeu* seemed to question. In the films he made after the war, in works as diverse as *Le Carosse d'Or*, *French Cancan*, and *Le Petit Théâtre de Jean Renoir*, it is no longer an ironic awareness that strikes us. Rather, it is a nostalgic effort to create a world in which classical theatrical modes are adequate modes of representation. And this nostalgic humanism leaves us with a nostalgia for the Renoir who was not afraid of his contradictions.

Prévert and Carné's
Le Jour se lève:
Proletarian Tragedy

Historical criticism of art and literature often contains the unstated assumption that a work of art finds its richest development when it expresses the basic moods, attitudes, and sensibility of the historical period that gave rise to it. The work that is out of season disturbs the critic, who can rarely find in it the full resonance he finds in a work that is, in some manner or another, in harmony with its era. In the work that seems to give voice to its epoch, every part of the whole points to a greater historical *geist* that gave birth to the work, while each part, in turn, is enriched by relations of mutual harmony. The fallacy of using historical data to elucidate the work (and vice versa) is that we consider only the richest works and then abstract from these works the homologies that we then claim characterize both the work and the period. Although these homologies may, indeed, neatly circumvallate the works we derived them from, the dangers of such a circular approach are obvious. Yet this circularity is a basis for rational coherence, and when several works from a given period present a common body of structures, themes, and attitudes, the critic may well be justified in analyzing these works in historical terms, if only for the multiple coherencies he can then find in them. With this caveat in mind we can turn from Renoir's ambiguities to Prévert and Carné's *Le Jour se lève*, a work of art that is a nearly perfect expression of an era's consciousness of itself.

In the broadest sense, *Le Jour se lève*, made in 1939, seems to epitomize the thirties' search for a tragic vision, or, in other terms, it is perhaps the richest expression that cinema has to offer of that era's feeling about its tragic impasse. For after the boisterous avant-garde experimentation in Paris in the twenties and early thirties, the later part of the decade was increasingly dominated by the belief that destiny had decreed decadence as France's lot. On the stage, Giraudoux gave expression to a tragic attitude that proclaimed the impossibility of altering what the gods had decreed or, perhaps more precisely, what history had determined. History, for many French artists and intellectuals, had become in fact a form of tragic destiny. In literature, both a Malraux on the left and a Drieu la Rochelle on the right could see only in revolution the hope of transcending those historical forces that had determined decline and degradation. In film, this antithetical pair, despair about the possibility of changing history's decrees and the call for revolt, found many varied expressions. On the one hand, the bleakest vision is the cynical pessimism of Feyder, Carné's teacher, exemplified in *Knight without Armour* (1937) when the Red Army seizes a machine gun from the Russian White Army and continues to assassinate prisoners with the same gusto with which the Whites had used the weapon. On the other hand, the belief in the power of revolt seems to vibrate through Renoir's marching crowds in *La Marseillaise* (1938), which shows the French people making their first, but perhaps not their last, revolution. It is, however, only in *Le Jour se lève* that tragic despair and revolt are completely expressed as two sides of the same anguish before history.

Carné and Prévert's first work together, *Jenny* (1936), as well as Carné's *Hôtel du Nord* (1938) foreshadow the dark vision we find in *Le Jour se lève*, but it is their *Quai des Brumes* (1938) that best demonstrates the coherence that underlies Carné's prewar work. Presenting the fundamental themes we find in the later film, *Quai des Brumes* portrays the impossibility of self-realization in a world where the attempt to love calls forth destruction in a nearly automatic fashion. The basic premise in this film, and in this respect we see a continuing surrealist influence, is that love is the liberating force that could free man from bondage to his mundane existence, were it not for a metaphysical form of destiny that crushes those outcasts who dare to hope for some other life. By *metaphysical* we mean that in *Quai des Brumes* the events that lead to destruction are determined not from within, by some kind of inner causality, but from without, by some transcendental force that insures that the protagonists never realize their love and liberty.

This metaphysical sense of destiny is common to both *Quai des Brumes* and *Le Jour se lève*, although *Quai des Brumes* presents a much less developed dramatic structure. In the latter film a deserter, played by Jean Gabin, arrives in a foggy port, designated as Le Havre, but representing a symbolic haven for this man in flight. He meets a girl, Michèle Morgan, and they spend a night together, the prelude to what might be happiness. But she is under the power of a strange tutor and has also consorted with a band of playboy gangsters, one of whom, now missing, was her lover. Her guardian, it appears, has killed her lover out of jealousy. When the guardian attempts to abuse her, Gabin beats the hypocritical tutor to death. Then, as Gabin is about to set sail, one of the gangsters, whom Gabin has twice humiliated, shoots him down in the street. The deserter's boat sails without him, bound for a freedom that he could never know.

Dramatic motivation in *Quai des Brumes* is thus provided by the most elementary instinctual reactions—jealousy, anger, revenge—though the psychological pivots in the plot serve primarily to justify the workings of a gratuitously evil destiny. For it is clearly this undefined but omnipotent force that weighs upon this world of outsiders who struggle without hope to know a moment of freedom and happiness. There is also what we might call a sociological axis to this film, for the gangster who kills Jean is a bourgeois, an idle and somewhat neurotic child of the middle class who can shoot down a man simply because he has been humiliated by him. The Prévertian vision of the bourgeoisie is further elaborated in *Le Jour se lève*, but one can see that this reflection of working-class struggle has already been integrated into the dramatic structure of *Quai des Brumes*. The bourgeois gangster is the agent that destiny uses to destroy this working-class hero, who by his desertion has refused the accepted order. Dramatic motivation and social mimesis thus dovetail in a single representation.

Quai des Brumes thus presents several of the constants of Prévert and Carné's tragic vision, especially the myth of love as a form of saving grace and, at the same time, the impossibility of love in a world given over to inexorable hostility. Pursued by the forces of an essentially gratuitous evil, Carné's heroes can only dream of escaping to a place that would be the negation of the present, where words such as *happiness* and *freedom* would have some meaning other than the expression of a vague refusal of the present.

What strikes one most about *Le Jour se lève* is the way in which Carné and Prévert considerably enriched their vision after *Quai des Brumes* by endowing the later film with several coinciding forms of dramatic determinism, so that we can speak of a complete form of tragic mimesis. In a general sense Prévert and Carné's romantic fatalism is still the overriding force that condemns the protagonist to destruction. But in *Le Jour se lève* they have also created a dramatic structure, based on purely cinematic devices, that establishes a determinism or a concatenation of events that lead to the hero's suicide. Using a series of alternating flashbacks and present-time sequences, they have invested the very fabric of everyday events with a sense of inexorability. Moreover, the social determinants in the film are more clearly defined. In fact, class determination enters here into tragic mimesis as another aspect of destiny.

The use of the flashback in *Le Jour se lève* is perhaps its most interesting structural aspect. The flashback is often considered a form of subjective representation, a device that can be used for the mimesis of a memory image. Of course, a cinematic image that supposedly represents the past differs in no way from one that represents a present, and the viewer cannot really view it as having any subjective properties at all. Rather, we view these images as another virtual present, one that preceded in chronological terms the virtual present that we take to be the present tense of the filmic narrative. In other words, a flashback nearly always functions in structural terms to create a narration, though, using literary analogies, the filmmaker may supposedly offer the flashback from the "point of view" of a character within the film. Point of view in film, however, usually exists only by analogy with a literary work. It is something of a convenient fiction, since, in point of fact, a filmic image is never modified by a supposed narrative point of view.

Carné and Prévert motivate their flashbacks by an appeal to memory association, for the film's hero supposedly recalls each past sequence. The present tense is given when François, the worker, again played by Jean Gabin, sits in his room, having just killed a man, and is besieged by the police. It is clear, however, that the significance of the flashbacks lies in their power to contrast, in terms of tragic progression, the past with the present moment that the past has determined. For the flashbacks follow one another in a dramatic progression that creates a sense of linear chronology and causality. In terms of classical tragic mimesis, one can see that each flashback presents a past agon, or confrontation, that causes the film to advance toward the present, toward the room in which François is trapped, the room the viewer has accepted as being situated in the present and to which, by necessity, all past events must then lead. For, in retrospect, simple concatenation is perceived as necessity. Each flashback can thus be likened to a classical peripeteia, the sudden change in tragic mimesis by which destiny inflects the course of events, though the film's final peripeteia takes place in the present moment. This is the assassination; we hear it in the film's first scene, and we must decipher its meaning as the film unfolds.

The film thus has an inexorable circular movement, leading from the room back through the past to conclude again in the room we see first at dusk, in a working-class area where an isolated hotel rises, sharply set apart from the other buildings. The opening, establishing shot sets the scene in the present, as does the following shot of a blind man going up the hotel's staircase. This blind man might well be destiny's harbinger, an analogue for François's blindness, for as he advances, a shot rings out, voices are heard, and a body tumbles down a flight of stairs. Like the blind man, the viewer can initially only wonder what is the significance of it all. The arrival of the police, François's evident despair, and the shooting that follows only point to imminent destruction. The filmic present tense is established as a moment of crisis that demands explanation; it cries out for causal antecedents.

The first flashback is, therefore, motivated by the need to establish narrative coherence, to find an answer for the opening enigma, and to allow an escape, in psychological terms, from what is given as an irremediable situation, from a dramatic dead-end. In the original version of the film, this transition is effected as François looks down on the street through bullet-shattered glass and supposedly recalls an earlier morning when he was able to take his bicycle and leave freely for work. The next image Carné filmed is François on his bicycle. The camera would thus appear to follow the drift of François's mind and go back in time to find that singular event that might have set in motion the chain of events leading to this moment of silence and broken glass.

In versions of the film that are presently available, the next shot presents the factory where François works as a sandblaster, encased in a uniform that looks like a deep-sea diver's. Françoise, an apprentice florist who, like François, is an orphan, wanders in one day while trying to make a delivery. It is a rather unlikely place for the erotic encounter that, according to surrealist mythology, is a promise of liberty and self-realization. This encounter of two disinherited children of the proletariat takes place under the same malevolent star that presided over the lovers' meeting in *Quai des Brumes*. Unlike his precursor, Jean, however, François wants to believe that this meeting could lead to some fuller existence, to some form of happiness that he had never believed possible before. His tragic flaw, if one can use such a classical notion here, is that he entertains the illusion that he might liberate himself from the daily oppression that binds him to his machine. His flaw would be quite simply his blindness to his true condition.

This encounter sets up the first, illusory promise of happiness that in turn gives rise to the ensuing agon, or confrontation. For Françoise is fascinated by Valentin (Jules Berry), the animal trainer whose language and manners mark him as belonging to another caste. When Françoise goes to a rendezvous with this artist, François follows her and watches as the trainer's assistant, Clara (Arletty), abandons him in the middle of his act at a café concert. After Clara makes rather frank overtures to François, he is drawn into a confrontation with Valentin in which he pits his worker's vitality and common sense against the artist's ability to twist language and hypnotize with words. François seems victorious in this first agon, for his physical superiority and his offer to give Valentin "a kick in the ass" appear capable of undoing the magic spell that the artist's words can cast.

The film's tragic rhythm then takes us back to the encircled room. This return serves to punctuate the unfolding present. The present has a continuous duration that is marked by François's chain-smoking as the night passes. The lit cigarette seems to underline the presence of life, perhaps of a last glimmer of hope as darkness gives way to dawn. However, each present-time sequence is also marked by a crucial event that seems to ensure the tragic ending. In this second sequence set in the present the police begin a fusillade in order to shoot down the room's door. François pushes a huge wardrobe against the door; as André Bazin noted, he has then in effect walled himself into his room.[1] He has set the seal on his destiny by turning his room into a crypt.

Next Carné again attempts to create a form of subjective representation in order to relate the next flashback to the present moment. A dissolve in which the two overlapping images of the wardrobe suggest a process of memory association seem to lead the viewer back to another, happier time. More importantly, the dissolve shows that the room is the locus for dramatic action as it unfolds through time. It transforms the room into a privileged space. The flashback also offers a respite in the tragic rhythm, for it begins on a Sunday when François can visit Clara and enjoy sexual satisfaction, if not sublime love. This is a "Sunday of life" when, free from the alienating labor of the week, François can find satisfaction within the limits of the possible. Sex, unlike love, demands only physical well-being and does not propose to alter the nature of things.

François cannot content himself with the limited satisfaction Clara might

1. André Bazin, "Le décor est un acteur," *Ciné-Club*, n.s., no. 1 (December 1949):4–5. Part of this important essay has been reprinted in Robert Chazal, *Marcel Carné*, pp. 146–49.

offer and is again drawn into an agon with Valentin. Valentin resorts to his almost demonic powers as a fabulist when he tells the astounded worker that he is Françoise's father. In this confrontation we begin to see that the worker's simple straightforwardness is not a match for malicious cunning, for when François learns that Valentin has invented the story, he can only give vent to rage, to helpless cries of disgust and dismay, signs of his incapacity to come to grips with the artist's destructive powers.

The flashback ends with a second respite, this time as François and Françoise seem to find a moment of harmony and understanding as they lie protected from the world by the transparent walls of a greenhouse. François gives in again to the illusion that things could somehow be other than they are. Within this respite lies the motivation for the final peripeteia, for the young girl, seemingly without guile, gives the worker a brooch, saying that it is the thing she most values. When François learns that Valentin gives such a brooch to every woman he sleeps with, it would appear that the artist's demonic powers have corrupted love itself. They have, in any case, made of Françoise an unblushing fabulist who offers lies when she tells what is conceivably true.

The following return to the present moment seems to mark, in rather classical terms, the beginning of tragic recognition. Dawn creeps into François's room as a crowd of workers gathers before the building. In *Le Jour se lève*, as in the earlier *Jenny* and *Quai des Brumes*, dawn is an ironically deceptive image of hope—one need only recall Gabin and Morgan as they stand in the old shack and watch the darkness and shadows being dissipated by a new day. Dawn becomes in *Le Jour se lève*, as the title ironically stresses, the image of the impossibility of hope, an image of the tragic awareness that seizes François when it is too late. The crowd, then, that gathers in the street and calls out for François might be likened to a chorus to whom François cries, in a tragic apostrophe:

> What are you looking at? What are you waiting for, all of you? I'm not a rare animal. What'd you expect? Are you waiting for me to jump? A murderer . . . A murderer's interesting, isn't he . . . . A murderer! I'm a murderer! A murderer. Murderers aren't unusual. They're all over the place. Everyone kills a little bit . . . but slowly so that you don't see it. It's like the sand . . . you get sand inside you! Inside! If you walk quick, you don't even see it. . . . Leave me alone . . . since I'm already alone. I'm not asking for anything from anybody. Get the hell out of here. I'm tired! tired!

tired! Used up. It's all over. I can't have confidence any more. It's all
over . . . [2]

Another dissolve using overlapping images of the wardrobe marks the
transition to the final flashback. This one takes place immediately before the
film's initial present-tense scene and thus completes the narrative circle.
Valentin enters François's room; this entry represents an intolerable foray into
François's inner space, something akin to a final piercing of his protective
cocoon. Debasing himself, using calculated words to cut François to the quick,
Valentin engages in a dangerous act that so provokes the worker that he nearly
throws the artist out the window. But Valentin cannot stop himself, and when
he makes ironic remarks about the brooch he finds there, François seizes the
gun that Valentin has brought and shoots his loquacious torturer. This final
peripeteia completes the chain of confrontations. The enigma is resolved, and
the narrative present can now only complete the ritual presentation of the
inexorable. Dawn has come when François lets his cigarette go out and the
police arrive with "gas" to smoke out their prey.

The final shots in *Le Jour se lève* present a remarkable example of
"analytical montage" at the same time they underscore a sense of tragic
elevation that is unique in film. François rises from his bed, for he is cold in the
early dawn. A close-up reveals with eloquent simplicity the presence of the
revolver. The next shot shows François taking the revolver and searching for
his heart with his hand. But we are never allowed to forget that the exterior
world is closing in on him. A slow pan shot follows a policeman on the roof as he
crawls toward the window that links the inner and outer world. The slowness
of the camera motion seems to underscore the deliberate pace with which
destiny moves in upon its victim. The camera cuts back to the room where, in a
final moment of tragic irony, François recalls his desire to gather flowers at
Easter with Françoise. A cut back to the roof discreetly masks François's
self-inflicted death. Only the sound of the shot is heard, a sound that the
policeman misinterprets in the same way everything François has done is
misinterpreted. The final image reveals his body while the alarm clock he was
winding at dusk rings as though to underscore the ironic distance that separates the present from the past—and the smoke from a tear-gas grenade marks
the obliteration of this anonymous man.

This circular structure of the tragic action is a reflection of the fatalism

2. Translated from film script of *Le Jour se lève* in *L'Avant-Scène*, no. 53 (1965):35. (All
translations are mine, unless otherwise indicated.)

that permeates Prévert and Carné's entire work. In *Le Jour se lève*, however, objects and the decor also enter directly into the web of tragic associations. As Bazin noted, every object in the film retains its everyday usage, but at the same time each "one is the instrument of a transcendental necessity that, on this night, haunts the material world that surrounds Gabin."[3] In more general mimetic terms, we can say that objects and the decor are denoted in their "typicality" as a sociological average that defines the social world the film represents. At the same time, the film's tragic structure appropriates the decor and objects and converts them, in semantic terms, by making them function connotatively to signify the tragic themes that run throughout the film. Objects, moreover, enter into analogical relationships with the events in the film; this in turn creates a series of analogies that reflect the tragic action. In *Le Jour se lève* we find, in fact, a kind of symbolic realism that seems to derive directly from nineteenth-century literary mimesis. As in Flaubert's works, objects and decor are given not only because they assure the ontological weight of the world represented, but also because they are ambivalent signs that reflect the thematic concerns that inform the work's development.

Take, for example, the film's first decor, the street in the industrial *banlieue*, with its working-class hotel that rises alone, starkly dominating the square with its streetcar tracks and cobblestones. Carné, it appears, first looked for a square in a lower-class neighborhood that had such an isolated building. Finding none, and it would be difficult to find a square with one building towering so abruptly over the others, he was obliged to construct a set that could both represent a typical suburban street and set forth those properties that are associated with the themes of isolation and singularity. The Dubonnet advertisement, the electric wires strung haphazardly, the cobblestones, these are all unique elements that represent what we call the sociological average. But they are also part of a decor that, while representing the quotidian, is transformed into part of the tragic mimesis or the representation of destiny. The isolated hotel is not simply a direct symbol of François's fate in the sense that it immediately represents it. Rather, its physical situation is analogous to his, and thus it connotes themes and emotions that are related to his tragic fate and are reflections of the larger workings of destiny. Or perhaps one might wish to say, drawing on the terms of literary modernism, that it symbolizes the essence of isolated elevation in itself while denoting an instance of this isolation.

3. Bazin, "Le décor est un acteur," p. 5; in Chazal, *Carné*, p. 149.

The workshop where François operates a sandblasting machine is another decor that enters into a web of associative meanings. We first see it through a tracking shot that goes along the row of workers, each with a blasting nozzle in hand, each insulated by a protective uniform. The workers are separated from each other, not only by their helmets, but also by the partitions that surround them, isolating each from the other in framelike cells. The decor suggests that each worker is a discrete unit in a series, an anonymous agent in a hellish region of deafening noise and fiery sand spray. When the camera comes to rest on François, we do not, of course, recognize him at first, for his work has shorn him of his identity. The decor therefore establishes an analogy between François's work and the chain of events through which destiny eventually seals him in his room, where, as he cries out to the crowd from his balcony, he is isolated and finally bereft of any identity:

> François? What's that? . . . François? Don't know him. . . . Don't know him! It's all over . . . there isn't any François. . . . There's nothing left anymore . . .[4]

Factory and room are interrelated decors reflecting the process that strips François of an identity, for the factory means a slow form of death as the sand destroys his lungs, while the room is the place of his final entombment.

A more complex example of the analogies that objects and decor maintain with regard to the film's action is offered by the greenhouse. Here Françoise, telling François that Valentin is not her father, agrees never to see the animal trainer again. In one of the most important shots in terms of its creation of symbol, the camera, situated outside the hothouse, frames the couple in the background while, slightly out of focus, flowers fill the foreground of the image. This shot, comparable to shots framing François through the window of his room, underscores how the decor separates the couple and the outer world, for they are literally encapsulated during this moment when they give themselves over to romantic fantasies. The hothouse is a world apart, a world of artifice and illusion that is signified as such by the way the camera places it in relief.

Moreover, the juxtaposition of the two photographic planes, of the flowers and especially of the girl, enters into another series of analogical relations. Here Françoise is depicted, in a metaphorical sense, as the *femme-fleur*, the woman-flower who is the representative of the surrealist love ideal, the object

4. Film script of *Le Jour se lève*, p. 35.

that can bring about the abolition of the distinction between the objective world of reality and the subjective world of desire. At the same time, the decor shows that she is part of the world of illusory, hothouse flowers that cannot exist outside this realm of artifice; this is made clear when, at the moment of the couple's encounter, the flowers that Françoise is carrying wilt in the factory's polluted atmosphere. This network of equivocal associations is further extended by the role flowers play in the couple's fantasy conversations. For François, the height of happiness would be to gather lilacs at Easter, whereas for the young girl, caught up in the fictions that Valentin has seduced her with, the epitome of joy would be to see winter mimosas on the Riviera.

The most important decor is François's room, the dramatic space where the present-tense drama unfolds. The room is the point of convergence for the causal chain that has led to the present, which we see especially in the way that many of the objects in the room are linked with the events that have led to the present crisis. To return to our suggestion that this kind of representation seems to derive from modernist literary mimesis, we might suggest that François's room functions much like Felicité's room in Flaubert's "A Simple Heart." In Flaubert's story the simple servant's room is situated on the top floor of her mistress's house, and its window opens up on the luminous fields around it. The room stands in a symbolic relationship with Felicité's destiny by foreshadowing her final mystical ascension. At the same time that the room is a metaphor for elevation, objects in the room also signify the story's central theme of worldly degradation. Every object mentioned in the room is associated with some event in Felicité's past (her church experience, her love for her mistress's children, and so forth) while the objects' decay represents through synecdoche the entropic processes that permeate Flaubert's world. Causal order and symbolic representation coincide in the portrayal of a room that has both a fictional specificity and a universal mimetic value.

As François's room becomes a place of confinement, isolation, and entombment, it is transformed into an iconic metaphor representing his destiny. An example is the way the image of the shattered window functions when François stands before it after the first round of gunfire. The jagged glass, set in relief by Carné's chiaroscuro lighting, frames Gabin's solemn face and emphasizes the distance that sets him apart from all those on the other side of the window. The decor here denotes the violence that has been unleashed against this trapped hero. It also signifies connotatively the unique moment in his life in which his hopes are broken, in which he has been separated from his fellows, isolated, condemned, and forced into solitude. The decor has thus a specific, realistic mimetic value as it shows the results of police violence. It also functions as a filmic trope to designate tragic fate and to show metaphorically the struggle the hero undergoes.

One should not confuse this notion of symbolic mimesis with the use of decor and objects as psychological and sociological indices that serve to specify the representation of a specific world, that denote how François is a neat, meticulous, rather athletic bachelor living in the most modest of circumstances.[5] Just as the objects in Felicité's room are a résumé of her past and thus represent the way the unfolding of events, the succession of disappointments, have transferred her room into a bizarre chapel, the objects in François's room are reflections of his past hopes and represent the way the inflexible causal order has led to the present, to his room's transformation into a shooting gallery. The teddy bear on his dresser, for example, which is hit by the first round of fire, stands as a symbol for the hope François once had. François took the toy animal from Françoise as a souvenir on the night he followed her to the café concert. The toy is thus associated with a key event in the worker's destiny. The bullet that strikes the teddy bear underscores that the object also signifies, over and beyond its own specificity, the destructive causal chain that has led to hope's ruin.

Nearly all the objects in the room function as various ironic reflectors of the way in which events have taken their destructive course. The bicycle parts, for example, recall François's promise to buy Françoise a bicycle for their Easter excursion; the alarm clock ironically calls for a new day after having ticked off the worker's last moments; the wardrobe contains clothes that each refer to a special moment in the past. It is, however, the room's mirror that is most richly charged with connotations. It is quickly shattered by the gunfire and can then reflect only a distorted image corresponding to the shattered world that lies about François. In it François sees himself both as he is and, metaphorically, as a destroyed being. It is thus not surprising that he should finally smash the mirror in anger, which is on one level an attempt to abolish this image of himself and, on another level, an act that analogically foreshadows his suicide. The shattered mirror contains within itself the contradiction of the tragic circle that leads to self-destruction as the only release from tragic awareness.

After one has considered the film's dramatic structure and its decor, a

5. Bazin is very suggestive in this respect. "Le décor est un acteur," p. 7.

complete exegesis of the film's mimetic project demands that one examine how the dramatic and thematic development in *Le Jour se lève* are interrelated with the film's ideological underpinnings. Carné and Prévert have used what we have called sociological determinants to ground their film in the class struggle that, in the late thirties, seemed capable of plunging France into civil war. It is for this reason that the film was banned as "demoralizing" in 1939 and that a right-wing critic, Robert Brasillach, devoted some of his most scurrilous remarks to the film in early versions of his *Histoire du cinéma*. Yet this ideological side is certainly one of the film's most remarkable aspects, for Prévert and Carné have succeeded in converting ideology into tragic myth while at the same time using tragic structure to convey ideology.

In mimetic terms, each character in *Le Jour se lève* exists as a projection of an ideological point of view that sees history as a form of necessity, though it should be stressed that neither Prévert nor Carné was an orthodox Marxist. Both undoubtedly hoped and perhaps vaguely expected that history would eventually bring about the triumph of the working class. But in the late thirties it seemed much more evident that history had decreed the subjugation of the working class to a bourgeoisie so decadent that it might resort to fascism to defend its power. It is from this perspective that one must understand why so many French artists saw the thirties as a tragic age.

Each character in the film presents a complex ensemble of attitudes and capacities that reflect this historical vision. Yet none of these protagonists is a simple allegorical figure. This is most evident if we compare Jules Berry as Valentin with the role that Prévert created for him in Jean Renoir's *Le Crime de Monsieur Lange* (1935). In this film Berry, as Batala, is simply a demonic capitalist who so mechanically exploits his workers that he becomes a rather comic figure. In *Le Jour se lève* Prévert has completely changed Berry's role by transforming the capitalist clown into a decadent, bourgeois artist who undertakes the gratuitous creation of evil. In both films Berry is a seducer, but in *Le Jour se lève* he seduces through the creation of illusions, the invention of fictions, that enable him to manipulate women much in the same way he forces his dogs to go through their routines.

We first see Valentin in the café concert, and it is more than a little revealing that his act is sandwiched between a ludicrous patriotic song celebrating the French Foreign Legion and an absurd cycle-riding xylophonist's routine. This is the world of degraded spectacle that mimics the high culture the bourgeoisie is no longer able to create. Valentin's refined language and manners—Clara claims he has a university diploma—only further emphasize, by contrast, the depths of his degradation. One might think in this respect of the grotesque street singer in Mann's *Death in Venice* who faces Aschenbach as his degraded double. Like Valentin, such an artist can only be presager of death and dissolution, for when he is no longer capable of genuine creation his only recourse is to join forces with pestilence and become a voice for ruin. Evil, then, is a surrogate for authentic creation.

Valentin, as an artist, thus defines himself in terms of spectacle, illusion, and, most especially, manipulation of language. This manipulation is the artist's ideological function, and in *Le Jour se lève* Carné and Prévert have linked Valentin's sadism and will to power to the more general ideological function of the bourgeois artist, namely, in Marxist terms, to mystify. It is through calculated mystification that he achieves his ends. Even if the viewer should reject the ideological vision that underlies this case of individual pathology, he can hardly deny that in a Marxist sense Valentin uses language without an object to construct illusions that keep the other in a state of subjugation. Language without a referent is either a lie or a fiction, according to its use. As a degraded artist, Valentin can only create lies—or fictions— used for the destruction of others.

François's shooting Valentin is an act of revolt against this mystifying, corrupting language. As a worker, François is defined in terms of acts, of doing, of his relation with things, and language for him is a simple tool that should be in direct contact with his everyday experience. This notion is humorously reflected in the implicit contrast Clara makes between François and Valentin when she says that she is tired of men "who talk so much about love they forget to do it." It is reflected more grimly in François's rage and disgust when he discovers how Valentin has used language to mystify him and even more so when finally, as a last defense against this language, François is goaded into destroying the source of this corrupting word. His act of shooting Valentin is essentially a desire to stop the flow of words with which he cannot contend.

Tragedy here also derives from ideological analysis in that François's identity contains a destructive contradiction within it. He must define himself in terms of his work; yet his work is destroying him. His relation to things is thus a destructive one that reflects both the hostile destiny that pursues him and the historical conditions that condemn a class of men to impossible conditions. The concrete instances of this contradiction—the sand that infects his lungs or the lead in the paint that once poisoned him—point to the universal contradiction that characterizes the relationship between one social class and the conditions that define its existence. François's self-destruction stands for the tragedy of the masses of men who are condemned to a slow death through their work.

François is not in a state of revolt, however, and one can scarcely see in him the prototype of the militant worker. He confronts his fate with good humor and even declares, though with a certain ironic detachment, that "work is freedom." Carné and Prévert have given us a portrait of the "good" worker who basically believes in the fundamental order of things as they appear to be. Another measure of his tragic destruction is, then, his loss of belief in this order, his coming to see that this order is inimical to all hope or confidence. Such is the meaning of his outcry when, addressing the crowd from his balcony, he shouts at them to leave him alone, telling them that he is tired and has no more confidence, that his job is available now for anyone who wants this "real little bit of happiness" with overtime. Disabused awareness is the pathetic mark of his tragic fall.

The dramatic agons are provided by the conflict between Valentin and François, which in turn reflects the Prévert-Carné vision of class struggle. In terms of dramatic progression, the two female protagonists serve to contrast the dynamics of conflict by their relation to each man. Françoise, the orphan who has been raised as a ward of the state, has no illusions about the possibility of any future in her relationship with François. When he suggests that they consider marriage—the conventional symbol of future happiness—she quickly dismisses the idea as foolish in their situation. In relation to Valentin, however, she shows herself a dupe, seduced by the artist's world of illusion and fictions, corrupted to the point that she tries to invent illusions for François, telling him a sentimental tale about the brooch. It is her mimicking Valentin that leads finally to François's loss of confidence and to his destruction.

Clara's relations with the two men complement the symmetry of Françoise's. Clara has succeeded in liberating herself from the spell that Valentin's language had cast upon her. He may once have "got her with mimosas," but she would now prefer the more tangible accomplishments that François might offer her. In terms of social class she is another hanger-on in the world of degraded art, and she thus stands opposed to Françoise, the proletarian florist, as Valentin stands opposed to Françoise. In mimetic terms, however, this contrast exists less as a reflection of ideology than as a reflection of myth, especially of the surrealist myth concerning archetypal women. The contrast between Clara and Françoise seems to mirror the kind of distinction that the surrealist poet Benjamin Péret, for example, made between the *femme-sorcière* and the *femme-enfant*.

The *femme-sorcière* ("the bewitching woman") represents the pessimistic side of love, for she is willing to accept the world as it is; Clara comes immediately to mind as an example of this type. On the other hand, the *femme-enfant* (the "child-woman") offers an image of what women could become in a world in which social forces did not oppose the realization of *l'amour fou* or sublime love. The *femme-enfant* offers an ecstatic revelation of what love might be, were it not for the destruction of love that forms of repression bring about, and thus, according again to the surrealist Péret, the child-woman represents "a value of revolt, since her possible happiness accuses the present and denies it any right to existence. By the very fact that she rises up as a presage of a time to come, she shows that obstacles encountered by sublime love are inherent in the social structure and, consequently, exterior to love itself. Her behavior in sublime love thus represents, in the final analysis, an indirect and, as it were, whispered call for subversion."[6] Françoise, the *femme-fleur* of surrealist myth, offers the revelation that the world might be other than it is, though she is at the same time the agent for tragic destruction. The love she reveals is the ground for tragic or impossible hope; this love is also the revelation of utopia and an indictment of all that stops its realization.

It is surrealism's vision of love and insurrection that allows us finally to see how *Le Jour se lève* sets forth the two sides of the anguish with which the artists of an era lived its seemingly tragic impasse before World War II. Underlying François's destruction is a belief in the impossibility of justice, which condemns every form of hope as an illusion. At the same time, the very intolerable blackness of this belief is the ground for a cry of rebellion and revolt. There is, however, no dialectical resolution of this tension between two poles of belief and sensibility, neither in the film, nor, in fact, in history. In *Le Jour se lève*, then, we find a classical form that is in the service of a radical ideology, a tragic despair that is grounded in utopian poetics. These are some of the tensions that make this film the most complete expression of its epoch.

6. Benjamin Péret, *Anthologie de l'amour sublime*, pp. 27–28.

The Existentialist
Moment

Bresson's *Un condamné à mort*:
The Semiotics of Grace

Stanley Cavell tells us in *The World Viewed* that the material basis of the movies is "a succession of automatic world projections" and, moreover, "that the projected world does not exist (now) is its only difference from reality. (There is no feature, or set of features, in which it differs. Existence is not a predicate.)"[1] Although the film semiotician might well ask how the projected world then comes to signify or to possess a semantic dimension, this view of film ontology is probably more widely held than any other. The view seems to lie, for instance, behind Robert Bresson's repeated rejection of the ideas that film can be a form of representation, that an actor's mimicry can have a role in film, or that film can use in any sense the notion of *mise en scène*. But Bresson, who hardly intends for his films to be a mere appropriation of an absent world, would have a ready answer for the film semiotician. According to Bresson, it is through the creation of a system of relationships among the projected images that the filmic world comes to have meaning. Bresson goes so far, in fact, as to deny that a single image can have a meaning, for if it does, it risks destroying the signifying system that the filmmaker must create:

> If an image, looked at apart, clearly expresses something, if it includes an interpretation, it will not be transformed by the contact with other images. The other images will have no power over it, and it will have no power over the other images. Neither action nor reaction. It is complete in itself [*définitive*] and unusable in the system of the cinematograph. (A system does not decide everything. It is a beginning toward something.)[2]

The cinematograph—Bresson has only disdain for the "cinema"—thus derives meaning from a system of relationships predicated on the interaction of all elements in a film.

1. Stanley Cavell, *The World Viewed: Reflections on the Ontology of Film*, pp. 24 and 72.
2. Robert Bresson, *Notes sur le cinématographe*, pp. 17–18. (All translations are mine, unless otherwise indicated.)

However, it is Bresson's final remark, in parentheses, that points to the need to think beyond the immediate visual system that orders a series of projected world views. For the filmic system can generate meaning only if the relations making up the system are semanticized in turn by a more general signifying context that is not directly present in the projected world. We would say, in fact, that the filmic signification is generated by the context provided by the film's narrative project, for narration is a privileged semanticizing agent for endowing the system of filmic elements with meaning. Perhaps it is in this sense that we might understand Bresson's remarks on how film can signify what most deeply concerns him: "Life must not be rendered by photographically recopying life, but by hidden laws in the middle of which one feels that your models move."[3] Models—Bresson has no use for the word "actor" either—must move in conformity with hidden laws that we might take to be the laws of narrativity or the narrative project that invests the filmic world with meaning. Thus the most fruitful critical approach to a film would be one that seeks to lay bare the film's fundamental narrative project, its hidden laws, so that all the elements in the filmic system can stand out in the full significance that they have derived from this semanticizing context.

The narrative project that endows the filmic system with meaning is rarely an autonomous structure, and perhaps it inevitably derives its semanticizing capacity in turn from the cultural context that gives rise to it. Even the most generically fixed narrative form is embedded in a cultural matrix that allows it to invest the image with a semantic dimension. In the case of a very complex film, such as Bresson's *Un condamné à mort s'est échappé* (1956), this cultural matrix is of the greatest importance. On the surface, Bresson's portrayal of a condemned prisoner's escape might appear to be an evocation of the French Resistance, for the film's opening titles tell us that *Un condamné à mort* is a "true" story dealing with the Montluc prison in which, of the ten thousand prisoners the Germans sent there during the Occupation, seven thousand died. On one level, then, it appears that the film is a historical adventure film, narrating how the prisoner Fontaine avoids death by escaping against impossible odds, and is thus a work that borrows its narrative conventions or signifying codes from a preexisting cinematic genre.[4] The strength—

3. Bresson, *Notes sur le cinématographe*, p. 78.
4. For a definition of the notion of codes, see Umberto Eco, *A Theory of Semiotics*. "One can then maintain that it is not true that a code organizes signs; it is more correct to say that codes provide the rules which *generate* signs as concrete occurrences in communicative intercourse" (p. 49).

and weakness—of genres is, of course, that they facilitate a quick recognition of the semantic codes the work uses and thus allow an easy "reading" of the film. But, as auteurists have stressed, the great director is one who uses the preexisting forms in order to shape his own vision. Perhaps the greatest directors, then, are those who use genres as a point of departure for the creation of new cinematic codes, and in this respect, it is evident that only the relatively inexperienced viewer would attempt to view *Un condamné à mort* solely in terms of the canons of the adventure genre. The film uses the adventure genre only a means for creating a new narrative structure, one whose significance is derived not so much from the heroic concerns of the Resistance, but rather from the cultural matrix provided by the Christian existentialism that was a dominant current in French intellectual life during the fifties.

It is, in fact, with a Kierkegaardian understanding of religious paradox that one must begin an interpretation of *Un condamné à mort*, for in one sense this is a film about an unmediated relationship between the particular and the absolute. The cultural context that grounds the narrative project is, in general terms, that system of existentialist religious values in which the oppositions of faith and despair, freedom and grace, or spirit and flesh establish a coherent semantic field. The film's full title is the first sign that we must look to this cultural matrix: *Un condamné à mort s'est échappé ou le vent souffle où il veut* (*A Man Escaped or The Wind Listeth Where It Will*). In semantic terms, titles often direct the viewer toward a context that offers the first key to meaning, and in the case of Bresson's film the double title orients us toward the fundamental series of oppositions that provide a general context. The film's visible action—the escape—is informed by an absent spiritual drama that stands in opposition to the present material drama of resistance and escape. (*Opposition* is used here in the technical sense of "a correlational opposition of pertinent features.") Fontaine's escape from the German prison, the manifest struggle for freedom in the world, is doubled by a spiritual determinism, for it is grace that allows him to overcome his captors. This opposition, a paradox in the eyes of the world, gives rise to secondary oppositions that both inform the narrative and generate secondary levels of meaning. For example, Fontaine struggles in prison to vanquish isolation and to achieve fraternal communion. This opposition derives its full meaning from its relationship to the religious drama, especially insofar as this opposition is part of the religious paradox: The prison actually allows these prisoners to overcome isolation and to enter into true communion. To give another pointed opposition, one might consider the relation between the material presence of evil and the despair to which it might lead, on one hand, and, on the other hand, the seemingly gratuitous faith that never abandons the hero, a paradox that is expressed existentially as a constant leap of faith.[5]

The film's narrative project is thus grounded in a rhythm that alternately turns on solitude and communion, the absurd and faith, and freedom and grace, in a series of related oppositions that endow all elements in the film with meaning. The first shots presenting Fontaine, detached from his fellow prisoners after he has been captured, begin the presentation of solitude, for he then attempts to escape alone from the automobile that is taking him and another prisoner to Montluc. He is recaptured, though the camera here emphasizes how little importance his physical flight has by refusing to follow him as he tries to flee. Fontaine is then handcuffed and struck with a revolver by an anonymous agent; the dull thud of the blow reveals how evil must be born concretely in the presence of flesh. Bresson pursues this descent into evil and isolation in the next series of shots, which suggest that Fontaine undergoes the solitude of the Passion. Fontaine is spat upon by passersby and, as the following ellipsis suggests, beaten by his captors. Isolation is thus lived as degradation of the flesh, though, as the comparison with the Passion reveals, this is the converse of the absent dream of grace and communion.

Isolation and evil, those absurd absolutes, give way in the narrative rhythm to Fontaine's first leap of faith, when he chooses to trust Terry, one of the men he sees walking in the courtyard, with the urgent message to the Resistance about his arrest and the Germans having seized their radio code. This leap of faith finds its complementary expression in the grace that allows Terry to bring Fontaine a pencil and paper; both Terry's act and the items he brings make possible the communion that might overcome the isolation imposed by prison walls. Communion as a transcending of the walls is realized paradoxically, in fact, when Fontaine uses the wall that separates him from a neighboring prisoner as a means of communication. They tap out messages to each other, and when the other prisoner tells Fontaine how to remove his handcuffs, we see clearly that communion, faith, and, as shown in this image, freedom are bound together as the constants that inform the narrative's structure.

5. Most of my references to Kierkegaard are drawn from *Fear and Trembling* and *Sickness unto Death*, as well as the *Journals*.

The narrative rhythm takes Fontaine back to solitude when he is moved to a cell on the top floor of the prison. His only neighbor here is Blanchet, the epitome of a man defeated by an absurd imprisonment and thus incapable, for the moment, of any kind of transcending communion. It is here that we see Fontaine closest to despair, as he speaks of his "frightening solitude." But it is also at this moment that we first see Fontaine and the other prisoners go down into the courtyard where, joined in their common humiliation, they enter into a silent communion as they empty their slop buckets. As the men go to gather up their pails, a brief chord from Mozart's Mass in C Minor stands in counterpoint to their abjection. In one respect, the music endows this humiliating routine with the solemnity of a religious service; at the same time, it recalls that the men's degradation, in spite of the daily drudgery that numbs the flesh and weakens the will, is the converse of the spiritual drama that stands behind every act. The music opens here onto the world of transcendence that stands in opposition to the material world of a drama that seemingly warrants only despair.

Mozart and the cesspool, like fraternity and torture, are two poles that structure Bresson's narrative project throughout the rest of the film. Equally important from this point in the narration until the end are the related poles of despair and lack of communion, on the one hand, and faith and willed action, on the other. Fontaine begins to use a spoon to remove fragments of wood from his cell door, a task demanding that he carefully dig away minute splinters, but also showing that he has assumed responsibility for his freedom. In opposition to this act of faith stands his neighbor's silence, the negation of communion, as well as the message given to him that Terry will be taken away and the news he receives of the condemnation of another prisoner. In existential terms, Fontaine has assumed his freedom, and by this act he has demanded the freedom of all men. In ethical terms, he has made freedom the universal value that vouchsafes all human activity. Though Blanchet quite correctly perceives that Fontaine's resistance could result in the punishment of all, Fontaine's continued affirmation slowly brings Blanchet out of his despair, for it opens a realm of future possibility in which Blanchet might again claim his dignity as a man and his worthiness as a self.

In religious terms, this affirmation is a paradox, recalling Kierkegaard's statement that faith surely implies an act of the will—even if grace be the most unmerited of gifts. This opposition of will and grace stands behind the scene in which Fontaine, now needing another spoon to finish dismantling the door, converses with the Pastor, who informs him that thanks to a miracle he has received a much-wanted Bible. Fontaine seems to know his own miracle of grace when he finds a much-needed second spoon lying on a ledge in the washroom. Yet this demonstration of grace is also a demonstration of Fontaine's determination to seize every available opportunity to continue his escape attempt, as Fontaine himself suggests when he later tells the Pastor, with a tone of remonstrance, that it would be all too easy if one were to let God take care of everything. Perhaps there is no way to resolve this paradox of freedom and grace, for, to borrow again from Kierkegaard, the man of faith is in such a relation to the absolute that nothing can mediate it. Freedom and providence stand semantically in opposition, and perhaps the great power of this film lies precisely in its power to maintain this opposition while showing how in Fontaine they are two manifestations of the drama of faith.

At this point the film's rhythm leads again to communion, for, having broken the door open, Fontaine can go into the corridor at night and bring a word of hope to a prisoner who has been permanently confined to his cell. The dialectic of communion and solitude then leads to destruction, for Orsini, the prisoner with the burning, sincere eyes, who has also been transformed by his contact with Fontaine, attempts to escape but is captured and executed. But now even Blanchet can see that the web of evil and grace is somehow connected, for it is Blanchet who tells Fontaine that Orsini had to fail so that through his failure he could tell Fontaine what he needs to get over the wall.

The final rhythm of this film is largely shaped by a series of leaps of faith, and by leap of faith we mean the Christian existentialist notion of an active affirmation of faith in the face of the absurd. For instance, Fontaine refuses to turn over a pencil he has, even though he can be punished by death if his captors find it. The absurdity of his act astonishes him, and yet Fontaine knows that this is another affirmation of faith and will. Even more important in this regard, once Fontaine has learned that he will soon be executed, is the arrival in his cell of Jost, the adolescent prisoner who has already become a traitor by volunteering for military service with the Germans. Bresson multiplies signs that point to Jost's being a potential German agent, for he alone talks to the German guard, and he admits that he thinks the Germans will win the war. Moreover, in a striking series of poses in the washroom, Fontaine's friends hover about Fontaine to warn him to beware of the boy. Communion, in the sense of the most elementary trust, between these two prisoners can only be a leap of faith. The paradox of faith is made even more complex in this instance, for, having revealed his plans for escape, Fontaine finds himself obliged to consider killing this child to preserve his own struggle against evil. Fontaine's unswerving faith thus leads him to the extreme situation where faith appears to resemble the evil that it strives to overcome.

The escape itself is the final leap of faith. It hardly seems an exaggeration to say that the physical leaps the two prisoners undertake are so many material analogues doubling the existential leap itself. This seems especially true of the final, determined jump; Fontaine hurls himself into space, sustained only by his improvised rope, as he goes from the inner to the outer wall. The leap triumphs over the absurd presence of evil as embodied in the wall, and it is a leap achieved through the fraternal communion that the two men have come to know. Jost's presence is a mark of grace, for it is only through his help that Fontaine, too weak to scale the final wall alone, can succeed.

The leap of faith here achieves that communion that few of Bresson's characters succeed in knowing, though for nearly all of them some form of human community would be a sign to the viewer of grace and salvation. In this respect one might consider how the religious community of *Les anges du péché*, Bresson's first major film, expels Anne-Marie during her novitiate. The expelling in turn leads to her sickness and death as she seeks to maintain furtive ties with the convent. Perhaps even more exemplary is Bresson's country priest in *Le Journal d'un curé de campagne*. He is isolated, scorned, and humiliated in the provincial community for which he should be the center of communion in every sense of the term. Like Anne-Marie, he finds transcendence only in death, though it is an isolated death born of sickness. For Bresson's heroes often live their estrangement as a form of humiliation of the body, as we see when his Mouchette finds her only human contact by being raped. She is so isolated that only in this violation of her flesh does she seem to find a moment of paradoxical communion, though this is only a prelude to her final despair and suicide. In nearly all his works, be it *Au hasard Balthazar*, *Jeanne d'Arc*, *Pickpocket*, or *Une femme douce*, Bresson's narrative turns in one way or another on isolation and humiliation, on estrangement and the impossibility of a desired community. Only in *Un condamné à mort* does transcendence seem to be realized in the flesh.

This discussion of the cultural oppositions that endow the narrative with significance allows us in turn to see how each individual element in *Un condamné à mort* acquires meaning within the semanticizing context provided by the narrative. Let us consider in greater detail Bresson's use of music, in this case Mozart's Mass in C Minor. On the level of immediate presence, the mass is present as a work of music and thus has meaning in terms of its own conventions and cultural codes. The naive viewer may, in fact, perceive this music only as a bit of fioritura, especially if he is accustomed to the standard filmic code by which film music often functions as a redundant marker, duplicating other elements of meaning within a shot or a scene. One will recall that in Bresson's film a chord or two of the mass recurs periodically, when the prisoners go down into the courtyard to empty their slop buckets or at the end of the film when Fontaine and Jost escape into the night. The music thus sounds at those moments when men find themselves together. Through this recurrence the narrative project appropriates the music and converts it into a signifier that has both its intrinsic meaning and a special meaning grounded in the filmic context. In *Un condamné à mort* the narrative principle of absence–presence specifically causes the music to signify the absent spiritual drama of communion that stands in opposition to the present drama of absurd degradation.

The religious drama of spiritual elevation is thus signified as doubling— though absent in physical terms—the action that we see on the screen. This oppositional relationship endows the music with a semantic dimension that is predicated on the music's intrinsic meaning but that fully exists only so far as the music is integrated into the narrative whole. Moreover, the music takes on full meaning only so far as it functions, if we may borrow a category from linguistics, as a paradigmatic option. Mozart's Mass stands, in other terms, in opposition to all other kinds of music that Bresson might have used, a patriotic piece or some kind of music signifying emotional distress. More importantly, it stands in opposition to the silence that exists most of the time. With no undue paradox we might say that it is the opposition between music and silence that endows silence with a semantic dimension, for in this context it comes to signify the absence of that revelation that the music offers. In a similar vein, the variety of natural sounds that Bresson uses on his sound track, such as the sound of a train whistle coming from beyond the walls, enter into a relationship with the silence and come not only to denote their source, but also to signify a transcendent world beyond the walls, an absent world that is the object of faith.

Another feature of the projected world for which it is difficult to find appropriate critical categories is the composition of this world achieved through lighting and the use of volumes, or, in other terms, the fact that the plastic values of Bresson's shots acquire meaning. Of course, the very fact that we perceive a projected world as being invested with these values indicates that some kind of fundamental conversion of the projected world has taken place. In theoretical terms, I should again maintain that it is primarily the narrative project that allows the viewer to see that a signifying intention lies behind framing, lighting, or composition, and that this transforming intentionality in turn allows the viewer to read these properties in function of the narrative context. It is again the narrative context that endows these purely "cinematic" elements (pure because they belong neither to the world nor to language) with semantic depth.

Bresson's composition of shots in *Un condamné à mort*, as in other of his works, is a more complex matter than in the case of many other directors, since he often draws upon well-known pictorial models. Like his use of music, then, his compositional values possess a semantic dimension that preexists the filmic context. The tensions Bresson creates between light and shadow in Fontaine's cell, the modeling he does with light volumes, are often based, for example, on the respresentational codes elaborated by baroque painters like George de la Tour or Philippe de Champaigne. The tension that exists between light and dark is thus already codified, for it designates a semantic space created by the opposition of flesh and spirit, free will and grace, or human and divine. The baroque code preexists the filmic context but is in turn appropriated by the film's action and integrated into the semantic whole. The film's primary narrative opposition of visible–invisible can thus appropriate the pictorial representational code and endow it with connotative values that are grounded in the film's narrative project.

Compositional values function, then, at several levels. They most immediately make up part of the image that sets forth the narration in its physical presence; at the same time, they signify through their own pictorial codes and through their being appropriated by the narration and given connotative values in the filmic context. Consider, for example, the shots near the end of *Un condamné à mort* when Jost and Fontaine climb through the skylight and edge along the prison roof, slowly making their way toward the precipice they must descend. The contrast between light and dark, in which Fontaine's face emerges intensely from the shadows, seems to suggest connotatively the spiritual drama of the escape while it also stresses the physiological tension caused by this nearly impossible enterprise. Moreover, the contrast portrays, in baroque terms, the drama between human will and destiny, in which man must triumph over darkness as he confronts the unknown in an unstable world. Fontaine does this literally when, after the descent, he enters the darkness and kills the German soldier who is standing guard. This baroque representatal value comes to signify the specifically Christian drama that the film narrates, and in this context the light and darkness are physical analogues for the drama of the visible and the invisible, the present and the absent, that underlies the film's narration. These levels are, of course, integrated into one mimetic whole in which the prisoners' progress is as much progress toward physical liberation as it is a defeat of the darkness and an arrival at the final communion.

The same kind of considerations we have given to compositional values can be given to Bresson's use of framing and the field size of his shots. The close-up, for example, functions paradigmatically in opposition to the four or five other options the filmmaker has when choosing field size. A great deal of discussion has been given to the meaning of a close-up, but it seems adequate to say that, according to standard film convention, it is most often used to designate a moment of psychological intensity or to signify a revelation. It stands, then, in opposition to the normal narrative shot, and its meaning is generated precisely by this opposition. Bresson, however, uses the close-up as his standard shot in *Un condamné à mort*. As Fontaine spends hours, for example, using a spoon to carve away the wood of his cell door, Bresson shows the prisoner's perseverance by means of a series of insistent close-up shots concentrating on the prisoner's hands, the spoon, and the wood. This deviation from standard film convention can be explained only if it can be integrated into the semantic totality generated by the narrative project, which is to say that the viewer must read this use of the close-up as the expression of an aesthetic intentionality that gives rise to a new filmic code. Within the specific context of *Un condamné à mort*, it is apparent that this use of the close-up presupposes the conventional use, for by making the close-up his standard shot Bresson is showing how revelation springs from the most minute acts and how every gesture Fontaine undertakes as he cuts away the wood is an intense expression of will. The close-up as Bresson uses it can thus become the standard shot for advancing the narrative at the same time it recalls, through its intensity, that there are no indifferent acts in the material world of the narration. Every act, even the most repetitive, routine gesture, betrays the invisible drama of grace.

Bresson has been called the most elliptical director in film history, and it is true that his use of ellipsis provides another example of how Bresson converts standard signifying elements of film discourse into a new filmic code. Ellipses are usually part of what one might call a secondary narrative code in that they denote an absent element of episodic experience, and standard film codification usually designates them by a dissolve. But consider the series of shots that begin with Fontaine's being recaptured, brought to the prison for the first time, pushed into a room in which we see, through the open door, a row of shovels, and then . . . and then nothing, for Bresson interrupts the action with a dissolve before showing Fontaine transported to his cell on a stretcher. On a first viewing this ellipsis can be very disconcerting, for the adventure-film genre that seems to inform the film would call for a direct confrontation between the hero and his captors, between the good and evil whose opposition serves to generate narrative meaning.

In *Un condamné à mort*, however, it is evident that the ellipsis is not simply used to designate economically some bit of episodic experience or to bring about dramatic concentration. Since the narration is as much informed by what is absent as by what is present, by the invisible world of grace as by the present material world, the ellipsis can be read as a connotative signifier, referring to the absent world that informs the unfolding narrative. The ellipsis opens onto the invisible. This orginal use of ellipsis allows readings such as Peter Schofer's: "In seeing black, in seeing non-action, and inhuman nothing-ness, we enter Fontaine's world; we transcend the physical and participate in Fontaine's unconsciousness."[6] It is not the physical contact between the prisoner and his torturers that is of the greatest import, and the ellipsis signifies that this cruel moment itself must be seen as referring to another drama, the drama of grace in which Fontaine, perhaps unconsciously, must hold onto his faith in the face of the absurd.

Bresson has disturbed more than one critic—most notably André Bazin—by his use of a spoken text or commentary that, in accompanying the image, often seems to be a redundant element offering a kind of semantic duplication.[7] Or perhaps one might say that Bresson seems to take pleasure in violating that canon of prescriptive film theory that requires that the image should have the primary responsibility for meaning in film. The origin of this prescriptive rule concerning the genesis of meaning dates back to the begin-

6. Peter Schofer, "Dissolution into Darkness: Bresson's *Un condamné à mort s'est échappé*," *Sub-Stance*, no. 9 (1974):60.
7. André Bazin, "The Stylistics of Robert Bresson," in his *What is Cinema*, trans. Hugh Gray (Berkeley: University of California Press, 1967), pp. 125–43.

ning of the use of sound in film. However, as several decades of successful films should have demonstrated, there appears to be no a priori reason why a film should not integrate an overlaid spoken text into its semantic structures.

It is a dubious proposition, in fact, that text or image can ever be in any real sense redundant, since their juxtaposition within a narrative context would appear to semanticize them in ways that go beyond either's meaning when considered alone. In *Un condamné à mort*, for example, when Fontaine is thrown into his cell and is then shown trying to pull himself together, his overlaid voice tells us, "Nothing broken, but I must not have been a pretty sight to see." The shot presenting Fontaine with torn clothes and a blood-covered face does, indeed, show that he is not a pretty sight to see. And if the viewer understands the spoken text as a mere interpretative commentary on the image, without considering their juxtaposition in the narrative context, then it might be taken to be redundant.

Yet this way of considering the spoken text hardly takes account of the way it functions within the specific context. Fontaine's spoken text is in the past tense. By its juxtaposition with the image it thus tells the viewer that the present image he sees designates a narrative past. It endows the image with a dimension of total completion or "pastness." This paradigmatic opposition of past–present is in turn appropriated by the film's primary narrative opposition of absence–presence. The voice, speaking from a present moment—since the act of enunciation can only occur in the present—thus signifies the presence of the word and the absence of the visual world or what we have called the material world of the physical narrative. We again confront a religious paradox, for the speaking voice essentially designates the pastness and thus the absence of what seems most physically present. The spoken word implies, then, the primacy of the absent spiritual drama, for the truly present drama is embodied in the word, and by *word* we might well understand the logos or Verb that reveals grace.

In conclusion, then, we might say that Bresson has informed his narrative by exploiting the ontological properties of the different elements of filmic discourse, for speech and image are not the same in this respect. Though present in a material sense, as a projection, the image signifies an absent world; the present instance of speech tells us the world is not only absent, but also in time past. The spoken word, even when recorded and mechanically reproduced, always surges forth as a present and, unlike the projected image, is as ontologically complete in its presence as if it were actually spoken. The full presence of the spoken word becomes significant, of course, only in the specific context of the narrative opposition of presence–absence that informs *Un condamné à mort*. In this context, Fontaine's speaking voice is semanticized in a way that has nothing to do with the immanent meaning of his words. The present voice of the absent speaker designates that locus of eternal presence, beyond the world, from whose vantage point the unfolding of *Un condamné à mort* can be seen as the work of the divine providence that has ordered the narrative. It is through such an understanding of film that Bresson has created one of the few truly Christian films that exist, and certainly no other film testifies so elegantly to the paradoxes of Christian existentialism.

The Existential Play
in Truffaut's Early Films

Art, one might argue, functions in two essential ways. First, it opens our experience, deranges our way of perceiving experience (including the experience of art itself), and changes the space within which experience may be represented or perceived. In this respect art is a form of discovery and a creator of the conditions of experience. It is a kind of knowledge. Second, once art has opened a space of representation or perception, it can become a testing ground, a realm of experiential probing, in which art may receive its informing impulses from sources other than itself and submit them to various forms of trial that allow us to evaluate the experience of these sources. In this function art derives its basic concerns from other realms but organizes them so that we can understand these other realms in their full import as experience. In this sense art may be a way of appraising experience. It is, then, a kind of praxis.

In the greatest works of art these two functions seem to condition each other, as, for example, in the early films of the New Wave filmmakers, in which the need to find new means of filmic representation was made imperative by a desire to portray and to probe the modern absurdist sensibility. Particularly important in this respect are the early films of François Truffaut, who, if he has become the exponent of a rather facile classicism in some of his later films, was perhaps the most inventive of all those young filmmakers whose works reflect the prevailing existentialist ideology of the late fifties. For it now seems clear that a fully adequate understanding of the New Wave must take account of the absurdist sensibility that conditioned the experiential limits of the early work of those directors—Godard, Chabrol, Rivette, and others—who, like Truffaut, came to maturity in an ideological climate in which the absurd was the fundamental category that underlay all attempts at representation in France.

Before turning to examine how Truffaut's early work is informed by what we are calling the then-reigning existentialist ideology, we should consider the limits that the notion of the absurd imposed on any artist who was open to this dominant sensibility. It seems to us that the absurd imposed three basic configurations that determined the limits of representation in both formal and thematic terms. First, the absurd was construed as a form of mere presence beyond which there could be no transcending telos or other type of motivation. The notion of absurd presence finds its classic expression in Sartre's vision of *being* as a superfluous, gratuitous presence, as well as in such notions as *dereliction, fallenness,* and *alienated being.* A second configuration is given by the notion of *rupture and divorce.* Camus's view of the absurd as the divorce between the cosmos and man's desire for a rational understanding of it is one example of the absurd as a form of rupture. But this notion is also at work in the existentialist view of man's radical freedom, by which he can constantly break with his past, or in the idea that man's identity is essentially a discontinuous series of assumed roles. The notion of rupture undermines all rational principles of representation, especially causality, and leads to a third configuration that we might call call "dysfunctionality" or the lack of congruent relations. The classic expression of this kind of absurdism is Beckett's description of an entropic world in which all the old modes of representation fail to function, in which they, in effect, come to represent the dysfunctionality of all attempts at representation. The notion of dysfunctionality leads in turn to various forms of self-referentiality; the work designates its consciousness of its incongruity, and irony thus becomes one of the fundamental modes of absurd consciousness.

These three configurations established the possibilities of representation for Truffaut's *Les 400 Coups* (1959), *Tirez sur le pianiste* (1960), and *Jules et Jim* (1961); at the same time, they demanded the formal inventiveness that constituted the New Wave's rejection of classical cinematography. Consider in this respect the very beginning of Truffaut's first feature-length film, *Les 400 Coups* (a bit of colloquial French that should be translated as "raising hell" or "going on a spree"). The mobile camera in the title sequence, going around the Palais de Chaillot—the home of the Cinémathèque—traveling down treelined streets, capturing glimpses of the Eiffel Tower, denotes Paris as the film's dramatic locus. But its very mobility, "read" against the canons of standard cinematography, designates the film's self-conscious quest for significance. Moreover, this aimless mobility, within the film's specific context, is converted into a metaphor for the indeterminate freedom that the film's hero, Antoine Doinel, enjoys. The camera's gratuitous movement thus foreshadows Antoine's goalless ramblings as he goes on sprees. The absurd, as designated by the camera's very movement, finds an analogous expression in the music played in this sequence. From the outset, the music establishes an ironic tension between image and sound, for the music is incongruously lyrical. This incongruity is another way by which the absurd is signified.

Thus the presence of a camera aimlessly set in motion, breaking self-consciously with the canons of traditional filmic representation and setting forth a world that has no immediate, inherent rapport with the film music, seems to confirm our assertion that the absurd informs the most basic formal aspects of Truffaut's early work. It is, of course, at the most primary level of mimesis that these absurdist configurations are most evident, since Truffaut's representation of episodic experience is grounded in plots that are essentially discontinuous series of causally unrelated events that reflect the radical, if often incoherent, freedom that Truffaut's characters enjoy. This discontinuity is grounded in an existentialist sense of human liberty, and it is also an expression of the absurdist view that man must live experience as a series of ruptures and that no definitive account of his experience can be given until man's flight into the future meets death. Death is the real or metaphorical terminus of all of Truffaut's early works.

In *Les 400 Coups* episodic experience springs from the boy Antoine's choices, fortuitous or intentional, that result in acts whose consequences ultimately go far beyond what a child might foresee, but for which he is entirely responsible. Antoine Doinel, conceived by accident out of wedlock and thus forced into a world that is indifferent to his existence, is something of a prototype of the existentialist hero, especially as he comes to discover that he must bear the responsibility for the least of his caprices. Whatever may be the autobiographical element in Truffaut's portrayal of Antoine's being branded a delinquent, it is clear that his manner of depicting the boy's stumble into crime and incarceration is grounded both in an absurdist sense of fortuitous being and in an existentialist view of the radical responsibility that is the converse of freedom. Sartre's description of our helpless dereliction and our paradoxical responsibility in the world gives a special insight into the existentialist understanding that Antoine is a victim of his own freedom:

> Someone will say, "I did not ask to be born." This is a naive way of throwing greater emphasis on our facticity. I am responsible for everything, in fact, except for my very responsibility, for I am not the foundation of my being. Therefore everything takes place as if I were compelled to be responsible. I am *abandoned* in the world, not in the sense that I might remain abandoned and passive in a hostile universe like a board floating on

water, but rather in the sense that I find myself suddenly alone and without help, engaged in a world for which I bear the whole responsibility without being able, whatever I do, to tear myself away from the responsibility for an instant.[1]

It is this tension between the boy's abandonment and victimization, on the one hand, and his free if unenlightened choices, on the other, that explains in part *Les 400 Coups*'s extraordinary power. Unwanted by his parents, a superfluous child in a world where no adults will, or perhaps can, help him, Antoine is nonetheless the author of a fate that is all the more cruel because it could not be predicted.

In *Les 400 Coups* the rhythm of episodic experience does, however, follow a regular pattern. The boy's activities, his accidental faults or spontaneous caprices, set up situations that result in his punishment. Each of these situations is in turn followed by a spree, a period of seemingly indeterminate freedom, during which Antoine plays or, as the title suggests, raises hell. The film begins on a humorous note; we see Antoine in a *lycée* ("secondary school") that appears to have been borrowed from Vigo's *Zéro de conduite*. Antoine, now at the age when eroticism is as much a subject of mirth as a mystery to be explored, looks at a pinup photo the boys are passing around the drab classroom. The consequences of this bit of schoolboy rowdiness set the pattern for the rest of the film, for it leads to Antoine's punishment by grammar exercise and to his decision, at his friend René's urging, to go on a spree and to play hooky the next day. The pattern continues when, on returning to school on the day after his spree with no excuse for his absence, Antoine blurts out to his teacher that his mother has died. This bit of spontaneity results in another punishment when his mother and adoptive father arrive at the school. Antoine again goes on a spree, feeling he can no longer live in a home where he is no more than a tolerated burden. The episodic rhythm finally results in Antoine's expulsion from school when, encouraged by his mother to do better scholastically, he reproduces in a school composition a passage from a Balzac novel he has read with such fervor that he has, unconsciously it would appear, memorized it. Expulsion is immediate, as is Antoine's decision to go on what becomes his longest spree when he goes to live in secret in an abandoned room in René's house.

This pattern of acts and consequences has thus prepared the viewer to

1. Jean-Paul Sartre, *Being and Nothingness*, trans. Hazel E. Barnes (New York: The Citadel Press, 1964), pp. 531–32.

accept that Antoine's petty thievery, his attempt to get some money by stealing a typewriter from his father's office, could result in the child's incarceration. One might construe the disparity between the child's act and its consequences as an indictment of those societal conditions that so easily allow parents to divest themselves of their child and that then offer no better way of dealing with the boy than imprisoning him, forcing him to consort with adult criminals, and finally interning him in a prison camp whose name, "observation center," seems the most cynical of euphemisms. This indictment is undoubtedly present, but beyond this Truffaut has shown how the concatenation of rather innocuous acts can lead to an absurd catastrophe in which there is no congruity between intent and consequence. And beyond societal deficiencies—though the bureaucratic order is replete with them—the structure of freedom itself seems somehow deficient. The boy is free to choose his acts, but these acts can turn against him and ultimately destroy his freedom. There is, then, more than a little romantic fatalism in this rather nihilistic vision of freedom. This paradox is, however, one of the defining features of this kind of existential nihilism: freedom appears inevitably to turn against itself.

This nihilism seems to lie behind the film's final spree, Antoine's escape from the observation center. The final shots are a powerful visual translation of the frenzy of flight, of an explosion of indeterminate freedom, as the continuous tracking-shot rushes forward with Antoine through the anonymous landscape. This is another visual metaphor for freedom. The child's flight is a desperate but gratuitous act that leads him to the sea, to the vast, mythic expanse that he has never seen before. In its limitlessness the sea appears to be the antithesis of all the constraints—school, family, and prison—that have limited the boy's freedom. But in itself the sea is also a limit to the boy's flight, an absurd barrier not unlike the wall in Sartre's short story of the same name. It is an absurd presence marking the limits of freedom.

The film's final freeze frame presents a still image that recalls the mug shots the police made of Antoine. In this respect the still image, in the cinematic context, designates itself as an image and denotes the inconclusiveness of the cinematic quest for significance. It, too, has seemingly run up against this absurd presence. Moreover, the image, in that it recalls the police photo, seems to offer a kind of summing up, a résumé that might attempt to fix the boy's identity, though in an absurd world of radical freedom this final résumé can be fixed only by death. And so the final image perhaps connotes death, the final absurd limit of all freedom. Here we see another aspect of the fatalism that decrees that the boy's acts can only generate a crescendo of catastrophes whose logical conclusion could be his death. When one turns to *Tirez sur le pianiste* and *Jules et Jim*, death is, in fact, the explicit limit that terminates both films.

In *Tirez sur le pianiste* Truffaut uses one of the more classic narrative devices in filmmaking, the flashback, in order to break up his linear narrative and create a sense of discontinuity in the narration of episodic experience.[2] He first presents his piano-playing hero as Charlie, the barroom pianist who beats out popular tunes, before portraying him as Edouard, the successful concert pianist whose wife commits suicide. Normal linear narration might have imposed what could be perceived as a causal framework on the character's development, but the flashback, by its very rupture of the narration, forces the viewer to perceive the relation between Edouard-Charlie as a kind of hiatus. Through the flashback Truffaut thus succeeds in portraying the discontinuity that underlies the absurdist view of the self. The flashback also produces a fracture in the narration that nothing can join together. Events are thus related as a disparate series of acts springing from a self fragmented in time. Perhaps nowhere does Truffaut more beautifully portray this fragmentation, however, than immediately after the flashback when we find Charlie and Lena now in bed. The repetition of shots of the couple, breaking their lovemaking and sleep into a mosaic pattern, seems to convey at once an image of their newfound joy and of its fragile dependency on this single moment in time, isolated from all those that came before or might come after it.

In *Jules et Jim*, on the other hand, absurd chance is incorporated into the fabric of the plot itself in such a way that not only does the plot set forth the dramatic action but its very structure also connotes the difficulty of choice in a world given over to absurd hazard. Consider, for example, the pivotal choice in the film, Catherine's decision to marry Jules. She makes this decision, as Truffaut stresses by the long scene set in the café, only after she misses a rendezvous with Jim. Later in the film Jim tells her, admittedly while under the influence of his own desire, that he would have counseled against the marriage; thus it appears that the turning point in the lives of these three is due, in part, to mere accident. In the first part of the film, Truffaut stresses how sudden, seemingly gratuitous decisions shape his characters' lives. For example, Jules and Jim suddenly decide to go to the Adriatic island where they

2. On the notion of discontinuity one can read with profit Gabriel Pearson and Eric Rhode's "Cinema of Appearance," in *Focus on "Shoot the Piano Player,"* ed. Leo Braudy, pp. 25–45.

see the mysterious female statue, the incarnation of the eternal feminine that Catherine represents; later, the three decide with no forethought to go on vacation by the sea together, where Jules finds himself drawn closer to Catherine. These ruptures, predicated on the characters' total freedom, emphasize that all choice, no matter how premeditated, is ultimately an absurd leap in which one encounters chance.

In the second half of the film, after the war has separated the Frenchman and the German, breaks in the narrative underscore that episodic experience is the product of chance encounters. Jim's return to Germany, for instance, might have ended with his sudden departure, had not Catherine returned at the precise moment he is walking out the door—a coincidence that seems to be ironically reflected in her facial expression as she peers through the window pane. Later, in France, they again come together through pure chance. Truffaut ironically emphasizes the role of chance in the final sequence by introducing it with a title, "Some Months Later," a narrative device that in this context can only signify the arbitrary workings of hazard. It hardly seems to be an accident, however, that Truffaut should place this final encounter in a cinema, for this oblique form of self-reference is another ironic foil by which film designates itself as the locus of chance encounters. Moreover, the newsreel of a Nazi book-burning also reveals that their encounter is due again to those historical vicissitudes that separated them during the war. For it would appear that it is Hitler's seizure of power that has forced Jules and Catherine to come to France and thus cross Jim's path once more. Chance thus leads from burning books to the flames that consume the remains of Jim and Catherine.

In *Tirez sur le pianiste* the absurdist configuration that gives rise to narrative ruptures also lies behind the gags and parodistic devices that constantly rupture the film's tonality: a gangster's mother who falls dead because her son tells a fib, an absurd song that needs subtitles even in the French version, Charlie's telling his prostitute girl friend to cover her breasts because the censor will not accept the shot (as indeed was the case in the American version), these and many other examples immediately come to mind. In fact, from the film's first sequence Truffaut establishes that he wants to use ironic ruptures to redefine our way of experiencing film so that we come to it as a locus of indeterminacy. In the first scene we see a character pursued by a car, running in the dark, in a nearly total blackness that is clearly an exaggeration of the tonality that is coded as a sign of mystery or danger in a conventional Hollywood film. The fight we see automatically sets up the expectation of a chase that must be motivated by a crisis. We would then expect the narrative structure to resolve eventually this opening crisis. But Truffaut shows our expectation to be a product of conditioned response, stemming from a desire that film characters be determined in their conduct by fixed narrative codes, their responses governed in accord with the conventions of genre.

In Truffaut's absurdist world characters are governed only by the dictates of the filmmaker's ironic self-consciousness, and thus his fleeing character can, in the most improbable manner, run into a street light, knock himself down, get up, and then begin a long conversation with a passing stranger who explains how he found marital happiness. The character then resumes his flight at top speed. This break with the codes of psychological verisimilitude and of standard narration signifies, from the film's outset, that we must read the film in terms of new codes predicated on those absurdist configurations that were establishing the limits for representation at the end of the fifties. Moreover, Truffaut's parodistic use of codes derived from Hollywood films and the *film noir* underscores how one perhaps inevitable consequence of an absurdist viewpoint is that the work comes to designate itself and to call into question the very potentialities of the medium.

In this respect, it is more than a little revealing to note that Truffaut has been a very harsh critic of *Tirez sur le pianiste*, perhaps in reaction to its failure to receive wide public acclaim. But *Tirez sur le pianiste* is Truffaut's most difficult film, much like many works of Godard in that it demands a constant recognition of its use of filmic codes and conventions and of its parodistic break with them. For it is a film that constantly tests the conventions of representation and their adequacy for representing what we might call conventional life.

The film begins and ends with the image of Charlie Kohler seated at his piano, grinding out popular tunes for the motley crowd that gathers to dance in this down-and-out bar. The film thus fails to advance beyond its opening situation; this is another way of designating a kind of absurd stasis in that the film cannot progress beyond this circular movement. This structural circularity also suggests the film's failure to advance beyond the conventions it uses for representation, at the same time that it narrates Charlie's failure to overcome his passivity or, more precisely, to engage himself in a project or to acquire a self. Yet the film is full of action in a conventional sense. It at first appears to be a gangster film, for we see Charlie help his brother Chico escape from the pair of pursuing crooks, Momo and Ernest. It then appears to borrow the conventions of boy-meets-girl romance as Charlie courts, in his fumbling way, Lena, the barmaid. The film's flashback, portraying Charlie-Edouard's conventional success as an artist, recalls the typical Hollywood newspaper tragedy: headlines proclaim that the concert artist's wife has committed suicide, and we know she kills herself because Edouard, in another conventional response, rejected her when he learned that she had slept with his impresario in order to launch his career. The film then borrows from the hero-as-tracked-man genre, the sort that Prévert and Carné perfected in the thirties. The best example of this borrowing occurs when Charlie interposes himself between Lena and the barman, Plyne. After using a telephone speaker to duel with this barman, who is also a sentimental idealist, Charlie is forced to plant an enormous knife between Plyne's shoulder blades because the barman is slowly strangling him to death. This accident assures that Charlie will remain a tracked man. Finally, *Tirez sur le pianiste* draws upon the Western, the genre to which, after all, it owes its ironic title. When Charlie retreats to the family cabin, where his brothers await the gunslinging gangsters, the prolonged shoot-out begins with Lena being gratuitously gunned down, the victim of the only accurate shot in an otherwise absurd gun battle.

It is this mixing of conventions and the resulting multileveled parody that were undoubtedly responsible for the rather hostile reception that was once given to *Tirez sur le pianiste*. The mixture of lyricism and parody, of gags and tragic seriousness, must be envisaged as another form of representation that signifies the absurd, the loss of certainty, the sense of discontinuity that underlie Truffaut's early work. The image of the gangster who twirls the pistol about his finger refers to the Western convention used to designate sure-fingered accuracy. In the narrative context, however, such a reference is a gag that does not seem consonant with the irrevocable death that follows, with the slow slide of Lena's body down the snow-covered hill. But it is precisely this rupture between cause and effect that signifies the existential gratuitousness that informs *Tirez sur le pianiste*. The gag, and this film is filled with them, is raised here to the level of a mimetic mode that signifies a metaphysical vision. If we may borrow an expression that is usually applied to the works of Ionesco and Beckett, *Tirez sur le pianiste* is often a metaphysical farce.[3]

The absurdist configurations that lie behind the shaping of episodic experience and the parodistic devices in Truffaut's early work also seem to determine his choice of themes. We can consider a privileged theme in these

3. Rosette C. Lamont, "The Metaphysical Farce: Beckett and Ionesco," *French Review* 30, no. 2 (February 1959): 319–28.

three films in order to gain an understanding of how the absurd orders the representation of character: throughout these films the theme of the characters' identity appears to be a key motif. It is the theme to which all other themes are related and from which the others derive their full significance. Antoine's freedom, for example, derives in one sense from his identity as a legitimized bastard. To be a bastard is, in effect, to exist free of a determining heredity, absolved of familial and social ties, capable of realizing oneself in complete liberty. Antoine does not, of course, have the maturity to think of himself as condemned to choose his own form of self-realization in an indifferent world. Yet as a bastard he is, like Stendhal's or Sartre's heroes, the prototypical free hero for whom there exist no predetermined structures of identity because there exists no father ready to emasculate him if he does not accept the ideal identity that the father would impose on him. This seems clearly to be the sense, for example, of the shots presenting Antoine's "father" in the kitchen; Antoine can only laugh at the weak cuckold who, wearing an apron, prepares supper while his wife "works late" at the office.

The bastard's accidental presence in the world is a metaphor for man's presence there, though the child can enjoy this gratuitous existence as a form of play until he must pass into the world of adults and assume their identity. In *Les 400 Coups* Truffaut brilliantly contrasts the world of children's magical freedom and the adult world of consciousness when he shows Antoine and René at the puppet show. Here the little children are enraptured, even terrified, by the magic presence of the theatrical world of play, whereas Antoine and René, in the not-so-innocent company of the little girl, are rather indifferent to the spectacle, already too adult to give themselves over to the puppets' illusory world of magical presence. Further, Truffaut shows during the theft Antoine commits how the child's assumption of adult identity leads to the assumption of radical responsibility for his existence. Antoine attempts to change his identity by transforming himself into an adult, and the slouch hat he wears during the theft is a sign of his seeking to change his identity. In a sense, of course, he does succeed in assuming another identity, but it is a catastrophic one, since it leads to his imprisonment and expulsion from society. One can see, then, that the child's changing his identity ultimately gives expression to Truffaut's fatalism, for the child's attempt to be an adult can only result in a form of fall, the fall into adulthood that leads to dereliction and abandonment.

In *Tirez sur le pianiste* Truffaut pursues this vision of absurd dereliction even further in his portrait of Charlie-Edouard, the piano player whose two names point to the discontinuous identity he lives as he seeks to deny the past. Charlie today, Edouard yesterday, he seeks to live the present as a rupture that refuses to give any existential weight to his catastrophic past, in which he sought his identity as a public image. In this sense Charlie has chosen to be the existentialist bastard who refuses all familial and hereditary links, though the film demonstrates, from beginning to end, the impossibility of escaping those ties. We first see Charlie when his brother Chico runs into the bar and, immediately drawing Charlie into their family's imbroglios, calls him Edouard as he asks for help to escape from the gangsters. Charlie's angry but comically incongruous response, "Call me Charlie," underscores how difficult it is to live one's identity as a negation of one's public image, or, in existential terms, to deny one's being-for-others.

In the existentialist's world of gratuitous presence we see that the converse to one's radical freedom is the way in which one must exist for others. There is a public dimension of identity over which one has no control insofar as it is determined by others. One might think of Sartre's portrait of the Jew in this respect. Like Sartre's Jew, the absurdist man is free to choose any identity and yet tied paradoxically to a being-for-others, an identity he cannot choose and cannot even really know.

Charlie-Edouard's dereliction turns on his impossible impasse: as Charlie he attempts to deny his being-for-others; as Edouard he had tried to exist only as a being-for-others. The first is, as the film demonstrates by the way the family clings to him and by the way others impose identities on him, a hopeless task, whereas to seek to exist only for others is a catastrophically inauthentic mode of being. The episode narrated by the flashback shows this inauthenticity from its very beginning. At the outset Truffaut shows Edouard acting out a role in the café in which his wife, Theresa, works. He plays at being a customer before a third party, who is, most appropriately, his future impresario, Lars Schmeel, the promoter who will in effect grant Edouard his identity as a public figure. This initial scene is emblematic of the way in which the couple live their relationship as a form of public ritual, even when they think they are playing roles only for themselves. Indeed, Truffaut's iris shot that closes this opening scene, isolating Schmeel's head over the couple's bed for a brief moment before the shot fades to the new scene, not only shows that the impresario has infiltrated their relationship in erotic terms but that his presence as a third party invests their relationship completely, granting them their identity as the publicly known couple.

In their bedroom, the other or third party is also present in the mirrors on the bedroom's walls, for it is against these mirrors that they project their images as they act out roles in so-called privacy. The mirror can seemingly embody the presence of the other and, perhaps, allow us some knowledge about our being-for-others. In the case of Theresa the mirror is the source of an identity that she cannot abide, as she reveals when she confesses her infidelity to Edouard: "Only you know, it's strange, what you did yesterday remains in you today. I look in the mirror, what do I see? Theresa? Your Theresa? No, no Theresa, nowhere, just a filthy rag."[4] The mirror offers Theresa an image of what she takes to be her being-for-others, her image as degraded flesh, for her body continues to have a public existence that no act of contrition can change and no act of denial can overcome. The mirror forces an enduring identity upon her, and it is only through suicide, through the destruction of her body, that she can bring about the rupture that will deny that humiliating image of herself.

Theresa is perhaps a victim of her own projection, for it seems that it is really quite impossible to coincide in any sense with one's public image. One view of the split between Edouard and his public image is given when Truffaut shoots the bedroom scene during which the couple quarrel and Edouard expresses doubts about his identity as a public success. The viewer first sees an image of Edouard that he takes to be the "real" image of the pianist, but the camera then moves, and the spectator discovers that he has been viewing a mirror image of Edouard. This split between the man and his double seems to signify the gap that always exists between a man's knowledge of his identity and his knowledge of that identity as it exists as his being-for-others.

Truffaut uses a number of ironic and sometimes comic devices to show how Edouard's being-for-others takes on multiple forms. Lars Schmeel, for instance, has a portrait made of Edouard so that through this image he can, as he says, possess the piano player. Lena keeps a large publicity poster in her room that seemingly allows her, too, to possess an image of the piano player, the public image of the conventional success she wants to admire. Edouard also tries to create publicly verifiable images of an identity when, for instance, he poses for photographs in the hope of creating a new image as an aggressive

---

4. My translation from the film. (All translations are mine, unless otherwise indicated.)

public figure who has overcome the timidity that others have told him is his essence. These multiple images are ironic doubles of the multiple identities that Charlie-Edouard has for others, and their very multiplicity points up the difficulty of ever knowing what one's image in the world might be.

Yet, in anguish, Edouard-Charlie seeks that knowledge and acts upon what others tell him. It is Lars Schmeel who tells Edouard that he is timid, which sends him comically scurrying in search of images of the nontimid so that he can correct his identity. Plyne, the barman, tells Charlie that he is fearful, which, in one of the more amusing ruptures in the film, leads Charlie to try out various ways of saying "I'm afraid," as if he might hear in his own ears a public intonation that would give him a sense of what he is. Happy to welcome Charlie-Edouard back into the family, his brothers offer him a hereditary identity—that of a born criminal, a true Saroyan—and with it a gun that seems necessarily to accompany his new role. It is revealing, too, that Lena-Helena, the illegitimate orphan whose name reflects her own uncertain identity, also wants to force Charlie-Edouard to act in accord with the identity she has determined to be his, that of a great pianist. The final result of this profusion of identities and the mishaps resulting from them is that the piano player withdraws from the world, determined to have no being-for-others, desiring to commit no act other than that most derisive non-act, beating on his tinny piano. Aznavour's stoical face, as he pounds on the piano keys, directly signifies a loss of self in this world where act and identity refuse to be in harmony.

Perhaps the most powerful ironic representation of this loss of self is given near the film's end, when the viewer sees Charlie, who, trapped in his parents' house by his accidental crime, must confront the futility of his attempt to change his identity. But now, having assassinated Plyne, having thus committed a disastrous act by intervening in Lena's quarrel, he has acquired another public image that should somehow be visible to him. He is, after all, a criminal. With unwanted gun in hand, he twice looks at himself in mirrors, as though searching for some sign of an identity, but all he finds is a cracked image of himself reflected in old, broken glass. The cracked double is an ambiguous sign, for it seems at once to set forth Charlie's loss of self, the destruction of any identity, and the impossibility of finding an affirmation of one's identity in the world. Moreover, the circular tracking-shot that follows Charlie around the room where he keeps vigil, leading him from his cracked image and then back to it, seems to stand in an analogical relationship with the film's circular movement that leads from the opening image of the piano to the final shot of the piano. The circular movements designate how the piano player is trapped in his own immobility, incapable of going beyond the search for an image, gratuitously derelict in a world of absurd presence.

The antithesis to this kind of immobile presence, lived as a refusal of one's being-for-others, also is to be found in the way Catherine seeks, in *Jules et Jim*, to renew her existence and invent new values at every moment. The absurdist configuration underlying this attempt at permanent creation is again that of rupture and discontinuity, as we clearly see when Catherine, dressing in a manner that recalls the boy in Chaplin's *The Kid*, can seemingly change even her sex at will. The question of Catherine's identity determines, in fact, the way Truffaut constructs his representational space throughout the film, for it is she who defines the limits within which the others attempt to find their own roles. This is evident from the very beginning, when Jules and Jim, attracted by the image of a statue whose enigmatic face is shaped like Catherine's, go to the Adriatic in pursuit of this mystery. In a sense they are drawn there by the power of eros, of the eternal feminine, of physical forces that are beyond their control, and all of these seem to be part of Catherine's identity. In this respect Truffaut has enriched his filmic axioms in that Catherine can deprive Jules and Jim of their freedom. As in Goethe's *Elective Affinities*, that classic study of passion's magnetism that Truffaut posits as an extrafilmic parallel to his work, Jules and Jim must contend with affinities that they are powerless to control.

Like the heroine in the Scandinavian play they attend that neither Jules nor Jim cares for, Catherine refuses all permanence and sees herself, as she says, "inventing life at every moment."[5] When Jules quotes Baudelaire's definition of woman ("Woman is natural, therefore abominable"), Catherine leaps into the Seine, a gratuitous act by which she shows that no label can be imposed upon her, no simplistic formula can give a résumé of her being. She sees herself as one and yet ever-different, like the water into which she leaps. This leap signifies a form of rebellion against all conventional restraints, including reason itself, and represents a kind of triumph over the absurd in which the irrational is held up as in itself a supreme value. In this respect, Catherine seems quite close to certain of her historical contemporaries and in particular to the Gide of *Les Nourritures terrestres* (1897) who, in proclaiming his hatred of families, sets forth an ethic of readiness, of willingness to try out all forms of experience. For in this post-Nietzschean world of nihilistic gratu-

5. François Truffaut, *Jules and Jim*, trans. Nicholas Fry, p. 36.

itousness the maximization of experience, as Camus described it for his "absurd man," becomes the only form of redemption.

Catherine is not only allied to water but also to fire, as we see when, immediately before the three go on their vacation by the sea, she decides to burn her letters and in doing so sets her robe on fire. It seems to be an ironic foreshadowing that Jim is there to put out the flames, for the film's denouement reverses this gesture, in metaphorical terms, when Catherine drives Jim into the water and finally quenches the flames of desire that have burned in them. Catherine's burning her letters is again a sign that she is another of Truffaut's characters who deny the value of the past; for, as Catherine says of her letters that contain her past, it is merely a matter of lies. But flames also burn those who live in them, and it would appear that Truffaut in this scene sets forth an implicit critique of that ethic of freedom that refuses all limits in the name of intensifying experience.

This critique becomes even more evident when one notes how Catherine's refusal of a fixed identity and her pursuit of freedom resolve themselves into a series of fetishes and rituals by which she constantly seeks to affirm her power of inventiveness and to prove her power over others. One might consider, for example, how Catherine refuses to allow Jim to place his hat on her bed, first when he comes for her baggage before their vacation, and later when he takes possession of the room in the chalet in Germany. A few other examples are Catherine's resolution to use the same bottle of vitriol wherever she may be, the search for rubbish she undertakes with the two men while on vacation, her refusal to speak on the telephone with Jim, or even her notion of "equilibrium" in sexual matters. This kind of constant ritualization and fetishism has no psychological significance in any conventional sense. Rather, these games and prohibitions are so many signs of how Catherine gratuitously converts objects and acts into rites endowed with an arbitrary taboo value. In this third film, then, Truffaut seems to present something of a critique of the absurdist view of identity. The quest for total inventiveness, denying any continuity in time, results only in a disparate series of gestures and disconnected rituals, until finally Catherine has no identity except that of an aging woman who has accumulated a repertoire of roles that are no longer adequate or even amusing.

The gratuitousness of man's presence in the world and the discontinuity of identity that underlie these films' vision give rise in turn to another essential motif. This is the motif of play, for it can be maintained that all of Truffaut's characters are essentially players and that the space of representation here is a ludic or play space. From an absurdist viewpoint, play is a privileged activity precisely because it needs no exterior or transcendent goal to give purposiveness to human action. Play is a self-contained activity that justifies itself by its very nature. As we see in the early films of Chabrol and Godard as well as of Truffaut, absurd man is almost obliged to be a player, for not only does play endow his being with at least a temporary justification, but, in a second and related sense, the disparate identities that he chooses to embody condemn him to be nothing more than a player, or an actor whose identity is nothing more than a series of roles.

In *Les 400 Coups* periods of play alternate regularly with periods of constraint and confinement. Constraint takes place in those enclosed spaces, such as the schoolroom, the dank apartment, the wire cage in prison, or the observation center, that are so many emblems of societal efforts to repress the child's desire. They are also so many emblems of the absurd enclosure that stands in opposition to the child's freedom, to his play instincts, to his sprees. Every time Antoine can escape from one of these places of confinement, he immediately begins to play. By himself, or in the company of his friend René, he uses his spree time as a play time in which going to the cinema, stopping traffic, playing pinball machines, or simply exploring Paris are moments of ludic freedom that allow acts to be gratuitously organized for their own sake, as play. The tension between enclosure and play is present throughout *Les 400 Coups*, though perhaps this tension finds its most revealing expression during the series of shots in which Antoine is in the amusement park rotor. The machine begins to spin and, as the centrifugal force pushes the riders to the wall, the floor falls away, leaving the riders pressed against the ride's inner walls. Here is an image of play in one of its purest states, for, as we see on Antoine's face, the apparent suspension of normal physical laws sets up a new state whose ludic justification is the pure exhilaration it offers. Yet Antoine also struggles against the forces that literally pin him to the wall, and the strain his face expresses shows us that the image is ambiguous. For he is pushed against the wall, forced into an immobility that seems to foreshadow the final freeze image in *Les 400 Coups*. Within play itself, it would seem, are forces that threaten the child, for, as we see here, play can result in a kind of oppressive confinement at the same time it remains an exercise in spontaneity.

What we have called the fall into adulthood marks for Antoine the loss of magical purity that play offers. In *Tirez sur le pianiste* Truffaut next portrays an adult player's failure to play in any authentic fashion. It hardly seems an accident, moreover, that Charlie-Edouard tries to define himself by playing the piano. As Edouard he attempts to use his playing to give himself a public role; as Charlie he uses it as a defense against the world, as a way of isolating and protecting himself. But in both cases it is noteworthy that Truffaut frames all shots of the piano player playing so that the piano is a barrier between the player and the world. Charlie's use of the piano in this respect is fairly obvious, but there is little difference when we see Edouard at the piano. In one shot hemmed in between large columns, the piano gives the impression of creating a kind of cell in which Edouard is locked. The piano player has thus perverted play, and what should be a form of affirmation in an absurd world becomes instead the walls of a prison house in which the self dies. Music—the purely ludic organization of sound—becomes for Edouard a means to an end, to the creation of an inauthentic social self, whereas for Charlie it becomes the means to the opposite end, the creation of a barrier around the self. Play has turned against itself and, perhaps as for Antoine, become a source of confinement.

It is in *Jules et Jim*, however, that Truffaut has developed his most complex testing of the notions of play in a world without constraint that seemingly allows the invention of any game one is audacious enough to contrive. Jules, Jim, and Catherine's attempt to redefine human relations and perhaps invent new values is, in fact, undertaken as a form of play, and the way they invent new relationships must be likened to games for which they invent the rules as they proceed. Before Catherine's arrival in Paris, we see that Jules and Jim are free spirits for whom life consists of nothing except games. The remarkable variety of shots at the film's beginning are so many images of play and play freedom.[6] As the credits are given, for instance, we see a quick series of shots in which Jules and Jim entertain themselves with various games— fighting a mock duel, playing dominos, racing, and so forth—that are a prelude to the games they play after their encounter with Catherine. It is, of course, Catherine who insists on defining the rules of those games. In the first part of the film, this is perhaps most evident when Catherine, after making a series of jokes that do not succeed in disrupting Jules and Jim's chess game, slaps Jules for a casual remark. On one level, she is merely petulant because the two men refuse to pay her any attention. But on another level, she is demonstrating her power to define all relationships, or the rules for the games

6. Compare Graham Petrie, *The Cinema of François Truffaut*, pp. 13–14.

they play. Truffaut stresses this aspect with the series of freeze shots that follow the slap, portraying Catherine's beautiful face in different expressions. Frozen, statuelike, each expression is like a different mask she wears for each play role she commands. Appropriately enough, it is at this moment that Catherine decides their vacation is over, for the ludic time of vacation has obviously run its course when the two men have found other distractions than Catherine's games.

In the second half of the film, Jim's decision to come to Germany to visit Jules and Catherine opens up a new period of play, for Jim comes to see if he, too, should marry or, in other words, give up the bohemian rules of the game that keep him from living with his mistress, Gilberte (though he spends each night with her). Jim finds that he is still magnetically attracted to Catherine. Since Jules, in a gesture of nearly monastic renunciation, has given up all hope of making Catherine happy, the trio tries to find a *modus vivendi* through play, through inventing new rituals that will allow them to come to terms with their desire by playing according to self-given rules. We see this play in all their activities, in the games Jules and his daughter, Sabine, enjoy, in their cavorting in the countryside, or in their cycling with Catherine's sometime lover Albert. After Jim and Catherine consummate their desire, directly under the sign of Goethe's *Elective Affinities*, it seems most fitting that the group invents a new game, "the village idiot," in recognition of the fact that the conventional local villagers consider this household to be full of lunatics. This also points up, however, that they are aware that the illusory harmony they institute is the play harmony of an arbitrarily accepted order, self-sufficient so long as it remains confined to the play space, the isolated Rhine Valley chalet.

When Jim leaves the play space, he is forced to confront choices, to commit himself to acts that have consequences that play acts seemingly do not. More precisely, Jim's flaw is that he can neither commit himself to the given rules for societal games nor accept the games that Catherine proposes. When he returns to Germany, he wants to leave as soon as he has arrived, but Catherine's arrival, after her spending the night with Albert (Albert equals Gilberte, according to her rules), merely starts the game again, with Catherine once more determining the rules.

The stakes of the game this time are a child, for it is apparently only by Catherine's conceiving that a play equilibrium can be established in Jim's favor—for Jules has already shown his capacity for paternity. Yet one also feels that the child would be a symbol of the plenitude that their game playing has not achieved. Jim again vacillates, for he has no heart for the kind of inventiveness Catherine desires, and when he learns in Paris that the child they finally conceived was stillborn, he can only conclude, "It is a noble thing to want to rediscover the laws of humanity; but how convenient it must be to conform to existing rules. We played with the very sources of life, and we failed."[7] Having lost at this game, Jim does take refuge in the safer conventions of the life he leads with Gilberte. Given Truffaut's almost obsessive concern with the family, however, their failure to create a child should be seen as a sign of the sterility of the gamesmanship, the inventiveness, and the desire for total freedom that have characterized their relations.

The rest of the film is then given over to portraying how Catherine's attempts to be an inventive player degenerate into neurotic compulsiveness, and lead, finally, to catastrophe. When, some time later, Jim encounters Jules and Catherine and they go for a drive in the country, her repetition of the adventurer's game (she remains at the inn with Albert, the man who has "played the part" for her so many times before) is a humorous but rather mechanical performance. When she later drives her automobile wildly about the square beneath Jim's window, careening about and honking its horn in the early hours, it seems clear that she is using her auto as a toy to express her freedom, as a toy in a new game to entice Jim, though this is as childish as it is neurotic. Then, in the mill house that spans the river, when Jim confronts Catherine with her failure to "invent love from the beginning," her menacing him with a revolver shows that she is now a desperate player who will stop at nothing to impose the games she desires. The film's denouement, then, is only the film's final confirmation that in her playing Catherine has not triumphed over the absurd, but rather, in Camus's terms, that she has chosen to collaborate with it.

In terms of Truffaut's career, it is important then to see how *Jules et Jim*, in differing in one important respect from *Les 400 Coups* and *Tirez sur le pianiste*, points beyond the New Wave towards his later works, like *L'Enfant Sauvage*, *Les deux Anglaises*, and *L'Histoire d'Adèle H*. The difference is, in the simplest terms, that *Jules et Jim* is a historical film. *Les 400 Coups* and *Tirez sur le pianiste*, like most New Wave works, set forth experiential situations that are contemporary with the aesthetic axioms—and the absurdist configuration—that inform them. They are, moreover, works that are, in an existential sense, to be experienced as a radically present world: open, unor-

7. François Truffaut, *Jules and Jim*, p. 92.

dered, and gratuitous in its lack of determination. In *Jules et Jim*, on the other hand, the film's experiential space is self-consciously given as a world past, and we are thus invited to make use of our knowledge of that past in experiencing the film. It is perhaps a bit ponderous to say that at this time Truffaut, like many other French artists in the late fifties and early sixties, encountered history and that *Jules et Jim* records his encounter. However, it is true that the historical dimension suggests an understanding of art and experience that points beyond the reigning absurdist ideology. To view experience with its historical dimension is to view it, potentially at least, in terms of a rational ordering, and one might well maintain that the sharpness of Truffaut's attitudes towards absurdist notions is heightened by his historical sense in *Jules et Jim*.

This historical dimension is certainly present in the documentary footage Truffaut uses to depict the rupture between the two friends that the war brings about or in the Nazi book-burning that they see in the cinema toward the end of the film. But it is also present in the way the film develops certain historical motifs that are, in fact, analogous to the absurdist motifs that run through the work. In more precise terms, the work begins during the heyday of modernist experimentation and shows how the modernist quest for the transvaluation of values ends, for Jim and Catherine at least, in the absurd plunge into the river. It is thus not at all an accident that Truffaut begins the film in the *belle époque*, during those "banquet years" before World War I, when artists and poets believed, with a naiveté that the war was to dispel, that they were capable of inventing new values and a new civilization. That Jules and Jim are to be viewed as part of the modernist movement is clear in a number of details, such as the way that Truffaut gives to Albert certain traits that recall the poet Apollinaire. Albert, like the poet, recognizes the great artists ten years before anyone else. Moreover, Jim evokes Apollinaire—the "impresario of the avant-garde"—when he describes a soldier who deflowered his fiancée through the mail. Apollinaire's importance in this context is that he was the central figure in the struggle between modernism and traditional values in Paris before World War I, and his struggle to balance invention with an understanding of the past stands in direct analogy with the struggle that Truffaut portrays in the film.

It is with this historical dimension in mind that we can clearly see that in *Jules et Jim* Truffaut sets Goethe against Picasso, an understanding of the limits of human possibilities against a belief in man's capacity to displace the values of the past—or, to return to the historical analogy, against the absurdist notion that man's radical freedom reduces the past to nothingness. But the only real survivor in any of these three films is Jules, and it is perhaps most significant that it should be the only father in the film, the only man to assure continuity, who can walk away from the crematorium. Moreover, he is the German whose renunciation allows him paradoxically to possess, and this renunciation, as Nietzsche said about Goethe, is perhaps to be seen as the only way to triumph over the absurd. The final image of Jules walking through the cemetery is, then, more than an image of dereliction and isolation; it is Truffaut's way of presenting an image of the death of modernist hubris.

Postmodernism

L'Année dernière à Marienbad:
The Narration of Narration

Resnais and Robbe-Grillet's *L'Année dernière à Marienbad* is perhaps the most interesting filmic example of how the creative displacement of artistic limits can go suddenly beyond critical theory and bring about an enigmatic opening in our experience of art. We can speak of an opening, since such a work compels the viewer to enter into an open experience that no critical awareness can immediately close off. Our categories for the perception of experience seem to be suspended, and yet, since we cannot deny the fascination of this work, it is imperative that we find new theoretical bases that account for the way this film entices our vision. This film is a seduction, then, not only of the unknown woman whom the narrator pursues throughout the film, but also of our vision. Like every seduction, the film draws us into an unknown realm where unfamiliarity is a source of both fear and pleasure, of both exhilaration and insecurity. The immediate effect is to bring about a desire for total possession, a need to grasp fully the film's paradoxical surfaces, to transform its strangeness into familiarity.

Perhaps the best starting point for a theoretical possession of *L'Année dernière à Marienbad* is to situate it immediately within the context of the postmodern artist's quest to redefine the relationships between art and perception, between the work and the work's understanding of itself, between mimesis and the limits of representation. By postmodern we mean those artists whose works, both novels and films, have since the late fifties broken with the modernist canons of representation. Writers as diverse as Beckett, Borges, and Pynchon, filmmakers as diverse as Godard, Robbe-Grillet, and Bergman, all seem united in a common refusal of the modernist belief in art as a form of revelation. They refuse to accept the possibility of mimesis as an unquestioned and unquestionable given; indeed, they seek to redefine the way in which the work can enter into relations with any form of referential reality or with itself.

166

Yet most critical commentary on *L'Année dernière à Marienbad* has attempted to understand the film within the canons of modernist theory. And it is more than a little interesting to note that Resnais and Robbe-Grillet, especially in their earliest comments on the work, were particularly guilty in this respect. Their comments, in fact, established the categories that most subsequent critics have repeated with little variation. By declaring *L'Année dernière* to be an extreme experiment in "subjective" cinema, they made of their work an essentially modernist attempt to find the means for directly representing some form of psychic reality. In effect, they suggested that the film was another variation on such modernist techniques as stream of consciousness or manipulation of narrative points of view. Seen in this light, *L'Année dernière* is a modernist attempt to find filmic epiphany, or the revelation of privileged psychic moments. By placing the emphasis on the film's revelation of immanent experience, rather than on the film's formal structures, the filmmakers as well as a good many later critics were able to take seriously the rather bizarre idea that the film takes place in someone's head.

This point is worth pursuing, for the desire to delimit the locus of mimesis by some privileged space is most characteristic of modernism—and of much of the early criticism to which Robbe-Grillet's work gave rise. In fact, it now appears that it was only because of such critical pressure that Robbe-Grillet theorized about his film in terms of "mental realism" or other modernist categories of "realism." But it is obvious that these categories belong to the theory of literary modernism, and, I believe, they can do little to account for the way we actually experience *L'Année dernière à Marienbad*.

Our first experience of the film is, in fact, a questioning born of our desire to find the locus of mimesis and to delimit the representational space. The film opens a region of experience and, in one sense, forces us to ask what images are about. Our first answer must be that the status of these images is ambiguous, for they blatantly refuse to obey the laws of verisimilitude and causal relation that we often take to be inherent in the nature of narration itself. This does not mean that they are irrational or that they can only be explained in terms of the kind of subjectivity represented in literature by an interior monologue.

In fact, it seems dubious that images can represent any kind of subjectivity by direct mimesis, for images never take place inside anyone's head. The images we see either occur in the world or, in the case of so-called mental images, occur nonspatially. Thus mental images cannot be *in* anything. In fact, one might be tempted to turn the relationship about and say that it is the perception of images that allows us to localize our heads. In any case, critics who resort to the metaphysics of inner and outer, of subjective and objective, to describe what images purport to represent have allowed outmoded philosophical categories to obscure the way in which images create the world they represent. *L'Année dernière à Marienbad* forces us to ask why we wish to speak in metaphysical terms about images or, equally important, why we wish to think of them in terms of literary categories such as *point of view*. It is by demonstrating the failure of such categories that the film opens up new possibilities for the experiencing of films.

Categories such as *subjectivity* and *point of view* have such surface plausibility that it is difficult not to wish to apply them. Thus Bruce Morrissette, one of the best-known critics of Robbe-Grillet's work, can unhesitatingly explain his films in the same terms that he uses to describe Robbe-Grillet's novels:

> It is well known that the theory and practice of *point of view*, in novels as in cinema, are closely tied to the metaphysics of each novelist or scriptwriter. Thus Robbe-Grillet chose at the beginning of his literary career to place himself on the side of Sartre and existentialist metaphysics and declared that every novelistic image must exist or come forth by being grounded in a narrating consciousness.[1]

Morrissette's point-of-view analogy annexes film to literary technique without questioning how this can be so. How can a film be grounded in a narrating consciousness when there is nothing in the structure of a projected image that allows it to be assigned to a consciousness? Language, to be sure, in the very process of enunciation, always presupposes a voice that offers the utterance and thus springs from what one can call a narrating (or narrative) consciousness, even if it is mediated by a third-person pronoun. But it is very difficult to see how the process of enunciation can be applied to the projection of images that, by their projection, create their autonomous world.

It is true, of course, that from its beginnings film has tried to grant itself the status of a literary work by using various conventions that designate the film as a transcription of a verbal narration. To take popular examples, one need think of the shot of the book and the narrating voice-over that open *Red River* or, more recently, the presence of the tape recorder at the beginning of

1. Bruce Morrissette, *Les Romans de Robbe-Grillet*, p. 226. (All translations are mine, unless otherwise indicated.)

Little Big Man. These naive conventions usually add little to the film and, in any case, in no way endow the film with a narrative point of view. More interesting of course are more complex films, such as *Citizen Kane* and *Rashomon*. In these works, too, it seems apparent that there is no existential bond between a narrator and the various narratives each film sets forth. Rather, the presence of a narrator serves only to designate each narrative as different from or complementary to the other narratives in the film. The narrator in the film thus serves an epistemological function, for his presence indicates that each individual narrative is a part of the quest for knowledge or truth that the total film undertakes. In *Citizen Kane* it is especially evident that the filmic world overflows, perhaps inevitably, what a narrator could really narrate from a limited point of view. Each narrative goes well beyond a single memory, not only in terms of remembered detail, but in terms of the very being of the image, its ontological fullness, its presence. Moreover, it is obvious that in this film the various narratives that make up the quest fit neatly together to form a linear chronology that purports, in the modernist sense of recapturing the past, to reveal the essence of a life.

Narration as a form of epistemological quest is central to our understanding of *L'Année dernière à Marienbad*, for it seems clear that the only narrative point of view present in the film is the one offered by the narrating voice, a first-person narrative that must be considered in juxtaposition to the world of images. However, we must first take into account one other approach to the film that has found a great deal of acceptance, the approach that takes *L'Année dernière* to be a dream. It does seem true that film can imitate dream images or, more precisely, that filmmakers have developed a series of conventions that allow us to accept certain kinds of images as a representation of dream. We are not disturbed when the autonomous world of the film is replaced by an oneiric world that, for purposes of narrative coherence, we then usually attribute to one of the characters within the film. *Wild Strawberries* and *8 1/2* come readily to mind in this respect, though both Bergman and Fellini have demonstrated in other works that they need not have recourse to dream conventions in order to use irrational images—irrational in terms of the canons of verisimilitude—for narrative purposes. Dream conventions often seem, in fact, a way by which a filmmaker integrates irrational ruptures into his narrative, for few directors are interested in the mimesis of dream for its own sake.

L'Année dernière à Marienbad is characterized by precisely the kind of ruptures that seem to designate the filmic world as a representation of dream. Yet dream convention usually demands that there be a filmic world against which the irrational images stand out as "dream," and this film world is not present in *L'Année dernière à Marienbad*. There are in effect no indices to designate one image as a "real" image and another, in contrast, as an oneiric image that must be attributed to one of the characters. The conventions *objective and subjective, inner and outer, substantial and oneiric*, are simply not present, and the film forces us to situate its images in some other space than that demanded by the modernist aesthetics of representation. *L'Année dernière à Marienbad* is, in fact, one of the seminal works for a definition of postmodern art, and only by turning away from such categories as *mental realism* and *degrees of reality* can we begin to understand the film.

If one of the postmodern tasks is to find a means by which to designate the work's functioning as a fiction, to force the reader or viewer to evaluate critically the mimetic constructs that seek to represent "reality," then it would appear that a work that lays bare its own genesis as a fiction best fulfills that critical task. The postmodern artist thus often strives to go beyond the ironic self-consciousness of the modernist to create a work of metanarration that can account for its own unfolding. Self-reference becomes a means by which the work designates its awareness of itself as a fiction. It is in this sense that we can call *L'Année dernière à Marienbad* a metanarrative that proposes a series of narrative hypotheses that finally coalesce into a past, a history, a plausible story. It is an exploration of the labyrinth, to use a favored postmodern metaphor, that designates both the quest for fiction and the fiction itself. And the representational space is the space of the labyrinth of the film itself, the space of the narration.

As the metaphor of the labyrinth points out, subject matter and motifs are metaphorical doubles for the metanarration itself. The quest for narration is thus an attempt to narrate a seduction at the same time it is a seduction—both of the woman who hears the tale and of the viewer who seeks to construct the fictional past out of the elements the film offers. The metaphorical equation of seduction-narration is another aspect of self-reference by which the narrative project designates its own functioning and telos. "X," the stranger who is the narrator-seducer, is then, in one sense, a surrogate artist who must seduce both viewer and woman through the creation of a story, through the elaboration of a preterit narrative that represents the creation of a "past of marble" that can authenticate the seduction.

In *L'Année dernière à Marienbad* Resnais and Robbe-Grillet have, in effect, "deconstructed" the myth of passion. One might well compare the film to the myth of Tristan and Isolde to see how the film uses the archetypical elements of myth to construct the metanarration. In his later works Robbe-Grillet prefers to call upon the popular myths of sex, drugs, secret agents, and the like for his narrative deconstructions. In his first film, however, he seems to have chosen the most perdurable of European myths as a basis for the film's motifs. *L'Année dernière*'s metanarration might be likened to the situation in which Tristan must convince Isolde of the reality of their passion by telling her its story, its legend, so as to create a past that can validate his present desire. In the film as in the myth, the passion depends upon a third party for its forbidden existence. The woman's companion, "M"—possibly a *mari*, possibly a *Marc*—thus fills the role of the interdictor against whom the narrative is directed. The goal of narration is thus given as a subversion of the order we find in the narration itself and, by analogy, in the hotel's rigid order as well. Our Tristan's task as metanarrator is to lead the object of his passion through the labyrinthine meanderings of his quest, through the halls and gardens, to an acceptance of the new order that he proposes in his narrative. His passion informs his narrative, for ultimately we see that the genesis of fiction is in the service of desire, just as desire or possession is another metaphor for the fiction itself.

The film's final seduction is to draw the viewer into the labyrinth so that he, too, participates in a narration that by laying bare its own genesis, its own functioning, reveals the dangers attendant upon the metaphorical seduction. In this respect Robbe-Grillet's own critical commentary can be useful, for he has always been aware of how the formal possibilities of constructing a representation have conditioned his novelistic or filmic vision. In the creation of *L'Année dernière à Marienbad*, the idea of negotiating a labyrinth seems to have been in his mind from the very inception of the film:

> I began with this idea: a form of itinerary that could be just as well a form of writing [*écriture*], a labyrinth, which is to say, a path that always appears to be guided by strict walls, but which nonetheless leads at each moment to impasses that then force one to go back several times over the same places, over greater or lesser distances, to explore a new direction, and to come again upon new impossibilities.[2]

One might well ask why the labyrinth has become a privileged metaphor for

2. Quoted in Gaston Bounoure, *Alain Resnais* (Paris: Seghers, 1962), pp. 79–80.

designating the postmodernist creation. It would appear that this metaphor can show the equivalence between the creator's quest and his creation as well as between the act of appropriating the creation and the act of understanding it. The work as a labyrinth is a circle that depends only on its own structures for its coherence; the reader or viewer is detached from all outside frames of reference and must explore the labyrinth in terms of its own presuppositions. And if the labyrinth's paths ultimately go nowhere, perhaps the labyrinth is a metaphor that denounces a naive acceptance of mimesis and warns that one enters only at one's own risk.

The film thus portrays the struggle that the narrating voice undertakes as it contends with the manifold hypotheses and possibilities its narration evokes. This struggle is mirrored in the relationship between the voice—the work—and the images. The images sometimes duplicate the narrative that the voice proposes as though they were offering a confirmation in an experiential world of the narrative hypothesis. At other times they serve as a framework that offers the narrating voice a concrete locus from which to speak. But they can also contradict the narrating voice and reject the narrative order that the voice would impose. The autonomous world of filmic space provides the arena in which the narrative voice must confront its desires as it seeks to negotiate the labyrinth.

The film's opening tracking-shot, accompanied by the sonorous voice repeating that once again the narrator is advancing through these halls, brings the viewer into the metaphorical labyrinth at the same time it sets forth the struggle in which the narrative voice will attempt to master the image. The plastic tensions and irrational patterns of the baroque decor are another analogy for an experiential world that the narrator must order. This order would seem to find an analogical presence in the various images presenting the formal, French gardens whose Cartesian rationality stands in opposition to the baroque profusion. The quest for narration might then be seen as the effort to suppress this labyrinthine exuberance and to create the seemingly ordered space of rational representation. Yet as the film's end, set in the geometric gardens, seems to show, such a rational order is also a maze. Indeed, the end is given in the beginning when we see the play within a play, or the theatrical performance, that sets forth the film's denouement. The play within a play here takes place in a Cartesian decor that points to the circularity of the representational order. The end is given in the beginning, so that every beginning is already a form of conclusion. Cartesian order turns in upon itself as another labyrinth that offers only an illusory openness onto some other referential realm.

The opening sequence is especially important, too, for establishing how every element in the film stands in analogical relation to every other element in this self-contained quest. In structuralist terms, the work self-consciously proclaims that all relations derive their meaning only from each other, for every element mirrors every other, as we see in the mirrors that line the walls and in which we often see the film's characters reflected. In this respect one is struck by the way the hotel's inhabitants are first presented in rigid poses, recalling the statues in the film that in turn double the characters themselves. One might also consider again the pictures that present the French gardens; they seem to point to an order beyond this baroque palace but in effect are but another image of the maze that designates the filmic world.

In the first part of the film, the various posed groups and couples also offer various bits of anecdotes that are doubles for the metanarration itself. One couple speaks of freedom; another group speaks of last year's weather; others speak of a certain "Frank" who the year before had apparently entered a woman's room and attempted to seduce her. All of these doubling fragments stand in analogical relation to the narrative quest, though the references to a certain "Frank" seem to allude to narration in an even larger sense. Through the paronomasia *Frank-Franz*, Robbe-Grillet appears here to be invoking, as he does more explicitly in his later film *L'Homme qui ment*, the patron saint of all postmodernists, Franz Kafka. (The inventor of the Castle, it should be noted, once vacationed in Marienbad with his fiancée.) Here we may again see another mirror image that refers to the narrative quest. In *The Castle*, Kafka's "K." loses himself in a proliferating textuality that never allows him to reach the Castle or the narrative to reach an end. Robbe-Grillet's Frank, a double for his own narrator, may have reached the castle, but narrative proliferation continues, and there appears to be no narrative finality that can vouchsafe the past, that can guarantee there was an entrance into the woman's room, that there *was* a last year at Marienbad.

Robbe-Grillet's narrator must therefore negotiate the various hypotheses that the narration generates much as K. must deal with the texts, suppositions, and hypotheses that emanate from the Castle's bureaucratic order, an order that is as problematic in its existence as is Marienbad's past. Let us consider in this respect how certain sequences function. Take, for example, the shooting gallery in which the men fire their pistols with such accuracy. These images are unaccompanied either by spoken text or by dialogue and thus seem to emerge as an unconnected possibility that bears little relation to the various hypotheses about "last year." On reflection, however, it is apparent that these images of men shooting methodically at targets show the controlled violence that underlies the order of this rigid world. Moreover, these images clearly foreshadow one of the major narrative hypotheses: that the passion the narrator feels for the woman could result in her death or in his. The eros that informs the narrative quest could bring about destruction. These images are thus related thematically to a hypothesis that could, if realized, destroy the entire search for a past and the authentication of desire.

These images of violence are related in turn to the various hypotheses concerning the woman's chamber—the locus of desire—and the kind of reception the narrator might have received there. The narrator first introduces the image of the woman's chamber by telling her that he came there one night. We then see the chamber in a series of flash frames that many spectators might take to be a flashback (as Resnais probably did) or perhaps as a flash forward, since this is the way these kinds of ruptures are usually coded. But, as later images of the room show, there is no single fixed image of the chamber, nor is there a fixed "past" chamber about which one of the characters might be thinking. Rather, there are the multiple rooms, with their varying decors, that offer themselves as hypothetical possibilities in the narrative construction of the past. The various chambers illustrate how difficult it is for the narrator to control the multiple experiential possibilities that besiege him, for each one forces him to modify his approach, to weigh other possibilities, and to struggle to maintain the inner coherence that will create the verisimilitude necessary for persuasion.

The first room, for example, is rather plain. In it we see a pile of shoes and a glass. These objects find their doubles in other parts of the narrative space and ambiguously relate the room to other aspects of the experiential world that the images propose. A second chamber contains no shoes, though it does contain a glass, while a third presents a more baroque decor in which a mirror reveals the woman's image as a kind of double to the other mirror images. Another chamber presents a painting, another image of the iconic double that recurs throughout the film, while the woman in these shots holds herself against the baroque mirrors that line the wall. This room in particular shows how the proliferation of possibilities risks destroying the narrative project. The narrator here insists that the room's door was closed and that the woman returned to the bed. The image shows quite clearly that the woman stays by the mirror and that the door is open. The room baffles the narrator, and his story seems unable to account for these plausible developments. And so the narrator breaks down, saying that he cannot remember any more. The room is thus the locus upon which the narrative quest is centered, for it is here that the full range of hypotheses are developed, ranging from rejection to death to joyous acceptance.

The various contradictory hypotheses represent what we might call the comedy of narration or, from another point of view, narration as a ludic function. The woman's multiple poses when she is dead, for example, seem to be a farcical aggression against the need for a single, coherent order. One readily thinks of Beckett in this respect, for these various hypotheses call to mind the epistemological games that Beckett's narrators play in *Watt* and *Molloy*. For Beckett's narrators the rules of the narrative game are given by the now-impossible metaphysics that once guaranteed knowledge, and narration now becomes a series of epistemological impasses in which one wonders if one can even know that one knows nothing can be told. Though Robbe-Grillet uses this same kind of speculation in his novel *Le Labyrinthe*, it would seem that *L'Année dernière à Marienbad* may well be the first film to have integrated into its structure this postmodern refusal of the certainty that traditional narration has been founded on. The systematic undermining of the various hypotheses that could make up a narration reflects the postmodern suspiciousness of fictions. Yet this destruction of narrative certainty goes beyond mere skepticism. It would seem that in the case of Robbe-Grillet it aims perhaps at the creation of an uncertainty principle that might become a new way of defining and representing experience.

In any case, the central figure in this constellation of uncertainties is the stone couple, the statue that stands in an analogical relation with the film's couple. The analogy is immediately established when the narrator invokes the statue for the woman as a form of evidence that might verify their common past:

> Remember: quite near us there was a group of stone figures on a rather high base, a man and a woman in classical dress, whose frozen gestures seemed to represent some specific scene. You asked me who these characters were, I answered that I didn't know. You made several suppositions, and I said that it could just as well be you and I.[3]

3. Alain Robbe-Grillet, *Last Year at Marienbad*, trans. Richard Howard, pp. 51–52.

As is the case with the very presence of the couple in the vacation palace, the camera offers images of the statue as a present *hic et nunc* that can support innumerable suppositions that might explain its existence. Every hypothesis is the beginning of a new narration about the past that can culminate in the present moment, for present identity—be it that of Pyrrhus and Andromache, Helen and Agamemnon, or of two strangers that a dog happens to meet— demands the creation of the narration whose causal chain will guarantee the existence of a substantial self through time. The need for an identity is, then, a generator of fictions, or at least of narratives, and in this respect the stone couple stands in a metaphorical relationship not only with the living couple, but with the entire narrative quest.

The relationship is perhaps made clearest in visual terms through one of the important changes that Resnais made in the script. By adding the suggestion that the couple had stopped before the sea, he was then able to add a tracking shot up and over the statue. The shot isolates a portion of a pond in such a way that the statue does seem to be standing before a vast expanse of water that could fill the entire visual field. The camera thus converts the narrative hypothesis into a visual reality that we know in a conventional sense to be false, for it is merely the change in perspective that has created the "sea." Yet in terms of pure perception the image has validated the hypothesis, and thus the narrative possibility is upheld as one that could apply to the statue. The autonomy of the image is of course responsible for the seeming truth of the shot, but by revealing how the image can change narration merely by the change in perspective, the camera undermines its own credibility in the game of narrative hypotheses. It can seemingly substantiate any supposition the narrator offers.

The alternative to this trickery seems to be given when the woman's companion appears and offers an explanation of the statue, an image of which the couple is contemplating in an engraving:

> Excuse me, sir. I think I can supply you with some more precise information: this statue represents Charles III and his wife, but it does not date from that period, of course. The scene is that of the oath before the Diet, at the moment of the trial for treason. The classical costumes are purely conventional.[4]

The introduction of a "historical" past, one based on dates and a publicly accepted chronology, is comic in its precision and yet as baffling in its disper-

4. Ibid., p. 69.

sion in time as any other form of explanation. Temporal layers overlap in a proliferation of dates and periods, and the statue's identity seems to dissolve into a series of pasts that can scarcely provide the unique series of events that will offer a necessary narrative order.

This is a film about last year, however, and in some sense one should be able to speak of the past. Robbe-Grillet has claimed, among other things, that the film takes place in the present and that it lasts exactly the time that it takes to see it.[5] In other words, there is no symbolic representation of time. We might say, then, that the film's time is the duration of the metanarration. The drama of narration lasts only as long as the narrator is undertaking the narrative quest. It takes place in a virtual present that is generated every time the film is projected.

In a sense, however, every narrative is a present act that aims, in phenomenological terms, at a past it seeks to reconstruct. One might even say that the past exists only as a present project that attempts to seize it. With this understanding in mind, one can turn then to the conclusion of *L'Année dernière à Marienbad*, where we find that the narration ends in the past tense, which seems to endow the entire film with a preterit dimension. It would seem that when the metanarration reaches its goal, one has effectively created or seized a past that exists in function of the present narrative project. In a sense, the metanarration is then sublimated into a "pastness" that is the aim of its quest. Once the woman-viewer has been seduced and led into the labyrinth of narration, then we can say that the story *was* as it *is* told. As Robbe-Grillet suggested, one is at Marienbad throughout the film, at the only Marienbad that can exist, which, however, is the one sought in the present by the narrative consciousness as it undertakes the quest to order a past.

From the moment the narrative voice shifts to the past tense, we know, as does the woman's companion, M, that she has accepted the seduction and that the stranger has created the past into which she will enter. All the elements of the myth of passion fall into place to create the mythic past that validates passion. The myth of passion and narration are one and the same in their metaphorical identity, for it is the narration that has created the legendary past, just as it is passion that has informed the narrative quest. And just as the other side of passion, according to the myth, is death, so the acceptance of a fixed past is entrance into the maze that can lead only to death. To fix a past, to order it as a finality, is to offer a death, since it is only as death that a past can be

5. Ibid., p. 13.

finally given. As Lucien Goldmann has pointed out, the film's final images are those of a cemetery.[6]

When we turn from a consideration of the film's motifs and their metaphorical relations, we may feel inclined to ask why Robbe-Grillet and Resnais should have taken so much effort to construct a convoluted work that ultimately designates only itself and its self-representing function. One might even claim that such a work should be branded a form of intellectual narcissism. Such a view would not be entirely beside the point, for any work that points out how it works to seduce the spectator, or the spectator's metaphorical surrogate, is a work that reveals itself as an erotic project. In the case of such a circular work, of a film that aims at itself in its narrative project, narcissism would be another term for the erotic circularity that animates the work. Yet this self-conscious narcissism is also another sign that the critical intelligence at work in a film like *L'Année dernière à Marienbad* is attempting to lay bare the mechanisms that realistic works seek to hide so that they do not destroy the illusion of representation. By revealing its narcissism *L'Année dernière* denounces in effect the seductions of mimetic conventions that hide their persuasion behind a metaphysics of substantial reality. By proclaiming its tentative hypotheses to be only forms of seduction, by revealing its codes, the construction of its myth, and its narcissistic gratuity, *L'Année dernière à Marienbad* forces us to evaluate all our responses to the guiles of mimesis.

In more positive theoretical terms, *L'Année dernière* points to Robbe-Grillet's more recent thought concerning the function of art. We have already said that the film springs from a series of epistemological games, and it is in fact this ludic aspect of art that has come increasingly to dominate Robbe-Grillet's theoretical views on his work, as it has dominated postmodern works in general. In retrospect, it seems clear that *L'Année dernière à Marienbad* is quite close to such works by Robbe-Grillet as *Projet pour une Revolution à New York* or *Eden et après*. All spring from a view of art as a closed game space in which certain combinative rules allow the genesis of fictions. The ludic functioning of art, as Robbe-Grillet now sees it, is another aspect of the postmodern rejection of various bourgeois forms of mimesis. He has, in fact, become quite explicit about how the "ideology of play" aims at the creation of new modes of representation that will liberate us from the repressive modes that characterize realistic art and what he sees as its concomitant bourgeois ideology:

6. Lucien Goldmann, *Pour une sociologie du roman*, p. 323.

Often I have thought that the disappearance of the old myths of depth [*profondeur*] has created a determining vacuum [*vide*]. What people call seriousness, that is, that which is underwritten by such values as work, honor, discipline, and so forth, belongs in reality to a vast code, one well situated and dated, outside of which the idea of profundity has no meaning. Seriousness supposes that there is something behind our gestures: a soul, a god, values, bourgeois order . . . whereas behind play there is nothing.[7]

Declaring that it is play that defines the field of our liberty in such a world, Robbe-Grillet goes on to say, "In short, play [*le jeu*] is for us the only possible way of intervening in a world that is henceforth deprived of all profundity."[8]

Already in *L'Année dernière à Marienbad* we find in the film's central ludic image a metaphor that is a double of the metanarration. The enigmatic game of pim, at which the stranger loses several times to M, sets forth an analogy with the narrative game of hypotheses. The stranger must defeat M in order to win the woman, and each failure at the game seems to be a metaphor for the narration's failure to carry out the persuasion. Moreover, the game stands as an analogy for the narrative quest in that the viewer can no more decipher the rules of the game than he can fix a past for the couple. The game's enigma designates the narrative's uncertainty, as narrative and game coincide in their drawing the viewer into a ludic space where the rules of the game must be worked out in the course of play itself.

The game's enigma also seems to designate the enigmatic opening in our experience of art that *L'Année dernière à Marienbad* has brought about. Robbe-Grillet's ideology of play may well be the basis for new modes of artistic experience. Certainly his and Resnais's work in film is among the most important postmodern work in this respect. By designating the conventions of realistic mimesis as myth—conventions such as causal necessity, depth or substantiality of character, psychological continuity, and so forth—and by using these conventions as he sees fit in his various combinative games, Robbe-Grillet in particular has displaced the perimeters of the space of mimesis. Perhaps most interestingly, he has also forced us to see that it is not only the subject and conventions of narration that are mythic, but also the narration itself. The myth of narration, which in France has become the dominant postmodern myth today, stands as one limit to the expansion of mimetic space, for the myth stands there as the self-conscious limit of every narrative project.

7. Quoted in *Nouveau Roman: hier, aujourd'hui*, 1:127–28.
8. Ibid.

Postmodern Dilemmas:
Godard's *Alphaville* and
Deux ou trois choses que je sais d'elle

Jean-Luc Godard is perhaps the most representative of postmodern filmmakers, at least so far as his works reflect the anguish and contradictions of an artist who, motivated by the highest ethical seriousness, has attempted to go beyond the impasse of his own beliefs. On the one hand, Godard has found himself forced to accept the postmodern canon that we might define as the view that mimesis can be no more than a representation of itself, a laying bare of its own genesis, or a critique of those conventions that would claim to represent some substantial reality transcending the act of representation itself. Every act of representation must designate itself as such or lay itself open to the charge that it is merely a naive construct having no consciousness of the way in which it creates the reality that it offers as a mere duplicata. Any work that purports to represent a transcendental reality ignores the fact that reality exists only as perceived in the act of representation.

On the other hand, Godard has struggled constantly to go beyond the solipsism that such a canon implies, for he believes that one of the hopes for man's survival lies in the discovery of new mimetic modes to adequately represent the social reality that Godard sees destroying us with increasing rapidity. The filmmaker must therefore search for new documentary modes that, lying beyond the antinomy *fiction–reality*, will allow the unmediated seizure of social reality and, with this new consciousness, political action. Godard's decision at the end of the sixties to embrace Marxism-Leninism, after he had become probably the most influential avant-garde filmmaker in the world, was thus a decision to repudiate the entire body of work he had created before that time. It seems clear, however, that his conversion to Marxism was motivated by the same ethical concerns that underlie much of his earlier work. Godard no doubt hoped that Marxism would enable him finally to come to an adequate form of praxis by offering an adequate means of accounting for the discrete and absurd phenomena that his camera had been recording from *A bout de souffle* (1959) through *Weekend* (1967). Marxism would offer a grasp of the totality that stands in such direct contrast to the discontinuous fragments that Godard had been able to film, for, in Godard's eyes, his work of the sixties could only be viewed as a series of failures. Yet, as each successive, self-consciously Marxist film has subsequently shown, Godard's attempt to use a Marxist conceptual framework has not enabled him to overcome his—and our—postmodern predicament.

Godard's instinctive reaction to this predicament has been to use ironic, or what we can call pop, modes of representation to compensate for what appears to be the impossibility of an unmediated seizure of reality. Pop art springs from a recognition that all forms of representation are ideological and mythological constructs. Having lost its belief in any form of "realistic" mimesis, pop sensibility then self-consciously creates works that are essentially ironic works about other works, ironic representations of representations, or mythic formulations of myths. This is most noticeably the case with Godard. At the same time his works attempt to represent the daily bric-a-brac and destructive trivia that make up our urban civilization, they are also films about other films. Humphrey Bogart and automobiles, Buster Keaton and brassieres, pop and documentary, these are the inextricably interrelated poles of Godard's imagination.

For this reason it seems to us that a study of two of his pre-Marxist-Leninist works that offer these two modes in a fairly pure state can contribute a good deal to an understanding of Godard and of the postmodern search for new mimetic forms. *Alphaville* and *Deux ou trois choses que je sais d'elle* are both films that deal explicitly with urban reality, *Alphaville* through "pop" modes, *Deux ou trois choses* through documentary. Moreover, both films deal explicitly with the rapport between image and language, the problem that throughout the sixties became increasingly central to Godard's work. In *La Chinoise* (1967) this problem is stated as one of confronting "clear images" with "vague ideas," an approach that seems to show that Godard believed in the possibility that the image might offer a direct appropriation of social reality if only there were an adequate linguistic means of making the images "talk." Having embraced Marxism, having found clear ideas and coherent language, Godard could reformulate the problem in *Pravda* (1969) as one of confronting clear concepts and confused images. One may well doubt that Godard can continue to accept this solution, for his images in *Pravda* suggest that the contradictions may well lie in the conceptual realm: his images show quite clearly that socialist workers can drink Pepsi-Cola and manufacture artillery shells for the North Vietnamese at the same time. In any case, the relationship of image and language is central to Godard's attempt to find new modes of representation, and this is quite clear as early as *Alphaville* (1964).

Marxism offers a language that is entirely adequate, in its own terms, for the representation of social reality. *Alphaville* and *Deux ou trois choses* both show how Marxism came as a logical solution to the crisis Godard had been living throughout the sixties, for both films present the city—Paris—as the crucible in which language is ground up, altered, emptied of meaning, and, finally, placed in the service of totalitarian repression. *Alphaville* presents Paris in a totalitarian future that is really a pop vision of the present, whereas *Deux ou trois choses* is an attempt to offer a documentary view of the present that contains within its ongoing mutations a nightmarish vision of the future. In either case there is a nearly obsessive ethical concern with language, for Godard believes that man's freedom is coextensive with his language's capacity for representation. According to the mother who replies to her child's question in *Deux ou trois choses*, language is the house man lives in. As a language, Marxism has, in a sense, come to replace Godard's ambivalent nostalgia for American cinema, so apparent in his portrayal of Fritz Lang in *Le Mépris* (1963). Lang is both the Olympian figure for whom classical European culture was an adequate means of accounting for human experience and the very embodiment of that era of American cinema when, in naive terms, there was total harmony between cinematic language and the experience it sought to represent. Godard's dedicating *A bout de souffle* (1959) to Monogram Pictures is thus both a form of nostalgia for a bygone language and a pop form of filmic self-reference.

Alphaville is Godard's most consistently pop film in this respect, and it does a great disservice to the film to try to interpret it as a vulgarization of Orwell or Huxley. *Alphaville* stands in much the same relation to American cinema as Lichtenstein's works stand in relation to comic strips, though the film has thematic elements that considerably enrich the purely pop dimension. For example, Alphaville, today's Paris and the intergalactic imperialist of the twenty-first century, is the city where language is reduced to functional constructs that the city's computer mastermind can deal with as it manipulates the city's inhabitants in the name of "logic." Godard's computer, Alpha 60, is

an image taken straight from popular mythology, in which science and the possibility for totalitarian thought control are closely linked. Cybernetics can only be the workings of the evil deity in the Manichean universe of popular mythology. At the same time, the computer's "Bible," a dictionary from which useless words are regularly pruned in order to reduce the range within which men can feel and think, reflects the anguish Godard feels before the increasing inadequacy of language to cope with technological society. In *Alphaville* we find that the limits of experience have come to be defined by comic-strip language.

The comic-strip side of *Alphaville* could be taken for a Brechtian form of "distanciation," for it is evident from the film's beginning that ironic distance must be maintained throughout the film. Otherwise, what is one to make of a film in which Lemmy Caution, the French Micky Spillane, drives into Alphaville in a Ford "Galaxy" (though it appears to be a Lelouch Mustang) that has just traversed intergalactic space? This city of the future is clearly contemporary Paris, though Raoul Coutard's camera offers us a night shot of the elevated metro that effectively transforms the present into a fantastic future worthy of a secret agent on a mission. After checking into a hotel, where this hard-boiled private eye passes himself off as a reporter for *"Figaro-Pravda,"* Lemmy is led by a brainwashed Seductress to his room. Pop references abound as Lemmy shows that he is worthy of his legend. He shoots an intruder after beating him up, pays homage to Humphrey Bogart by reading *The Big Sleep* while doing target practice on a *Playboy* foldout, and, *de rigueur*, drinks whisky. Science, comics, and film provide us with other pop references as we learn that Lemmy is on a mission to inquire into the activities of a Professor von Braun, known as Leonard Nosferatu before he was banished by the Outerlands and began his work in Alphaville. Moreover, it appears that Lemmy was preceded on this mission by Dick Tracy and Guy Leclair, the French Flash Gordon, both of whom may have perished in the ghetto of Alphaville reserved for deviates. It is evident that we are in a world of purely ironic pop mythology where Lemmy Caution, pop hero equipped with only his .45 as a weapon against malevolent fate, is pitted against the absolute evil that pure logic and intelligence, endowed with no human qualities, generates with gratuitous malice.

At this point we might well ask ourselves in more specific terms what is the importance of pop conventions as they are used as a postmodern mode of representation. Godard's work is undoubtedly permeated by a certain admiration for the naive harmony that exists between certain popular modes of representation and the world they mythically present. Godard is quite serious when he expresses his esteem for John Wayne. At the same time, Godard is in revolt against the destruction that popular myths work on language and image. No filmmaker shows greater anguish when confronting the popular mythologies and those forms of popular discourse that manipulate us and undermine our capacity for perception. The discourse of comics, magazines, popular films, and advertising images, a discourse of simple violence, sexual exploitation, and created desires, is, for Godard, the discourse of a totalitarian world in the original sense of the word. It is a totalizing discourse that excludes all others as, in its total coherence, it places all language in the service of an economic system that functions with no other end than its own perpetuation.

Godard's revolt thus raises the following question: when confronted by a totalizing discourse and the myths it produces, how can one find a language that this discourse cannot appropriate and subvert? It is now only too obvious that the antidiscourse of the counterculture could be quickly integrated into Madison Avenue's advertising myths—as Godard seems to show in the sequence in *Weekend* (1967) in which his hippie guerrillas depend literally for their sustenance on bourgeois tourists. One strategy of revolt is to destroy this totalizing discourse by forcing it to designate itself as myth, or, as Roland Barthes has demonstrated in *Mythologies*, to transform popular myths into self-designating myths. We can begin to understand the functioning of pop art and its irony when we see that the destruction of popular myth can be brought about by mythologizing these myths in their turn:

> It thus appears that it is extremely difficult to vanquish myth from the inside: for the very effort one makes in order to escape from its stranglehold becomes in its turn the prey of myth: myth can always, as a last resort, signify the resistance which is brought to bear against it. Truth to tell, the best weapon against myth is perhaps to mythify it in its turn, and to produce *artificial myth*: and this reconstituted myth will in fact be a mythology. Since myth robs language of something, why not rob myth.[1]

Barthes's analysis of contemporary popular myths, calling in the fifties for artists to produce pop art several years before pop art became one of the major forms of postmodern contestation, points to a way of understanding how pop is a mode of artistic resistance.

Myth is a form of discourse and can be analyzed in fairly simple semiotic

1. Roland Barthes, *Mythologies*, trans. Annette Lavers, p. 135.

terms. Let us consider first a relatively simple mythic image, a soup can or, as in *Alphaville*, a whisky flask, images that might be called minimal units in an iconic, mythic discourse. In itself such an image is semantically poor, since it is merely a sign possessing its immanent sense (or denotation) that refers to nothing beyond what is represented. Its meaning is limited to "a simple container, holding a certain liquid of given properties." A myth is created when this simple iconic sign, joining signifier and concept, is transformed into a signifier that refers to a larger, mythological discourse. When the image of a soup can is reproduced in the context of an advertising poster, or when the image of a whisky flask is used in the context of a gangster film, the image's meaning is appropriated by a mythic function, and the image comes to signify a realm that transcends the object's immanent meaning. The soup can, to use this rather celebrated example of banality, comes to signify the world of supposed convenience, ease of living, and painless culinary expertise that modern capitalism packages for us. Lemmy Caution's whisky flask, especially in a French context, is even richer in mythic connotations—think of all the whisky that is consumed in New Wave films. Among other things, it refers to the mythic realm of fast living, modernism, amoral adventurism, and to a rejection of provincial modes of life, as well as to the sophistication, manly force, and spontaneous living the mythic realm offers.

When the image of a soup can is reproduced in a context that can add self-reference to its mythic signification, such as in a painting, or when a whisky flask is used as a signifier in the context of a film that self-consciously signifies the entire realm of detective films, then a third link is added to the semiotic chain. In effect, the artist has taken the mythologized sign and appropriated its sense so that it refers back to the realm of mythology. The referential chain turns back upon itself and denotes its own functioning. The myth is still there, but its status has been made clear; thus the myth is ultimately reduced, through its designation as pop, to a nonsignifier.

Images of objects, or iconic signs, are not the only elements of discourse that can be converted into mythological signifiers. Consider, in this respect, the comic-strip hero or, as in *Alphaville*, the secret agent or detective. In himself, be he Steve Canyon or Lemmy Caution, the hero functions as a narrative agent in a simple, linear intrigue. As the agent of narration he is endowed with those properties that allow him to resolve the narrative problems generated, usually, by various evil forces whose function is to create conflict and bring about suspense. But myth quickly appropriates this simple narrative function and converts the narrative agent into a signifier that designates a very complex mythological realm. The detective, the secret agent, this socially marginal figure, comes to designate a mythical realm where a popular *übermensch* signifies the necessity for violence; the superiority of white men over evil, inferior races; and the justification of basically petit bourgeois ethical notions about retribution and justice. At the same time, he represents the joys of vengeance, murder, sadism, gratuitous violence, and degraded eroticism. It is perhaps because of this mythic realm that so many pop artists have been attracted to the comics. In no other form does the ideology of the lower middle class express itself with such abandon.

Lemmy Caution is thus both a mythologized, mythical figure and a hero in the service of the language that can destroy totalitarian repression. These two aspects overlap, for as a signifier of myth, Caution destroys his own mythic functioning. Yet Godard obviously believes that the primordial violence that Caution represents can be put in the service of a revolt against "repressive logic" or, more properly, against the conventions for representation that high culture prescribes. Caution is thus an ambivalent figure, both a creation of pop irony and a subversive force that defines itself as sheer energy in revolt against the canons of repressive culture. This ambivalence characterizes much of pop art, for it is evident that many pop artists have seized the pop mode as a means of fighting against the dominant artistic conventions of official culture. The ironic glorification of popular myth thus turns not only against the myths themselves, but also against the enshrined cultural values of modernism. To offer one example, let us consider the way the pop artist can use the cartoon-strip hero or the one-dimensional tough guy of popular detective films. The glorification of the cartoon strip, for example, is especially emblematic of the postmodern artist's refusal to accept modernist psychologisms as the basis for characterization.

This desire to reject various narrative codes and mimetic conventions has an ideological aim. Brecht seems to have foreseen this postmodern rejection of depth of character, or what we might call the modernist myth of profundity, when he noted that cinema by its very nature was evolving modes of representation that would be antithetical to bourgeois notions concerning mimesis:

> In reality, cinema needs exterior action and not introspective psychology.
> And it is in this sense that, by provoking, organizing, and rendering auto
> matic certain needs on a mass scale, capitalism acts in a quite simply revo
> lutionary manner. By concentrating exclusively on "exterior" action, by

reducing everything to processes, by no longer recognizing a mediator in the hero or in man the measure of all things, it is demolishing the introspective psychology of the bourgeois novel.[2]

Godard has gone at least one step beyond this notion of process as the basis for characterization, for in many of his films his characters try to find their identity in a preexisting popular model that is derived from film—usually with disastrous consequences. Belmondo's imitation of Bogart in *A bout de souffle* and the way the "band" imitates Billy the Kid in *Bande à part* reflect both Godard's refusal of psychologism and his use of pop as a form of ironic critique. With Lemmy Caution, however, Godard has for the first time used a popular hero whose mythic existence completely determines his identity. Caution is also Godard's only successful hero.

Lemmy Caution is not entirely a comic-strip hero, as we see when he tells us that not only is he on a mission, but he is also making a *Journey to the End of the Night*. This reference to the novel by Céline, whom Godard had already consecrated in his pantheon of culture heroes in *Une femme mariée* (as well as by quoting long passages from Céline's work in *Pierrot le fou*), shows that Caution is more than an agent for ironically celebrated violence. He is another of Godard's characters who carry a heavy valise full of the debris of past culture and who never hesitate to pull out the famous quote when necessary. In effect, they carry with them the language of the past and try, usually in vain, to wield it as a defense against the present. Few critics writing in English have noted that a great deal of Caution's speech, especially when he confronts the computer, Alpha 60, is made up of famous quotations. When asked what he felt on passing through galactic space, Lemmy summons up Pascal, "The silence of these infinite spaces frightens me." He becomes a Bergsonian hero when Alpha 60 asks him what is his religion: "I believe in the immediate data of consciousness." And he quotes Eluard, the surrealist poet, when he declares that it is poetry that turns night into day.

The function of this language seems double. On the one hand, within the context—Lemmy Caution attacking Alpha 60 with Bergson and Pascal—the pop myth is underscored and even further emphasized by the immediate incongruity. Within this pop context, on the other hand, the language itself is set in relief and designated as the language of culture. The language is used to signify, not what it means in itself, but rather the myth of culture itself. There

2. Bertolt Brecht, *Sur le cinéma*, p. 180. (All translations, including those from Godard's films, are mine, unless otherwise indicated.)

is no doubt that Godard has a great deal of sympathy for or, more precisely, respectful nostalgia about, the monuments that high culture preserves in testimony to its ability to account adequately for human experience. His films are full of references, usually ironic but often nostalgic as well, to this enshrined culture, to Homer and Vivaldi, to Mozart and Rembrandt. But it is a mark of Godard's postmodern sensibility that he takes his distance vis-à-vis official culture by using it only as a form of self-reference and thus mythologizing it with self-conscious irony.

The most problematic aspect of *Alphaville*, however, is that this film does seem to propose a language that is adequate, at least in that it offers a form of resistance to Alpha 60. This is the poetic language of Eluard's *Capitale de la douleur*. Lemmy receives a copy of Eluard's work from Henri Dickson, the old and tattered secret agent who appears to have preceded Caution on his mission to Alphaville and who dies, in a form of suicide, by trying to copulate with a Seductress. As he dies, Dickson tells Lemmy to overcome Alpha 60 by causing it to destroy itself. Language is the key to this mission, for the computer must be short-circuited by a language that defies the rational order of its circuitry—presumedly by the language of poetry, or by the language of surrealism, the poetry of antirationality.

One way in which to look upon Godard's use of Eluard and surrealist poetry is to consider Lemmy Caution on one level as something of a surrealist hero. Surrealism's essential goal, as Breton said, is to find the mode of expression adequate to unite the subjective world of desire with that exterior world which, when reified by the categories of bourgeois rationality, becomes known as objective reality. If one follows this interpretation, then one might consider Caution, as some critics have, as an agent in the service of desire, as a representative of a rebellious id that seeks to destroy the repressive superego, or Alpha 60, and its repressive order. Without taking such an allegorical view, one might simply see that Godard is using surrealism to vouchsafe his own rebellion against the ossified modes of representation he finds in bourgeois culture. Moreover, it would seem that Godard is exalting, in a Marcusean sense, a language of negation that proclaims the primacy of human affectivity in the face of functional thought. Eluard's importance here, then, is to suggest that there is a language that can express desire as a form of liberation.

From another point of view, however, surrealism is a language of the past that believed in the adequacy of the expressive means at its command.

Surrealism is a modernist movement precisely in that it saw language, among other means of expression, as being equal to the task of expression that the surrealists set it. Language as well as the image could express, according to Breton, the "true functioning of the mind," an optimistic view that we have already suggested might be considered as another version of the modernist credo of epiphany. Surrealist revelation is, of course, different from other modernist forms of revelation in that it promised more than a mere expansion of our perception or a triumph over time. It aimed at a transformation of the nature of our experiential reality, and in this aim surrealism joins those heroic ideologies of the twenties and thirties for which Godard at one time felt a good deal of nostalgia. In *Le Petit Soldat* (1960) Bruno wishes he could return to the thirties when, for instance, the Marxist revolutionary Malraux or the fascist revolutionary Drieu la Rochelle could find an ideological discourse that was both heroic and historically relevant. In *Les Carabiniers* (1963), however, we see that a revolutionary ode by Mayakovski does not stop Michelangelo and Ulysses from assassinating a member of the Resistance, and we may well doubt that Godard's transforming his whisky-drinking secret agent into a surrealist poet is anything other than another ironic strategy, than another homage to a language of the past.

The liberation of desire does, however, lead to a demonstration of the harmony that might result if image and language could coincide in a moment of adequate expression. We see this in the montage of shots in which Caution and Natasha seem to dance together as she recites an accompanying text that, though reflecting motifs taken from Eluard, seems to come from Godard's pen. Juxtaposed against a series of intercuts that show the arrival of the police, this montage creates an image poem in which Godard, echoing surrealist myth, shows the couple to be the locus of salvation:

> More and more I see the human predicament
>   as a dialogue between lovers.
> The heart has but a single mouth.
> Everything by chance.
> Everything said without thinking
> sentiments drift away
> Men roam the city.
> A glance, a wind.

This sequence ends with Natasha looking out into the city, with *Capitale de la douleur* pressed against the window. She seems to enact an Eluard text by pressing "her forehead against the pane" ("le front aux vitres"), as if she were looking through the transparency of adequate language in which desire and expression would be in harmony.[3]

This lyrical evocation of what might be a moment of adequate expression quickly gives way to a pop denouement in which the secret agent is the avenging force who brings about the final judgment on Alphaville, destroying the diabolical scientist, the computer, and all the malignant, mythic powers that the recurring formula, $E = mc^2$, signifies. This pop eschatology points to the dilemma Godard faces in having recourse to popular mythology. Pop art is ultimately a form of antimimesis that designates the "dysfunctioning" of received codes of representation. In *Alphaville* Godard has placed in question those codes that in effect limit our perception of urban reality, but ultimately his representation only turns on other representations, designating them for what they are and thus demystifying them. *Alphaville* is a successful film precisely because it accepts the limits imposed upon it by preexisting popular myths and then subverts that discourse with an irony rarely found in film. Yet for Godard this subversion of discourse could only be the first step in the creation of new forms of discourse that could adequately account for the destructive urban reality that is proliferating like a cancer. There are no Lemmy Caution figures to save us from the Alphavilles we have constructed—only bewildered filmmakers who, having recognized that we do not even see what is about us, must struggle to find ways to represent our own reality to us. *Alphaville* is thus the negative moment in a creative project that demands that one next attempt be made to find a way to overcome our lack of adequate discourse.

That attempt came two years later, in 1966, when Godard made *Deux ou trois choses que je sais d'elle*, a film that is immediately linked to *Alphaville* because it purports to represent an urban reality that Godard characterizes as resembling increasingly an enormous comic strip. Though *Deux ou trois choses* is an attempt to create documentary modes of representation, it bears much in common with *Alphaville*. Godard's documentary Paris often seems to be a product of science fiction, a city in which machines have become autonomous beings that, like strange insects, appear bent on imposing their will as they wander about the urban landscape. Night shots of Paris in *Alphaville* bring out the dehumanizing anonymity of urban structures. In *Deux ou trois choses* what Godard calls the "gestapo of structures" no longer hides its

3. See Eluard's poems in *L'Amour la poésie* (now published in *Capitale de la douleur*).

destructiveness. As red, white, and blue dump trucks and cranes crawl across devastated building sites and freeways, as jackhammers beat a din into our ears, we realize that in this film even more than in *Alphaville* he has turned "familiarity into awareness." He has stripped the quotidian of its inconspicuousness through what Brecht called "alienating the familiar." Yet once one has revealed the aberrations inherent in the daily experience of the urban dweller, there remains the task of explaining them.

Deux ou trois choses is a film that relentlessly pursues the familiar, the banal, the ordinary, in an effort to find modes of representation that can go beyond mere revelation of the incongruous. To accomplish this Godard does center his film on a narration, for the film purports to relate a day in the life of a suburban housewife who practices part-time prostitution in order to pay for the necessary luxuries that the society of affluence expects her to consume. There is perhaps an element of pop in this choice of a topic taken from a weekly magazine, *Le Nouvel Observateur*, and this element is perhaps part of a larger ironic stance Godard adopts toward the necessity of providing any narrative line at all in a film that seeks to lay bare the essential structures of urban society. Yet it is also evident that prostitution has obsessed Godard since he began making films. Prostitution, whether presented directly, as in *Vivre sa vie* (1962), or indirectly, as in the portrayal of the Seductresses in *Alphaville*, is more than a banal fact of social reality. For Godard it is a privileged metaphor that expresses a fundamental truth about the nature of contemporary social relations as well as about the degradation the individual must suffer when he seeks to accommodate himself to those relations.

The attempt to describe a typical day of a lower-middle-class housewife who sells herself in order to buy Vogue dresses, pay the electricity bills, and meet the payments on her husband's car is the point of departure for the investigation of a web of relationships that are connected at least metaphorically, if not by some network of absolute laws. Godard's working premise is, however, that there must be an *ensemble* or "totality" that, were he able to find the proper modes of representation, would be revealed as underlying all the disparate phenomena his camera lays bare. Language itself seems to point to some unity underlying the discrete appearances we see. For instance, Juliette, the prostitute-housewife, lives in a *grand ensemble*, a huge complex of suburban apartments where, as in so many boxlike dormitories, the inhabitants of the city are "together" when they are not at work. The *ensemble* is thus a new form of urban organization that capitalism has produced. *Ensemble* also means "together," the parts united as a whole, and yet the paradox of the *grand ensemble* is that men are housed together but are separated from each other in ways that would have been inconceivable in older forms of urban organization. In this *ensemble* the camera reveals only disparate parts, no wholes. How does one go from this fragmentation to what Godard notes is the mathematical sense of *ensemble*, to the total structures where the basic human units are governed by laws that go beyond them, precisely because these are *lois d'ensemble*, or laws that govern a total set of individual phenomena?

Godard thus starts with the hypothesis that such laws exist, though at the same time he knows that he will be able to reveal those laws only through the invention of cinematic modes of representation that can grasp them. Ultimately, we might well suspect that Godard, again caught up in the postmodern dilemma, really believes that these laws will exist only as a function of new modes of representation. His camera constantly lays bare images of incongruity and destruction. Yet there appears to be no underlying explanation, no laws, no linguistic mediation that can account for them. Much of the frustration that *Deux ou trois choses* produces comes from the tension the camera creates. Godard's camera unmasks the appearances of banality and forces the viewer to face a chaotic world that is, in effect, his daily world. But the viewer—and the filmmaker—want to find a significance in them that transcends mere chaos.

Godard sees language as bearing a heavy burden in this task. One has the feeling that at times he wants indeed to shift the burden from the camera to the spoken word, though Godard's interrogation of language is also one aspect of the postmodern questioning of the possibilities of all forms of representation. In fact, it is this constant questioning of language, this constant juxtaposition of clear but inarticulate images with confused concepts, that endows *Deux ou trois choses* with its most persuasive force. To accomplish this interrogation Godard has borrowed, in an entirely self-conscious way, certain Brechtian concepts of acting. Each actor, reciting his role and questioning his words, often joins the narrator in this process of weighing the adequacy of language.

Juliette (Marina Vlady) is the most important character in this respect, since we follow her from her morning chores, throughout her day's activity, until she and her husband go to bed in their housing-project apartment ("HLM" or *hôpital de la longue maladie*, as it is called in *Alphaville*). Godard first introduces Marina Vlady as an actress and then, repeating the same words he used to describe her as an actress, immediately introduces her again as

Juliette, his fictional protagonist. From the outset, Marina underlines the Brechtian character of this refusal of traditional mimetic illusion by telling the spectators that her task is "to speak like quotations of truth. Papa Brecht used to say that. That actors must quote." Godard's refusal of fictional or theatrical illusion reflects his basic interrogation of the very possibility of filmic representation. This basic questioning therefore aims at more than inducing a critical state of awareness in the viewer.

First, the explicit joining of the real actress and the fictional protagonist points to a specifically cinematic dilemma Godard must face as a documentary filmmaker. By its very nature cinema converts every image it offers into a sign that in the filmic context becomes charged with semantic density to varying degrees. The postmodern filmmaker, and Godard in particular, is often painfully aware that film offers no neutral view of some reality that preexists its filmic appropriation. The very fact of filmic appropriation means that the filmed object is converted into an iconic sign. A real actress, even if she retains her identity in the film (which in point of fact she does), becomes a protagonist who has, in a broad sense, a symbolic function. In one sense film automatically converts the real into the symbolic material of fictions even though the image continues to denote the real. In nearly every film he has made, Godard has shown his awareness of this problem through ironic forms of self-reference that both underscore the fictional nature of the work and attempt to destroy the generation of fiction. With regard to his refusal to generate fictions one might consider his part of the collective work *Loin du Vietnam* (1967). In this documentary he refused to do more than film himself musing on the impossibility of filming images that could have any relevance, or rather, the only pertinent images he could show were those depicting the anguish of the filmmaker trying to find images that might be more than private fictions. In *Deux ou trois choses* Godard accepts this dilemma by beginning the film with a self-referential demonstration that shows how the film converts the real into the symbolic, how Marina Vlady remains Marina Vlady at the same time she becomes a filmic sign and a fictional protagonist.

Marina-Juliette can thus both act and reflect on her roles as an actress as well as a fictional protagonist. Godard allows her to participate in the questioning of the possibilities of representation, particularly with regard to the language she uses. Juliette has at least three voices in this film, or, if one prefers, she speaks on three levels. On one level she speaks as a fictional housewife-prostitute, in a nonreflexive manner. On a second level she examines her language and uses a self-reflexive language. This level leads to a third where she tests her language against her environment, which often shows how absurdly incongruous her language is with regard to the images that present her situation. The film thus becomes a documentary or a self-denying fiction about an actress representing herself as she struggles to represent a fictional character to the second degree.

To see how these three voices interrelate, let us examine the scene that takes place in the Vogue shop where Juliette goes to select a dress that she will pay for later with her afternoon's earnings. Godard immediately places the very possibility of language in question by increasing the noise level so that one must strain to hear the words above the roar of automobiles and machines. In decibels, the sound is probably no louder than the noise one might hear in a good many Parisian streets. It is, however, considerably louder than the background noise allowed by cinematic convention for the naturalistic mimesis of daily reality. By disregarding this convention, Godard does more than merely represent a sociological average concerning street noises. He endows the sound with significance not only by making communication impossible, but also by violating the code for naturalistic mimesis. Through this violation, the noise becomes a sign that designates the malfunctioning of the entire mimetic project. This malfunctioning is also underscored by the moments of absolute silence that Godard uses to punctuate the bedlam. The opposition of noise and silence sets up the context in which each comes to represent a form of failure, both in the world and in the attempted representation of that world.

Against this backdrop Juliette inquires about the various dresses offered for sale. Her first speech constitutes the nonreflexive level of discourse. Our first impression is that at this level Godard is making a more or less straightforward documentary, since her speech seems to reflect the daily language of a typical housewife. It is the language of utter banality. Godard also uses the other actresses in the shop to create the impression that this is a documentary. For example, in this scene a salesgirl turns to the camera and, as if replying to some sociological questionnaire, tells us, "I'm leaving at seven o'clock. I have a date with Jean-Claude at eight. We go to a restaurant, sometimes to a film." The camera's presence is thus acknowledged, as an agent that solicits language. But Godard's interest in their speech goes beyond a merely documentary interest in the typical. He is using Juliette, the shop-girls, and the prostitutes to reveal the limits of consciousness that everyday language seems to impose. One is reminded of the Seductresses in *Alphaville* and their mechanical "I'm very well, thank you, not at all." Like these pop characters, the Parisian shopgirls are locked in trivial forms of discourse that are totally inadequate to deal with the environment that surrounds them or with the degradation they undergo in their daily life. Language is here used to signify its own inadequacy, not through its primary meaning, but by its semantic nullity.

In contrast with this language stands Juliette's examining her language and her role from within. As she examines dresses, Juliette weighs the language she must use: "Yes, I know how to speak. . . . All right, let's speak together [*ensemble*]. . . . Together . . . it's a word that I like very much. An *ensemble*, that's thousands of people, a city perhaps." Implicitly, refusing theatrical illusion, she uses language reflexively. There is a poetic tension in this metalinguistic quest, for the noise level increases, and at the same moment her speech is juxtaposed against a quick shot of a freeway exit framed against a clear, blue sky. The tension between image, noise, and language continues as Juliette faces the camera and speaks to us directly. Now there is no attempt to produce theatrical illusion, as the actress questions the possibility of mimesis itself. Godard thus presents his actress as she tries to cope with the language she must speak: "No one today can know what the city of tomorrow will be. A part of the semantic richness that belonged to it in the past . . . it's going to lose all that, surely . . . surely . . ."

We see the third level of language appear at this point, when Marina-Juliette begins to spout a verbiage that undermines itself by its incongruity. This language might be called the language of culture, or at least a pastiche of the language that is offered to us by the official explicators of social and cultural life. Juliette in this speech begins to undo her meditation with the word *perhaps*, coming after the certainty she expressed with *surely*: "Perhaps . . . the creative and formative role of the city will be assured by other means of communication . . . perhaps. . . . Television, Radio, Vocabulary and Syntax, knowingly and deliberately . . ." The sudden insert of the paperback cover of *Psychologie de la forme*, taken from the inexpensive Gallimard "Ideas" series, shows that Godard is, as in *Alphaville*, again ironically playing with what we have called the myth of culture. Juliette's language seems to have become a canned imitation of the language of the paperback culture that is marketed everywhere in the same manner as Vogue dresses. This language, too, seems radically inadequate in this clamor and tumult where a pretty robot can give a résumé of her life by saying that, basically, she does "a lot of banal things."

Juliette is not alone in this testing of language or in her failure ultimately to represent her coming to terms with her role of representing herself as an actress. Godard, a French intellectual who consumes far more paperbacks than his actress-housewife, forces his own language as filmmaker to confront the cinematic image. This critique of language becomes quite explicitly a critique or a questioning of the relationship between the image and the word in the café sequence in which Godard's camera, using extreme close-ups, transforms the swirling foam that forms on the surface of coffee into something that could be likened to an image of the cosmos or perhaps of the intercellular world that the cinematic "biologist" tries to study. In any case, the camera has taken one of the most banal objects of daily reality and converted it into an ambivalent sign that Godard, in his role as filmmaker, tries to translate into verbal language. Much like Juliette questioning her language from within, Godard thus begins this scene by asking how he, a documentary filmmaker, can give an adequate account of the simplest object, be it a women's magazine or the surface of his coffee.

Godard's instinctive reaction is to draw upon the cultural categories that the culture of the past, that culture marketed in paperbacks, proposes. As his camera focuses on an "object," his commentary rapidly becomes something of a parody of his own search:

> Perhaps an object is what allows to connect . . . to go from one subject
> to the next, thus to live in society, to be *ensemble*. But, since the social
> relation is always ambiguous, since my thought divides as much as it unites,
> since my speech brings near through what it expresses and isolates by what
> it does not say, since an immense gap separates the subjective certainty I
> have of myself from the objective truth that I represent for others, since I
> never cease finding myself guilty whereas I feel innocent. . . .

The coffee foam and black surface fill the wide screen, and Godard's language seems to have all the relevance of a dialogue lifted from an intellectual comic strip. Mixing Baudelaire's ironic lines from "Au lecteur" ("mon semblable, mon frère . . .") with a nonsense use of Sartrian categories of *being* and *nothingness*, Godard throws out a pop mixture of cultural clichés that can barely be heard above the noise of a pinball machine. The iconic sign successfully resists any attempt at verbal translation, while Godard's verbiage finally turns back upon itself, designating itself as inadequate.

Throughout *Deux ou trois choses* the symbols of culture—paperback covers, famous quotes, even the idea of questioning language itself—that Godard uses as compositional elements are essentially self-referential and, as signifiers, thus turn back on themselves to designate their own failure to mean. This attempt to mythologize the myth of culture finds an ironic analogue in the presence of Bovard and Pécuchet, Flaubert's mad cataloguers, in the long scene that takes place in the café where Juliette's husband waits for her. Compilers of the word in every form it has taken, Bovard and Pécuchet cull one sentence after another from books in an attempt to create the absolute book, the total encyclopedia. Here the cultural myth of adequacy turns against itself as its absolute impossibility is made clear. Moreover, Bovard and Pécuchet's attempt to find a means to represent the totality of culture seems to be an ironic analogue to Godard's own attempt to represent the *ensemble* of urban reality.

Godard's ironic self-depreciation thus continually undermines his own mimetic project. In this respect, it would appear that he cannot really rid himself of his postmodern disbelief in any form of cultural absolute except, perhaps, that of impossibility. In spite of his stated desire to be a cinematic sociologist, we feel that he does not believe in any motivated form of representation. Every attempt at mimesis is belied by the gratuity that underlies the effort to organize a discourse purporting to offer a unique truth. There is no unique reality to which mimesis would conform, but only so many arbitrary representations of reality that are, in effect, only so many different constructs. Thus Godard offers the sequence taken in the service station as another self-conscious demonstration of the impossibility of finding the discourse, the exact organization of images and language, that will reveal the essence of even the most banal of Juliette's daily experiences (and what is more Flaubertian than this quest for essence?).

Godard begins this sequence with another ironic demonstration of the ambiguity of "signs," for an advertising sign that reads "Mobil Protects" is juxtaposed with a shot of a car whose fender has been bashed in. It seems as if Godard must first assure us that language is corrupt before he can go on to show that cinematic forms are also inadequate. This sequence then breaks down into a series of disparate juxtapositions of advertising signs, Juliette, her car, her husband, and so on, while Godard wonders aloud how he can relate them so that signification will emerge from the filmic discourse. Though each image may have an immanent sense, Godard's Joycean desire to encompass the totality, his attempt to find a significance that transcends the details that should make up an *ensemble*, leaves him grasping nothing: "Why all these signs among us that end up making me doubt language and that submerge me under meanings, by drowning the real instead of separating it from the imaginary?" Godard's premise, perhaps in a nearly Hegelian sense, is that the real must be more than the mere aggregate of disparate signs and images presenting service stations and Austins, trees blowing in the wind, and a pretty housewife who prostitutes herself. Yet his camera, with diabolical consistency, seems determined to prove the contrary.

Deux ou trois choses que je sais d'elle is, then, a documentary about a filmmaker and some actors who tried to make a film about life in contemporary Paris. It is obliged, however, to be only the attempted representation of that representation. The documentary founders on Godard's epistemological uncertainties, not the least of which might be the necessity of infinite regress. For if the validity of an act of representation can only exist in function of another act of self-representation, then this act of automimesis can only exist in function of another act of representation to the third degree, and that only by another to the fourth degree, *ad infinitum*. In the face of this uncertainty and failure, Godard's recourse is to use ironic self-consciousness, which in turn leads him back to the creation of pop modes. There is no infinite regress, since Godard's representation, by representing itself in its circularity, by designating itself as failure, turns itself into another pop mode of mimesis. *Deux ou trois choses* is ultimately as much a pop work as *Alphaville* in that it mythologizes its own postmodern myth of the impossibility of discourse.

Yet this self-representation of failure is also an ethical act. To represent failure is, by implication, to proclaim the need for a praxis that would create a world in which the lost harmony of language and referent would be recovered. Failure here is a form of praxis, but it is a difficult one, and perhaps now we can see why Godard came to prefer his own version of Marxist commitment to the politics of pop. Nonetheless, Godard's disasters cry out for a world where human discourse is adequate to man's needs. Or, as Godard himself expresses it in *Deux ou trois choses que je sais d'elle*:

> The birth in man's world of the simplest things, man's taking possession of them with his mind . . . , a new world where men and things will know harmonious relations. That's my goal. It is as much political as poetic. It explains, in any case, the rage to express. Whose? Mine.

Afterword:
Is Film a Language?

Can one say that film is a language? This question seems never to lose its potential for arousing theoretical debate, and contemporary semiotic concerns have given the question a new meaning. It is a question, moreover, that has been brought up, at least implicitly, during the course of this study and hence deserves a brief answer, if only to the end of using this question to ask about the nature of film discourse. As a conclusion to a study of French film, this question is especially relevant, since French discussions of the subject have been a curious and constant source of confusion for discussions of film language in English. The problem lies in the way French discussions have been translated or interpreted, for the notion of *langage cinématographique* invariably comes across as "cinematic language," "film language," or something of the sort. But *langage* does not have quite the same meaning as "language," for French makes a distinction between *langue* (literally, "tongue") and *langage*, which is the distinction between *langue* or language as a specific verbal system or a series of differences that can be formalized at various levels, and *langage* or the repository of usages and techniques that make up a means of communication or, in a broader sense, any sign system. Thus contemporary French theoreticians will often say that film is not a *langue* (it cannot literally be broken down into phonemic, morphemic, and other formal levels of linguistic structure), but it is a *langage*.

If film is a language in this sense, if it is a communications or sign system, then one should be able to find, according to semiotic reasoning, some way of describing the way the system functions and perhaps of formalizing at various levels the structures that make up the system, much in the way linguistics describes a language in terms of phonemic, morphemic, syntactic, and other levels of organization. However, the next problem such a mode of reasoning encounters is the well-known fact that film is a form of discourse that supposedly incorporates a heterogeneous series of codes or, if one prefers, other discourses: spoken and written language, the code of the reproduction of moving images, the cultural codes within the images, music, etc. The *etc.*

199

here is not a form of condensation. It indicates that film is an open discourse or *langage* that can incorporate all manner of discourses, can transform an indefinite number of types of elements into signifying structures. There would appear to be no a priori limitations to this capacity, though at a certain point we might hesitate to continue to speak of "film" were a director to go beyond certain limits in adding new elements to film discourse. (Suppose, in the name of total realism, a director were to arrange for a few stray bullets to fly into the audience during a war film. . . .) This capacity for transformation does pose problems for the theorist. How is he to define or formalize a system that appears to be open-ended? Can he formalize only a posteriori? If this were the case, would the theorist in reality be only a critic working, as it were, on idiolects?

Perhaps we have not found the right description of filmic discourse if we pose the problem of film communication in the above manner. In fact, perhaps the well-known heterogeneity of filmic discourse is a bit of a myth, a useful analytical myth at times, but a myth nonetheless. As we hope to have shown in the course of the preceding essays, film has the capacity to make of all the various elements incorporated into the work a single signifying whole; this whole signifies in function of a central mimetic project that institutes a unified discourse. When we view a film we are rarely aware of any heterogeneity, unless we make a conscious effort to analyze the film's separate signifying elements according to some conceptual model, much in the same way the linguist isolates the various elements in language of which we are not necessarily conscious when we speak. This analogy with the linguist is perhaps not entirely satisfactory, since the linguist works on a single, verbal substance, whereas in film multiple substances are involved and the messages can be complex. Language, however, is rarely univocal. . . .

An objection should present itself here, as it probably already has several times in the course of this book, especially to the reader who is an advocate of "expanded cinema." What about the nonnarrative film? How can it be called a language or a *langage* or a sign system? Of course, many apparently nonnarrative films, documentaries or didactic films, for instance, are in reality narrative films that use an implicit narrative to semanticize their elements. The semantic content of such films is (usually) rather poor, since it derives from narratives that are imposed on the material precisely in order to create a film discourse. Often there is a redundancy of signifiers with regard to what is signified; the ultimate example of this is the advertising film.

With regard to the "poetic" film, on the other hand, our essay on Man Ray should indicate the problems one faces in attempting to endow iconic figures with the same semantic depth as verbal figures. However, the kind of film our advocate of expanded cinema might be thinking about is not really a poetic film, but rather the abstract film that offers the animation of figures, colors, volumes, motifs, and so forth. Alternatively, he might think of an abstract film that orchestrates images taken from the real world, but does so in order to transform them into formal patterns and plastic constructions. I would agree that it is often difficult to speak of a sign system in these cases, but I would also say that it is difficult to call many of these works films in that they are not mimetic projections of the world. They are kinetic art works that really differ in no way ontologically from paintings except to the extent that they have endowed their artistic patterns and motifs with motion. The semiotician may wish to speak of the *langage* of painting and sculpture, but that is not the point here. The point is that most of what is called expanded cinema is not cinema at all, or at least not in any ordinary sense of the word, and ontologically belongs to another realm.

To return then to the question of film as discourse or as communication system, let us concede for the moment that all discourse can be formalized a posteriori, but that the question of finding an a priori syntax remains open. (Perhaps this would explain what I see as the relative failure of transformational grammar.) Let us examine a much simpler case of verbal and filmic communication and see what properties they might share. Consider the enunciation "he sees it," for example. Film can surely communicate the same semantic content by the rather simple convention of showing a character looking at something and then cutting to the object seen. At this level at least two filmic images plus a cut seem to have the same communication function. In this example, verbal language can seemingly be converted into images, and the images in turn can be translated into verbal language. The problem with this kind of analysis is that it is invariably far too simple. How would the image account for the tone of voice, intonation and pitch, stress and accent, that might endow the sentence with a multiplicity of secondary meanings? Moreover, how could any number of words exhaust the multiple meanings that necessarily accrue to an image, meanings given by camera angle, lighting, framing, objects within the frame, composition, and the like? Moreover, if we insist on talking about "meaning," how can we talk about it except in terms of a semantic content that must have language as its basis?

Perhaps one answer to these questions about meaning is that the material presence of the image somehow exceeds the notion of meaning, that there is always a superfluity of presence of the world in the image that goes beyond the film's semantic structures. Our relationship to that presence may be neuter, or it may be affective, but the presence does not have meaning until it can be converted into a discourse that we can articulate. This view of film frees us from the temptation of "extreme semiosis" of the sort that characterizes, in a very enticing way, the early work of Roland Barthes: the temptation to see the world as being made up of sign systems referring to other sign systems, so that finally everything can be converted into a translucent language. The world consists then only of signs. On the other hand, it would also appear that everything in the image can be transformed into a signifying element if we find the right question to put to the material presence in the image. In the image, as in the world, things remain gratuitous until we interrogate them. This would be the "meaning" of Godard's showing images of trees in the sequence in *Deux ou trois choses* when he asks about the possibility of meaning in the mere presence of the objects he films. In this case, as sheer presence, they do not signify. As interrogated objects, they seem to signify at least that interrogation that is the beginning of the genesis of meaning.

In terms, then, of communicative functions, film and language share some common properties—and do not share others. Since the image cannot, or at least has not yet, been endowed with pronouns, it seems dubious that film can communicate such statements as "I see it," "you see it," or "we see it." Language cannot offer us the presence of a/the world, nor can it amalgamate as many signifying elements into a simultaneous whole as can film. Film can incorporate language, but the converse does not seem to be true. To continue a list of differences and similarities would be interesting, but pointless, since it seems that there is no exhaustive list of properties that can delimit either what film and language have in common or what they do not have in common.

Theorists have attempted to formulate a syntax of film in terms of analytical units larger than the image. Usually these attempts to establish, for example, the syntagmatic units of film are in effect attempts to establish the grammar of the narrative possibilities of film. Insofar as language can also narrate, it might appear that film and language would share a certain "grammar" at this level. Undoubtedly they do, though this brings us back to the problem we mentioned earlier: to wit, can one find an a priori grammar that would define the essence or the structural possibilities of a given form of discourse? I frankly doubt that this is the case, though, as much structuralist criticism in France shows, the formulation of such a grammar is a perpetual temptation. A posteriori models can of course be constructed for narrative syntax, each having its own degree of coherence and its own rules for pertinence. The degree of rigor we demand for such models is in fact a reflection of how closely we wish to see defined the rules for the particular narrative game involved.

My point in making the last statement is to bring us back to the conceptual underpinnings of the book and to remind us that if language and film have something in common that strikes me as especially important, it is that they are, as Wittgenstein says about language, a series of games, of ludic spaces, each game having its own grammar or rules that we can define as precisely or as loosely as we need for our own purposes once we have examined the game. Language has no essence, however, and film, it would appear, has none either. Facing this problem of essence in his attempt to understand the nature of language, Wittgenstein framed a series of metaphors stressing the ludic nature of language, the plurality of games in language corresponding to the plurality of uses, situations, "life-forms," that make up the way we use language. One might be tempted to say that for Wittgenstein, there is no *langue*, no single system, only *langage*, the multiple, overlapping games that we learn to play as we acquire knowledge of a language. There is no a priori way, then, of knowing what the essence of games is or even that there is an essence *game*:

> Consider for example the proceedings that we call "games." I mean board-games, card-games, ball-games, Olympic games, and so on. What is common to them all?—Don't say: "There *must* be something common, or they would not be called 'games' "—but *look and see* whether there is anything common to all.—For if you look at them you will not see something that is common to *all*, but similarities, relationships, and a whole series of them at that. To repeat: don't think, but look![1]

What do we see when we look at language and film? We see what Wittgenstein calls many shared family resemblances, or many shared properties, but no exhaustive group of properties common to both. We see that film and language are made up of many overlapping games, some of which can be played only in film (farce like Chaplin's and Keaton's cannot exist outside of film),

1. Ludwig Wittgenstein, Philosophical Investigation No. 66, *Philosophical Investigations*, p. 31e.

some of which can be played in both (detective stories, romances, lessons in fire prevention), and some of which can be played only in language (Kant's *Critique of Pure Reason*—one could reproduce the text on film; yet would we call that reproduction a film?).

In the development of film these games are often repeated and become quickly codified. Genre films, for instance, are constructs for which the rules are well known, and so they can be quickly, rigidly formalized and pose no problem of "reading" for the average viewer. The viewer need not, of course, articulate these rules for himself every time he sees a Western, no more, in fact, than he need think about the rules when he sees a basketball game, or than, when speaking his own language, he needs to consult a grammar book to see if he is using his language meaningfully. On the other hand, new filmic games are invented, just as developments in language bring about new ludic spaces for which the rules are different. The language of nuclear physics or of computer science exists as a set of rules that must be mastered by apprenticeship, and many viewers would feel, with good reason, that the same is true of films by Alain Resnais, Marguerite Duras, or Alain Robbe-Grillet.

A study of the sort we have just completed is then, in a metaphorical sense, something of a historical grammar of the rules that have evolved in a given national cinema, and the plurality of critical approaches used here corresponds to the variety of filmic games we have encountered. The historical dimension of filmic literacy should not be underestimated. The literate user of language can read a text adequately only if he knows how the rules governing the production of the text have evolved and how those rules have been used, consciously or passively, by the writer of the text. In the same way, the literate viewer of film needs to have the total "language" of film at his command if he is to see how a filmmaker may make use of what has already been codified. In this respect the general rule of structural linguistics is reversed: diachrony does exist as a meaningful dimension of the playing of games—the production of meaning—in units of discourse that are larger than the mere word. To offer simple examples in film, a lateral "wipe" in a film today can only be read as an ironic reference to an earlier mode of film discourse, and an iris dissolve must inevitably connote Victorian sentimentality. Film exists then as a *langage*, as the entire corpus of works that make up "cinema" and that are in effect the various games and their rules that have evolved since the Lumière brothers made their first projection of moving images in 1896. This corpus exists as a virtual repository of meanings that one might well call the dictionary of film.

This repository of meanings can of course be contained in no single dictionary, any more than a single dictionary could exhaust the possible meanings that language can generate. Film and language are alike, then, in that as discourse they are capable of generating an infinite number of meanings. The infinite genesis of meaning is another aspect of the ludic nature of both, for the creation of meaning in discourse is a form of play, and no discourse will ever be exhausted by the play it allows. Jacques Derrida, an exemplary postmodern thinker in this respect, offers insight into the play behind the genesis of meaning when he says that discourse today, shorn of any transcendental center, refuses any totalization of its meaning:

> If totalization no longer has any meaning, it is not because the infinity of a field cannot be covered by a finite glance or a finite discourse, but because the nature of the field—that is, language and a finite language—excludes totalization. This field is in fact that of *freeplay* [*jeu*], that is to say, a field of infinite substitutions in the closure of a finite ensemble. This field permits these infinite substitutions only because it is finite, that is to say, because instead of being an inexhaustible field, as in the classical hypothesis, instead of being too large, there is something missing from it: a center which arrests and founds the freeplay [*jeu*] of substitutions.[2]

It is not Derrida's view of the history of metaphysics that interests us here. We have quoted him at length to show how he joins Wittgenstein and Saussure in discussing the genesis of meaning using the model of a chessboard—a field of infinite substitutions in the closure of a finite ensemble—using the model of the closed space of play where man has the freedom to create those meanings he needs. This is perhaps the most interesting point of intersection of film and language, for, as discourse, film bears a large responsibility for generating those meanings that go to make up our contemporary culture. The task of interpreting those meanings is infinite, but the student of film should find this openness of filmic discourse to be only one more challenge, a call to his own creative liberty in playing the game of interpretation.[3]

2. Jacques Derrida, "Structure, Sign, and Play," in *The Structuralist Controversy*, ed. Richard Macksey and Eugenio Donato (Baltimore: Johns Hopkins Press, 1972), p. 260. Reprinted in Derrida's *L'Écriture et la différence*, p. 423.

3. Derrida notes in the quoted essay that this view of the "freeplay" (or *le jeu*) of infinite interpretations is at odds with our desire to root discourse in an origin that would guarantee its meaning: "There are thus two interpretations of interpretation, of structure, of sign, of freeplay.

The one seeks to decipher, dreams of deciphering, a truth or an origin which is free from freeplay and from the order of the sign, and lives like an exile the necessity of interpretation. The other, which is no longer turned toward the origin, affirms freeplay and tries to pass beyond man and humanism, the name man being the name of that being who, throughout the history of metaphysics or of ontotheology—in other words, through the history of all of his history—has dreamed of full presence, the reassuring foundation, the origin, and the end of the game" (*The Structuralist Controversy*, pp. 264–65). Do we not really live both impulses at once, especially insofar as we, as critics, participate in the play that generates meaning? Yet we would also claim that our interpretations rest upon a "reassuring foundation."

Selected Bibliography

Agel, Henri. *Le cinéma français: René Clair*. Lyon: Centre culturel du cinéma et de la télévision, 1953.

———. *Miroirs de l'insolite dans le cinéma français*. Paris: Editions du Cerf, 1958.

Alquié, Ferdinand. *Philosophie du surréalisme*. Paris: Flammarion, 1955.

Alter, Jean. *La Vision du monde d'Alain Robbe-Grillet*. Paris: Seuil, 1967.

Amengual, Barthélemy. *Clefs pour le cinéma*. Paris: Seghers, 1971.

———. *René Clair*. Rev. ed. Paris: Seghers, 1969.

Analyse des Films de Jean Renoir par des Elèves de l'I. D. H. E. C. Paris: Institut des Hautes Etudes Cinématographiques, 1966.

Analyse des Films de René Clair par des Etudiants de l'I. D. H. E. C. Paris: Institut des Hautes Etudes Cinématographiques, 1965.

Aragon, Louis. "Qu'est-ce que l'art, Jean-Luc Godard?" *Les Lettres françaises*, no. 1096 (September 1965).

Armes, Roy. *The Cinema of Alain Resnais*. New York: A. S. Barnes, 1968.

———. *French Cinema Since 1946*. 2 vols. 2d ed. Cranbury, N.J.: A. S. Barnes, 1970.

Artaud, Antonin. *Oeuvres complètes*. Vol. 3. Paris: Gallimard, 1961.

———. *Le Théâtre et son double*. Paris: Collection Idées, 1969.

Bardèche, Maurice, and Robert Brasillach. *Histoire du cinéma français*. Nouv. ed. Paris: André Martel, 1948.

Barthes, Roland. *Le Degré zéro de l'écriture* and *Eléments de sémiologie*. Paris: Gonthier, 1964.

———. "Le message photographique." *Communications*, no. 1 (1961).

———. *Mythologies*. Paris: Seuil, 1957. American ed., translated by Annette Lavers, New York: Hill & Wang, 1972.

———. "Rhétorique de l'image." *Communications*, no. 4 (1964).

Bataille, Georges. "La 'Vieille Taupe' et le préfixe *sur* dans les mots *surhomme* et *surréaliste*." *Tel Quel*, no. 34 (Summer 1968).

Bazin, André. *Jean Renoir*. Paris: Editions Champ Libre, 1971.

———. "Los Olvidados." *Esprit*, no. 186 (January 1952).

———. *Qu'est-ce que le cinéma*. 4 vols. Paris: Editions du Cerf, 1958–1962.

Bazin, André, and Jacques Doniol-Valcroze. "Entretiens avec Luis Buñuel." *Cahiers du cinéma*, no. 36 (June 1954).

Beilenhoff, Wolfgang, ed. *Poetik des films*. Munich: Wilhelm Fink, 1974. (Translations of Russian formalist writings on film.)

Bellone, Julius, ed. *Renaissance of the Film*. New York: Collier Books, 1970.

Benayoun, Robert. *Erotique du surréalisme*. Paris: Jean-Jacques Pauvert, 1965.

Benveniste, Emile. *Problèmes de linguistique générale*. Vol. 1. Paris: Gallimard, 1966.

Bernal, Olga. *Alain Robbe-Grillet: le roman de l'absence*. Paris: Gallimard, 1964.

Bertolucci, Bernardo. "Versus Godard." *Cahiers du cinéma*, no. 186 (January 1967).

Blanchot, Maurice. "Le demain joueur." *Nouvelle Revue Française* 32, no. 172 (April 1967). (An essay on surrealism.)

Borgal, Clément. *Cocteau, Dieu, la mort, la pensée*. Paris: Le Centurion, 1968.

Bory, Jean-Louis. *Des yeux pour voir*. Paris: 10/18, 1971.

Bourgeois, Jacques. "L' évolution artistique de René Clair." *La Revue du cinéma*, n.s., pt. 1, no. 2 (November 1946).

———. *René Clair*. Paris: Editions Roulet, 1949.

Bradbury, Malcolm, and James McFarlane. *Modernism*. New York: Penguin Books, 1976.

Braudy, Leo. *Jean Renoir: The World of His Films*. Garden City, N.Y.: Doubleday, 1972.

———, ed. *Focus on "Shoot the Piano Player."* Englewood Cliffs, N.J.: Prentice-Hall, 1972.

Brecht, Bertolt. *Schriften zum Theater*. Vol. 7. Berlin: Suhrkamp Verlag, 1964.

———. *Sur le cinéma*. Translated by Jean-Louis Lebrau and Jean Pierre Lefebre. Paris: L'Arche, 1970.

Bresson, Robert. *Notes sur le cinématographe*. Paris: Gallimard, 1975.

Breton, André. *L'Amour fou*. Paris: Gallimard, 1937.

———. *Anthologie de l'humour noir*. Paris: Jean-Jacques Pauvert, 1966.

———. *Arcane 17*. Paris: 10/18, 1965.

———. *La Clé des champs*. Paris: Jean-Jacques Pauvert, 1967.

———. *Position politique du surréalisme*. Paris: Jean-Jacques Pauvert, 1962.

———. *Les Vases communicants*. Paris: Gallimard, 1955.

———. *Manifestes du surréalisme*. 1946. Reprint, Paris: Collection Idées, n.d.

Briot, Robert. *Robert Bresson*. Paris: Editions du Cerf, 1957.

Brosse, Jacques. *Cocteau*. Paris: Bibliothèque Idéale, n.d.

Brown, Frederick. *An Impersonation of Angels*. New York: The Viking Press, 1968.

Brown, Royal S., ed. *Focus on Godard*. Englewood Cliffs, N.J.: Prentice-Hall, 1972.

Brunius, Jacques. *En marge du cinéma français*. Paris: Arcanes, 1954.

Burch, Noel. *Praxis du cinéma*. Paris: Gallimard, 1969.

———. "Reflexions sur le sujet." *Cahiers du cinéma*, no. 196 (December 1967).

Caillois, Roger. *Les Jeux et les hommes*. Paris: Gallimard, 1958.

Cameron, Ian, ed. *The Films of Jean-Luc Godard*. New York: Praeger, 1969.

———. *The Films of Robert Bresson*. New York: Praeger, 1969.

Canziani, Alfonso. *L'ultimo cinema francese*. Urbino: Argalià Editore, 1964.

Cardinal, Marie. *Cet été-là*. Paris: Julliard, 1967. (On Godard's *Deux ou trois choses*.)

Cardinal, Roger, and Robert Short. *Surrealism: Permanent Revelation*. New York: E. P. Dutton, 1970.

Cauliez, Armand-Jean. *Jean Renoir*. Paris: Editions Universitaires, 1962.

Cavell, Stanley. "More of The World Viewed." *Georgia Review* 28, no. 4 (Winter 1974).

———. *The World Viewed: Reflections on the Ontology of Film*. New York: The Viking Press, 1971.

Charensol, Georges, and Roger Régent. *Un Maître du cinéma: René Clair*. Paris: La Table Ronde, 1952.

Chazal, Robert. *Marcel Carné*. Collection Cinéma d'aujourd'hui. Paris: Seghers, 1965.

Chirpaz, François, and Janine Chirpaz. "Carné ou la rencontre impossible." *Esprit*, no. 244 (November 1956).

Clair, René. *Cinéma d'hier, cinéma d'aujourd'hui*. Paris: Collection Idées, 1970.

————. *Réflexion faite*. Paris: Gallimard, 1951.

Clouzot, Claire. *Le cinéma français depuis la Nouvelle Vague*. Paris: Fernand Nathan-Alliance Française, 1972.

Cocteau, Jean. *La Difficulté d'être*. Paris: Editions Paul Morihien, 1947.

————. *Entretiens autour du cinématographe*. Paris: Editions André Bonne, 1959.

————. *Journal d'un inconnu*. Paris: Grasset, 1953.

————. *Opéra*. Paris: Le Livre de Poche, 1959.

————. *Opium*. Paris: Stock, 1930. Reprint, Paris: Le Livre de Poche, n.d.

Cohen-Séat, Gilbert. *Essai sur les principes d'une philosophie du cinéma: Introduction Générale*. Paris: Presses Universitaires, 1946.

Collet, Jean. *Jean-Luc Godard*. Paris: Seghers, 1963.

Crisp, C. G. *François Truffaut*. New York: Praeger, 1972.

Culler, Jonathan. *Structuralist Poetics*. Ithaca: Cornell University Press, 1975.

Curtis, David. *Experimental Cinema*. New York: Universe Books, 1971.

Dali, Salvador. *La vie secrète de Salvador Dali*. Translated by Michel Déon. Paris: La Table Ronde, 1952.

Delahaye, Michel. "Les Tourbillons élémentaires." *Cahiers du cinéma*, no. 129 (March 1962). (On Truffaut's *Jules et Jim*.)

Denoël, Jean, ed. *Jean Cocteau et le cinématographe*. Paris: Gallimard, 1972.

Derrida, Jacques. *L'Écriture et la différence*. Paris: Seuil, 1967.

Dort, Bernand. "Godard ou le romantique abusif." *Les Temps Modernes*, no. 235 (December 1965).

Dubourg, Pierre. *Dramaturgie de Jean Cocteau*. Paris: Grasset, 1954.

Eco, Umberto. *La Structure absente: Introduction à la recherche sémiotique*. Translated by Uccio Esposito-Torrigiani. Paris: Mercure de France, 1972.

————. *A Theory of Semiotics*. Bloomington: Indiana University Press, 1976.

Ehrmann, Jacques, ed. *Game, Play, Literature*. Boston: Beacon Press, 1968.

Estève, Michel. *Robert Bresson*. Paris: Seghers, 1962.

Fanne, Dominique. *L'Univers de François Truffaut*. Paris: Editions du Cerf, 1972.

Gardiès, André. *Robbe-Grillet*. Paris: Seghers, 1972.

Garroni, Emilio. *Semiotica ed estetica*. Bari: Editori Laterza, 1968.

Gautier, Xavière. *Surréalisme et sexualité*. Paris: Collection Idées, 1971.

Gilson, René. *Jean Cocteau*. Paris: Seghers, 1969.

Godard, Jean-Luc. *Jean-Luc Godard*. Edited by Jean Narboni. Paris: Pierre Belfond, 1968.

Goldman, Annie. *Cinéma et société moderne*. Editions Anthropos, 1971.

Goldmann, Lucien. *Pour une sociologie du roman*. Paris: Collection Idées, 1964.

Graham, Peter. *The New Wave*. New York: Doubleday, 1968.

Greene, Marjorie. "Robert Bresson." *Film Quarterly* 13, no. 3 (Spring 1960).

Grossman, Manuel L. "Jean Vigo and The Development of Surrealist Cinema." *Symposium* 27, no. 2 (Summer 1972).

"Le groupe Dziga-Vertov." *Cahiers du cinéma*, no. 238–39 (May–June 1972). (Maoist attack on Godard's latest work.)

Harcourt, Peter. *Six European Directors*. Baltimore: Penguin Books, 1974.

Huizinga, Johan. *Homo Ludens*. Translated by Cécile Seresia. Paris: Gallimard, 1951.

Jakobson, Roman. *Questions de poétique*. Paris: Seuil, 1973.

Joly, J. "Between Theater and Life: Jean Renoir and *The Rules of the Game*." *Film Quarterly* 21, no. 2 (Winter 1967–1968).

Kast, Pierre. "Une fonction de constat. Notes sur l'oeuvre de Buñuel." *Cahiers du cinéma*, no. 7 (December 1951).

Kerans, James. "Classics Revisited: *La Grande Illusion*." *Film Quarterly* 14, no. 2 (Winter 1960).

Kihm, Jean-Jacques. *Cocteau*. Paris: Bibliothèque Idéale, 1960.

Kyrou, Ado. *Buñuel*. Paris: Seghers, 1970.

———. *Le surréalisme au cinéma*. Paris: Editions Arcanes, 1953.

Labarthe, André. *Essai sur le jeune cinéma français*. Paris: Le Terrain Vague, 1960.

Lannes, Roger. *Jean Cocteau*. Paris: Seghers, 1968.

Langer, Susanne K. *Feeling and Form: A Theory of Art*. New York: Charles Scribner's Sons, 1953.

Leprohon, Pierre. *Jean Renoir*. Paris: Seghers, 1967.

L'Herbier, Marcel. *Intelligence du cinématographe*. Paris: Editions Corréa, 1946.

Lherminier, Pierre. *Jean Vigo*. Paris: Seghers, 1967.

Lotman, Juri. *La Structure du texte artistique*. Translated by Anne Fournier et al. Paris: Gallimard, 1973.

MacBean, James Roy. *Film and Revolution*. Bloomington: Indiana University Press, 1975.

MacCann, Richard Dyer, ed. *Film: A Montage of Theories*. New York: E. P. Dutton, 1966.

Martin, Marcel. *Jean Vigo*. Paris: Anthologie du cinéma, 1966.

Mast, Gerald. *Filmguide to The Rules of the Game*. Bloomington: Indiana University Press, 1973.

Mast, Gerald, and Marshall Cohen. *Film Theory and Criticism*. New York: Oxford University Press, 1974.

Matthews, J. H. *Surrealism and Film*. Ann Arbor: University of Michigan Press, 1971.

Metz, Christian. *Essais sur la signification au cinéma*. 2 vols. Paris: Klincksieck, 1968, 1972.

———. *Langage et cinéma*. Paris: Larousse, 1971.

Miesch, Jean. *Robbe-Grillet*. Paris: Editions Universitaires, 1965.

Mitry, Jean. *Esthétique et psychologie du cinéma*. 2 vols. Paris: Editions Universitaires, 1963, 1965.

————. *René Clair*. Paris: Editions Universitaires, 1960.

Monaco, James. *The New Wave*. New York: Oxford University Press, 1976.

Mondragon. "Comment j'ai compris *le chien andalou*." *Ciné-Club* 2, no. 8–9 (May–June 1949).

Morin, Edgar. *Le cinéma ou l'homme imaginaire*. Paris: Gonthier, 1958.

————. *Les stars*. Paris: Seuil, 1972.

Morrissette, Bruce. *Les Romans de Robbe-Grillet*. Paris: Editions de Minuit, 1967.

Nouveau Roman: hier, aujourd'hui. 2 vols. Paris: 10/18, 1972.

Oxenhandler, Neal. *Scandal and Parade*. New Brunswick: Rutgers University Press, 1957.

————. "*Marienbad* Revisited." *Film Quarterly* 17, no. 1 (Fall 1963).

Péret, Benjamin. *Anthologie de l'amour sublime*. Paris: Albin Michel, 1956.

Petrie, Graham. *The Cinema of François Truffaut*. New York: A. S. Barnes, 1970.

Piazza, François. "Considérations psychanalytiques sur le 'chien andalou.'" *Psyche* 4, no. 27–28 (January–February 1949).

Pluchart, François. *Pop Art & Cie*. Paris: Editions Martin-Malburet, 1971.

La Politique des auteurs. Paris: Editions Champ Libre, 1972. (Interviews.)

Pornon, Charles. *Le Rêve et le fantastique dans le cinéma français*. Paris: La Nef de Paris, 1959.

Poulle, François. *Renoir 1938 ou jean renoir pour rien?* Paris: Editions du Cerf, 1969.

Quéval, Jean. *Jacques Prévert*. Paris: Mercure de France, 1955.

————. *Marcel Carné*. Paris: Editions du Cerf, 1952.

Ray, Man. *Self-Portrait*. Boston and Toronto: Little, Brown, 1963.

Rebolledo, Carlos, and Frédéric Grange. *Buñuel*. Paris: Editions Universitaires, 1965.

Régent, Roger. "René Clair ou le paradoxe théâtral." *La Revue Théâtrale*, no. 32 (1956).

Ricardou, Jean. *Le Nouveau Roman*. Paris: Seuil, 1973.

————. *Problèmes du nouveau roman*. Paris: Seuil, 1967.

Rivette, Jacques. "Du côté de chez Antoine." *Cahiers du cinéma*, no. 95 (May 1959). (On Truffaut's *Les 400 Coups*.)

Rivette, Jacques, and François Truffaut. "Nouvel entretien avec Jean Renoir." *Cahiers du cinéma*, no. 78 (December 1957).

Robbe-Grillet, Alain. *Pour un nouveau roman*. Paris: Editions de Minuit, 1963.

Roud, Richard. *Jean-Luc Godard*. 2d ed. Bloomington: Indiana University Press, 1970.

Sadoul, Georges. *Histoire du cinéma mondial*. 1949. 9th ed., rev. and augm., Paris: Flammarion, 1972. (Parts of this work appeared as *French Film*. 1953. Reprint, New York: Arno Press, 1972.)

————. *Vie de Charlot*. Paris: Editeurs Français Réunis, 1957.

Salachas, Gilbert. "*Les Quatre Cent Coups*." *Téléciné* 13, no. 83 (n.d.).

Salès-Gomès, P. E. *Jean Vigo*. Paris: Seuil, 1957.

Sartre, Jean-Paul. *L'Imaginaire*. 1940. Reprint, Paris: Collection Idées, 1966.

————. *L'Etre et le néant*. Paris: Gallimard, 1943.

————. *L'Existentialisme est un humanisme*. Paris: Editions Nagel, 1946.

Sémoulé, Jean. *Bresson*. Paris: Classiques du cinéma, 1959.

Siclier, Jacques. *La femme dans le cinéma français*. Paris: Editions du Cerf, 1957.

Smith, John M. *Jean Vigo*. New York: Praeger, 1972.

Sontag, Susan. *Against Interpretation*. New York: Delta, 1967.

————. *Styles of Radical Will*. New York: Farrar, Straus & Giroux, 1969.

Spanos, William V. "The Detective and the Boundary: Some Notes on the Postmodern Literary Imagination." *Boundary 2* 2, no. 1 (Fall 1972).

Starobinski, Jean. "L'autorité suprême." *Nouvelle Revue Française* 32, no. 172 (April 1972). (Essay on surrealism.)

Stauffacher, Frank, ed. *Art in Cinema*. San Francisco: San Francisco Museum of Art, 1947.

Talbot, Daniel, ed. *Film: An Anthology*. Berkeley: University of California Press, 1966.

Taylor, John Russell. *Cinema Eye, Cinema Ear: Some Key Film-Makers of the Sixties*. New York: Hill & Wang, 1964.

Teush, Bart. "The Playground of Jean Vigo." *Film Heritage* 9, no. 1 (Fall 1973).

Truffaut, François. "Une certaine tendance du cinéma français." *Cahiers du cinéma*, no. 31 (January 1954).

————. *Le cinéma selon Hitchcock*. Paris: Robert Laffont, 1967.

————. "Rencontre avec Luis Buñuel." *Arts*, no. 526 (27 July 1955).

Tudor, Andrew. *Theories of Film*. New York: The Viking Press, 1973.

Walles, C. G. "The Blood of a Poet." *Kenyon Review* 6, no. 1 (Winter 1944).

Wittgenstein, Ludwig. *Philosophical Investigations*. Translated by G. E. M. Anscombe. 2d ed. New York: The Macmillan Co., 1958.

Wollen, Peter. *Signs and Meaning in the Cinema*. Rev. ed. Bloomington: Indiana University Press, 1972.

Worth, Sol. "The Development of a Semiotics of Film." *Semiotica* 1, no. 3 (1969).

Zimmer, Christian. "Totalisation du vrac." *Les Temps Modernes*, no. 252 (May 1967). (On Godard's *Deux ou trois choses*.)

Special Issues of Periodicals

L'Age du cinéma, no. 4–5 (August–November 1951). (On surrealism.)

Cahiers du cinéma, no. 7 (December 1951). (On Buñuel.)

Cahiers du cinéma, no. 78 (December 1957). (On Renoir.)

Cahiers du cinéma, no. 123 (September 1961). (On *L'Année dernière*.)

Cahiers du cinéma, no. 138 (December 1962). (On the New Wave.)

Cahiers du cinéma, no. 185 (December 1966). (Film and novel.)

Ciné-Club, n.s., no. 1 (December 1949). (On Carné.)

Communications 8 (1966). (L'analyse structurale du récit.)

Communications 15 (1970). (L'analyse des images.)

Etudes cinématographiques, nos. 20–21, 22–23 (1963). (On Buñuel.)

Etudes cinématographiques, no. 38–39 and no. 40–42 (1965). (On surrealism.)
Etudes cinématographiques, no. 51–52 (1966). (On Jean Vigo.)
Etudes cinématographiques, no. 57–61 (1967). (On Godard.)
Image et son, no. 157 (December 1962). (On Buñuel.)
Positif, no. 42 (November 1961). (On Buñuel.)
Premier Plan, no. 4 (1959). (On Resnais.)
Premier Plan, no. 13 (1960). (On Buñuel.)
Premier Plan, no. 14 (1960). (On Prévert.)
Premier Plan, no. 19 (1961). (On Vigo.)
Premier Plan, no. 22–24 (1962). (On Renoir.)
Premier Plan, no. 42 (1966). (On Bresson.)
La Revue des lettres modernes 5, no. 36–38 (Summer 1958). (Cinéma et roman.)
Sub-Stance, no. 9 (1974). (Film theory, criticism, ideology.)
La Table Ronde, no. 94 (October 1955). (On Cocteau.)
Take One 2, no. 10 and no. 11 (1971). (On Godard.)

Film Scripts

Buñuel:
  L'Age d'Or and *Un Chien andalou*. *L'Avant-Scène du cinéma*, no. 27–28 (1963).
  L'Age d'or and *Un chien andalou*. Translated by Marianne Alexandre. New York: Simon & Schuster, 1968.
  Scénario "*Un chien andalou* par Luis Buñuel and Salvador Dali." *La Révolution surréaliste*, no. 12 (15 December 1932).
Carné:
  Le Jour se lève. *L'Avant-Scène du cinéma*, no. 53 (1965).
René Clair:
  Entr'acte and *A Nous la Liberté*. *L'Avant-Scène du cinéma*, no. 86 (1968).
Cocteau:
  Le Sang d'un poète. Monaco: Editions du Rocher, 1948.
  Two Screenplays. Translated by Carol Martin Sperry. New York: Orion Press, 1968.
Jean-Luc Godard:
  Alphaville. Translated by Peter Whitehead. New York: Simon & Schuster, 1966.
  2 ou 3 choses que je sais d'elle. Paris: Seuil, 1971.
Jean Renoir:
  La Grande Illusion. Paris: Seuil, 1971.
  Grande Illusion. Translated by Marianne Alexandre and Andrew Sinclair. New York: Simon & Schuster, 1968.
  La Règle du jeu. *L'Avant-Scène du cinéma*, no. 52 (1965).
  The Rules of the Game. Translated by John McGrath and Maureen Teitelbaum. New York: Simon & Schuster, 1970.
Alain Robbe-Grillet:

L'Année dernière à Marienbad. Paris: Editions de Minuit, 1961.

Last Year at Marienbad. Translated by Richard Howard. New York: Grove Press, 1962.

François Truffaut:

Les aventures d'Antoine Doinel. Paris: Mercure de France, 1970.

The 400 Blows. Edited by David Denby. New York: Grove Press, 1969.

Jules et Jim. Paris: Seuil, 1971.

Jules and Jim. Translated by Nicholas Fry. New York: Simon & Schuster, 1968.

Jean Vigo:

Zéro de conduite. *L'Avant-Scène du cinéma*, no. 21 (1962).

Index